VOLUME FOUR

Landscape and Landscape Imagery in R. M. Rilke

BITHELL SERIES OF DISSERTATIONS
VOLUME FOUR

Landscape and Landscape Imagery in R. M. Rilke

JOHN SANDFORD

Lecturer in German in the University of Reading

INSTITUTE OF GERMANIC STUDIES
UNIVERSITY OF LONDON   1980

ISBN 0 85457 096 9

Printed by W. S. Maney & Son Ltd, Leeds, England

FOR MY PARENTS

CONTENTS

CONTENTS

PREFACE

I would like to record my gratitude to the Editorial Board for recommending publication of this thesis in the Bithell Series of Dissertations. I am also most grateful to Mrs Ann Weaver for the painstaking care with which she sub-edited my revised manuscript.

The text as it appears here is substantially that of the original; material by and on Rilke that has appeared in the intervening years has not led me to want to make any significant changes to what I wrote in 1972. I have, however, shortened the original in order to conform with the guidelines for the Bithell Series. Some of the less important sections of the original version have been removed: in particular those on the concept of 'home' in Rilke; on seasons, times of day, weather, and the sky; and on Rilke's 'minor' landscape experiences. Relevant material from them has been incorporated elsewhere in the text. A few other minor abbreviations and excisions have also been made, but the bulk of my material and, I hope, the overall development of my argument remain intact.

ABBREVIATIONS AND NOTES

Full details of all works referred to may be found in sections A and B of the Bibliography. References to Rilke's writings are abbreviated as described in section A of the Bibliography. Secondary literature is referred to simply by the author's name; where more than one work by the same author has been used, the reference also includes the first distinctive word(s) of the title. Notes are to be found at the end of each chapter.

INTRODUCTION

Und was Du schaust
und erbaust,
liebst und verstehst:
*ist alles Landschaft,
durch die Du gehst.* (SW, III, 397)

Rilke is not normally thought of primarily as a 'landscape poet', and it is not the
purpose of this study to try to claim that he is one. My aim is rather to examine
those landscapes and landscape elements that do occur in his works and in his
correspondence in order to see what the recurrent concerns are that emerge from
his experience and depiction of them. In the lines quoted above, written by Rilke
at the turn of the century, 'Landschaft' signifies the total environment, the realm
of the Non-Self, from which the Self distinguishes itself by experiencing ('schaust')
and ordering ('erbaust') it. The problems of landscape in Rilke are precisely those
of this relation of the individual to the whole, of *Ich* and *Nicht-Ich.* The question
of the place of the individual in the world, of Man in the universe, is a basic theme
that his work shares with much modern poetry, but it is essentially an abstract
question, and as such intangible and elusive. In the poet's landscapes this abstraction
becomes concrete and tangible: a recognizable symbol of the universe is presented;
a comprehensible sample of the much larger problem is made available, and serves
to illustrate it more clearly.

A clear pattern of preferences underlies the portrayal of the relations between
Self and Non-Self, and between part and whole in Rilke's landscapes. In all cases
undue dominance of any of these elements is rejected, and the ideal is seen as a
higher unity in which the parts paradoxically enjoy increased individual integrity.
Thus the stifling dominance of the whole in the sentimental pantheistic scenes of
the early years as well as the chaotic self-assertion of the parts in Malte's Paris are
both rejected in favour of the gently 'tamed' hillsides of the Valais or the many
parks that Rilke knew, where, through Man's (i.e. the Self's) agency Nature (i.e.
the Non-Self) has been made more truly and lastingly itself, and has thus entered
the aesthetic realm of 'Bezug'.

More than anything it is the biographical fact of Rilke's 'homelessness' – his
constant wandering from place to place, and his concern at setting up a meaningful

1

relationship with each new environment – that makes landscape significant for him. Some of the most famous lines of his poetry exemplify his rootlessness, and for all their wider metaphysical implications such statements as 'daß wir nicht sehr verläßlich zu Haus sind / in der gedeuteten Welt' in the First Duino Elegy, 'Wir sind die Treibenden' at the beginning of the twenty-second of the first group of Sonnets to Orpheus, or the picture of 'die Fahrenden', the fleeting itinerant acrobats of the Fifth Elegy, are all apt images springing from the poet's personal experience. Rilke's search for a home, for a meaningful and stimulating environment, is the key to his experience and description of landscape. The successive stages of his landscape experience are manifestations of this search for a home, and in his poetry they become symbols of a much more fundamental search for a meaningful place in the universe.

The main body of this study – Parts One and Two – deals with the two main aspects of the 'poet's landscapes': firstly the *places* (Russia, Paris, Spain, etc.), and secondly the *features* (parks, mountains, islands, etc.). Part One is based principally on statements contained in Rilke's letters; Part Two, which is divided along thematic rather than chronological lines, is based more on his poetry. By way of conclusion, Part Three attempts to put the results of this investigation into a wider context. It discusses the implications of the concerns that emerge from Rilke's landscapes for his thought as a whole, and in particular suggests that his experience and depiction of landscape can throw helpful light on his complicated and obscure aesthetic theories and ideals.

PART ONE: PLACES

Many of the landscapes that Rilke experienced were of prime importance in the formation of his poetic vision, sometimes 'teaching' him a new approach to the world, and always exemplifying and confirming ideas and feelings that had previously found little or no symbolic equivalent. Broadly speaking they fall into three groups, corresponding respectively with ideas of unity, disunity, and a reintegration transcending both the former situations. The unity of the early years was largely the result of unquestioning subjectivity, and manifested itself in a cloying superabundance of mood. It is a feature of all the landscape experiences that culminate in that of Russia. The second stage begins in Worpswede — where the first is, however, still dominant — and very quickly culminates in the landscape of Paris, reaching its most extreme point in the disintegrating world of *Malte Laurids Brigge.* The final stage, beginning in Paris and finding an initial climax in Spain, is experienced most decisively in the Valais. Increasingly clearly Rilke finds in these landscapes both expressions and confirmations of ideas of relationship between part and whole, Self and Non-Self, 'inner' and 'outer' worlds. In the first period the second parts of these pairs are dominant, whilst the first parts take over in the second period, and the third period is characterized by the search for and creation or discovery of an ideal balance in which both exist with equal justification — a balance in which the sought-for 'home' is finally attained.

One should naturally beware of oversimplifying the infinitely subtle and complex interplay of factors that characterizes any human development. It is not always possible to define accurately the crucial 'Wendepunkte' at which a decisively new stage is embarked upon, and with Rilke there is the added peculiarity of his capacity to live two very different stages of his evolution at one and the same time, so that a new and different attitude could join, rather than replace, the old one, and the two proceed side by side, with now the one, now the other taking the upper hand. During the Paris years in particular both the middle and the final periods tended to coexist in this way — a duality that manifests itself in Rilke's ambiguous attitude to the city, and in the 'Umschlag' theories of *Malte Laurids Brigge.*

The landscapes dealt with in detail in the following pages all had a measurable

3

effect on Rilke's development, and occur as recognizable locations in his poetry. They do not, of course, represent the sum total of his landscape experience, which also included various cities and areas of countryside in Germany, Austria, Provincial France, North Africa, and Scandinavia, and even extended to a glimpse of Greece from a boat in 1911. These, however, were 'minor' landscapes, providing Rilke with images that he later used, and that can be more or less definitely traced back to a specific place. (This is most notably the case with the 'Klagelandschaft' of the Tenth Elegy, which clearly echoes Rilke's experience of the Nile valley in early 1911.) These 'minor' landscapes are, however, incidental to Rilke's search for a 'home' with its attempts to define more clearly the place of the Self in the midst of the Non-Self.

1

THE LANDSCAPES OF RILKE'S LIFE

Prague

In a letter written less than a year before his death Rilke described, as in many other letters of this period, the immense significance that the landscape of the Valais had had for him. In most cases where he mentioned parallels to this experience it was the outwardly similar landscapes of Spain and Provence that he referred to, but here he looked at his more inward reactions and found that only one other environment had inspired him to poetic expression with quite the same intensity — that of his native city, Prague:

Abgesehen von jenen früheren jugendlichen Versuchen, in denen die Einflüsse meiner Prager Heimat sich durchsetzen wollten, hatte ich mich nie mehr hingerissen gefühlt, eine erlebte Umgebung unmittelbar im Gedicht zu rühmen, sie zu 'singen'. (B, 932; 20 March 1926 to Eduard Korrodi)

In his wording here Rilke reveals something of his attitude in the later years to the Prague period: he almost dismisses his first poems in the word 'Abgesehen' and then goes on to talk of them as 'jenen jugendlichen Versuchen', attempts, he implies, that have failed, for they are poems in which the influences of his home environment 'sich durchsetzen *wollten*'. Yet at the same time, whatever its result, the impetus to write is acknowledged as one of considerable force — he feels himself to have been 'hingerissen' by the demands of Prague to be praised by the poet.

Prague and the surrounding countryside of Bohemia are the first landscapes to appear in Rilke's poetry, and, in general, his later dismissal of these early experiments seems justified; they are, on the whole, decidedly inferior poems, unoriginal, pretentious, and full of trite sentimentality. What is striking from the point of view of landscape is the sheer volume of topographical description. In his juvenilia Rilke was almost entirely a landscape poet, and, as he suggests in the letter just quoted, the only other period when he wrote so consistently and at such length in his poetry about one particular landscape was that of his stay in Switzerland, at the other end of his life.

The peculiar social situation of the German writer in Prague at the end of the nineteenth century was probably of greater significance for the early Rilke's poetry than the actual physical environment of the city, but, as appears even more clearly in the works of Kafka, the two cannot be wholly separated.[1] The rarefied, isolated atmosphere of Prague German culture and Rilke's rather affected attempts to overcome this in a sometimes distinctly condescending Slavophilia go together with the more general air of the *fin de siècle* in European literature to create the climate through which he saw and portrayed his early Prague landscapes, of which the *Larenopfer* of 1895 are the main collection. Prague was nevertheless not the 'big city' experience for Rilke that Paris was to be, and when Politzer talks of it as being the first European city to show themes of 'anguish and alienation, solitude and bewilderment' (p. 49) he is using terms much more appropriate to Kafka's Prague, or to Malte / Rilke's Paris, than to the Prague of René Rilke. Demetz states the case somewhat better when he says:

Der Prager deutschen Dichtung, jener Stadt-Literatur par excellence, der Rilke, Kafka und Werfel entstammten, mangelte jede Kommunikation mit der Natur. René Rilke erlebte seinen Frühling zwischen den Mietkasernen auf den städtischen Friedhöfen. . . . Während die national-deutsche Dichtung Böhmens inmitten einer köstlichen Landschaft nach einem gültigen Kunstwerk strebte, entstanden im Düster der Stadt Werke der Weltliteratur, die an Naturarmut kaum zu übertreffen waren. (*Prager Jahre*, p. 108)

For all their restriction to the streets and confined spaces of the city these poems contain nothing of the 'Angst' of *Malte Laurids Brigge;* with a few exceptions the city is never seen in terms of claustrophobia; the confined spaces are sometimes mentioned, but rarely dwelt upon, and are even found to be positively poetic:

Auf der Kleinseite

Alte Häuser, steilgegiebelt,
hohe Türme voll Gebimmel, –
in die engen Höfe liebelt
nur ein winzig Stückchen Himmel.

Und auf jedem Treppenpflocke
müde lächelnd — Amoretten;
hoch am Dache um barocke
Vasen rieseln Rosenketten.

Spinnverwoben ist die Pforte
dort. Verstohlen liest die Sonne
die geheimnisvollen Worte
unter einer Steinmadonne.   (SW, I, 9f.)

Far from lamenting the narrow streets and courtyards, Rilke turns his attention more often than not to the rooftops of Prague, to the open skyline of churches and towers and the glint of sunlight in distant windows. This feeling of openness, expressed in such poems as 'Vom Lugaus' (SW, I, 13), was doubtless inspired to a large extent by the dominating feature of the Prague landscape: the Hradčany castle on its hill, with all the views this offered even in the centre of the city. It provided the subject of one of the more successful and better known of the *Larenopfer* poems:

Der Hradschin

Schau so gerne die verwetterte
Stirn der alten Hofburg an;
schon der Blick des Kindes kletterte
dort hinan.

Und es grüßen selbst die eiligen
Moldauwellen den Hradschin,
von der Brücke sehn die Heiligen
ernst auf ihn.

Und die Türme schaun, die neueren,
alle zu des Veitsturms Knauf
wie die Kinderschar zum teueren
Vater auf.   (SW, I, 10f.)

This, like many of the other Prague poems, shows nothing of 'anguish and alienation, solitude and bewilderment' — if anything, there is a naive sense of integration and delight, of being 'at home' in Prague. The significance of this poem is emphasized by Demetz, who calls it 'ein gutes Beispiel jener wirklichkeitsgesättigten Verse, die sich später zum Dinggedicht verengen' (*Prager Jahre*, p. 120). The river, also present in 'Der Hradschin', seems to be a kind of guarantee that the countryside is all around, and indeed visible from the heart of the city; some of the poems are about boat-trips (e.g. SW, I, 47, 60), and in the essay 'Ein Prager Künstler' (SW, V, 469) — about Emil Orlik, though it could, in many respects, be about Rilke himself — it is the Moldau that leads the eye out into the Bohemian countryside beyond the grimy suburbs, which, in the 'Naturalistic' poems

6

such as 'Hinter Smichov' (SW, I, 46f.) represent the nearest approach that Rilke finds in Prague to the 'Großstadt' locale of *Malte Laurids Brigge*. The description of Prague with which the essay on Orlik begins is one of Rilke's few detailed prose portrayals of the view of his native city, and it captures much of the atmosphere that he felt to be contained there:

Die giebelige, türmige Stadt ist seltsam gebaut: die große Historie kann in ihr nicht verhallen. Der Nachklang tönender Tage schwingt in den welkenden Mauern. Glänzende Namen liegen, wie heimliches Licht, auf den Stirnen stiller Paläste. Gott dunkelt in hohen gotischen Kirchen. In silbernen Särgen sind heilige Leiber zerfallen und liegen wie Blütenstaub in den metallenen Blättern. Wachsame Türme reden von jeder Stunde, und in der Nacht begegnen sich ihre einsamen Stimmen. Brücken sind über den gelblichen Strom gebogen, der, an den letzten verhutzelten Hütten vorbei, breit wird im flachen böhmischen Land. Dann Felder und Felder. Erst ein wenig bange und ärmliche Felder, die der Ruß noch erreicht aus den letzten lauten Fabriken, und ihre staubigen Sommer horchen hinein in die Stadt.

There then follows a description of the Bohemian countryside (SW, V, 469). Here again it is the rooftops of Prague, the towers and gables, that draw the poet's attention, but also he is interested in the city's past, which these buildings envelop. He evokes an atmosphere of rich historical association: Prague is seen as a city in which, paradoxically, the process of decay itself is somehow captured and preserved. Such an environment must clearly have been a strong stimulus to the neo-Romantic decadence of the young poet[2] and an important source of inspiration for the strange religiosity of the *Stunden-Buch*, for, as Demetz points out:

Die eigentliche historische Erbschaft, die diese Stadt ihren Dichtern vermachte, war die mystische Ekstase. Unter den hundert Glockentürmen geriet jedes Gefühl in die gefährliche Nähe religiöser Verzückung. (*Prager Jahre,* pp. 108f.)

The pervasive atmosphere of decay and dissolution, and the concomitant concern with death, are apparent in the recurrence of one of the most remarkable and characteristic landscape features of these early Prague poems: the city's cemeteries. These feature prominently in the *Zwei Prager Geschichten* of 1897-98,[3] and recur also in the *Larenopfer*. In both of these works it is the 'VII. Friedhof', the 'Wolschan', in which Rilke is particularly interested,[4] whilst a poem entitled 'Im Sommer' tells of a boat-trip on the river to the cemetery of Zlichov (SW, I, 47). The Jewish cemetery too is the subject of a lengthy poem written in 1896 (SW, III, 156ff.). The morbid fascination with what Demetz calls 'die nekrophile Topographie seiner Heimatstadt (*Prager Jahre*, p. 126) is reflected in a remarkable passage from the *Florenzer Tagebuch* of 1898, where the inhabitants of Prague are pictured in such a way that the whole city seems to become a giant graveyard; they are people

welche das ganze Leben lang ihre eigene Vergangenheit leben. Wie Leichen sind sie, welche nicht Frieden finden und deshalb in heimlicher Nacht immer wieder ihr Sterben leben und über die harten Grüfte hin aneinander vorübergehen. Sie haben nichts mehr; das Lächeln welkte auf ihren Lippen, und die Augen trieben mit dem letzten Weinen wie auf abendlichen Flüssen hin. Aller Fortschritt in ihnen ist nur, daß ihr Sarg zermorscht und ihre Gewänder zerfallen und sie selbst immer mürber und müder werden und ihre Finger verlieren wie alte Erinnerungen. Und davon erzählen sie sich mit den lang verstorbenen Stimmen: so sind die Menschen in Prag. (T, 13

The interest of the early Rilke in cemeteries, paralleled later by Malte Laurids Brigge's obsession with hospitals, is the most distinctive expression in landscape terms of this neo-Romantic vision of Prague as a kind of vast necropolis – the cemeteries almost become symbols of the whole city. Here he reveals the beginnings of his later much less physical interest in the problem of death. In his fascination in particular with the phenomenon of spring and summer in the cemeteries (e.g. SW, IV, 124f., and SW, I, 47) – for it is these seasons, rather than the outwardly more appropriate autumn and winter, that he usually portrays in the 'cemetery works' – he is already expressing, again in landscape terms, something that later grows to become the problem of the unity of life and death with which he was very much concerned in his maturity, and that finds similar expression in the 'Gleichnis' involving spring and death at the end of the Tenth Elegy.

At the end of September 1896 Rilke left Prague and moved to Munich, the first of the endless series of *déménagements* that characterized the rest of his life. He did return to Prague, but his visits were short and few in number, becoming more infrequent as time passed. He never attempted or intended to return 'home' to settle in the city, and he mentioned it very rarely in his letters. When he did so his feelings were mixed, but fundamentally negative, as in the following passage addressed to Clara during a short stay in November 1907, where the shift of emphasis from environment to Self that has taken place in Rilke is clearly expressed. In his childhood, he feels, Prague had overwhelmed him, had 'used' him, whereas now it appears 'gedemütigt', 'kleiner', 'reduziert'. Its sentimental associations, though, are still too strong to allow him complete independence from this city of his birth; he is thus at the same time saddened at Prague's 'humiliation', he is both attracted and repelled – a 'feindsälige Verwandschaft' exists between him and the city; for all its loss of 'Schwere' it is still as 'schwer' a place as ever, and his conclusion can only be one of confusion, of 'Unbegreiflicheit und Verwirrung':

... wird man eines Tages hier sein und auch dieses sehen können, sehen und sagen, von Vorhandensein zu Vorhandensein? Wird man seine Schwere nicht mehr zu tragen haben, die immense Bedeutung, die es annahm, da man klein war, und es war schon groß und wuchs über einen hinaus; damals gebrauchte es einen, um sich zu fühlen. Da war ein Kind, und alles das fühlte sich an ihm, sah sich in ihm, groß und phantastisch gespiegelt, wurde hochmütig und schicksalsvoll seinem Herzen gegenüber. Das alles darf es nun nichtmehr sein. Herabgesetzt unter sich selbst, zurückgekommen wie einer, der lange Gewalt getan hat, ist es irgendwie beschämt vor mir, bloßgestellt, eingeschlossen, als widerführe ihm nun Gerechtigkeit und Ausgleich. Aber ich kann mich nicht freuen, *das* schlecht behandelt zu sehen, was einmal hart und hochfahrend gegen mich gewesen ist und sich nie herabließ zu mir und mir nie erklärte, welche Verschiedenheit zwischen uns gesetzt ist, welche feindsälige Verwandtschaft. Es macht mich traurig, diese Hausecken, jene Fenster und Einfahrte, Plätze und Kirchenfirste gedemütigt zu sehen, kleiner, als sie waren, reduziert und völlig im Unrecht. Und nun sind sie mir in ihrer neuen Verfassung ebenso unmöglich zu bewältigen, wie sie es damals als Hoffärtige waren. Und ihre Schwere ist ins Gegenteil umgeschlagen, aber wie sehr ist sie, Stelle für Stelle, Schwere geblieben. Mehr als je fühle ich seit heute früh die Gegenwart dieser Stadt als Unbegreiflichkeit und Verwirrung. (B 07-14, 7f.; 1 November 1907 to Clara)

Prague was the setting of Rilke's childhood, and, on the whole, he did not wish to be reminded of his childhood, of his early years dressed as a girl, of his subjection to the prejudices and whims of his mother, of the years at the Military Academy, and he was embarrassed by the thought of the facile effusiveness and affectation of his early poetry. When he revisited Prague it was this stifling sense of a wasted childhood that affronted him and prevented any uninhibited appreciation of the city: 'schade, daß nun Prag kommen mußte, kaum zu atmen, dicht von abgestandenem Sommer und unbewältigter Kindheit', he wrote in 1910,[5] and again, a year later, he said:

Dies hier richte ich nach Prag, wahrscheinlich werden Sie noch nicht zurück sein, fast wünsch ichs Ihnen, denn Prag war mir kaum zu atmen heuer, es hat immer noch die Luft meiner Kindheit. (B, 291; 28 September 1911 to Hedda Sauer)

The finality of Rilke's break with Prague appears in a passage where he compares it to a sloughed-off skin that he has now hopelessly outgrown:

Nun gestern mußt ich denken, ich wär die Libelle und man setzte mich wieder aufs Abgestreifte. Ach Prag: das Gefühl ist zu lang geworden, der Kopf geht nichtmehr hinein, von den Flügeln gar nicht zu reden. (B Taxis, 24f.; 21 August 1910)

The landscapes of Prague accordingly play little discernible part in the poems of the later years; perhaps the 'Klagelandschaft' of the Tenth Elegy is in some ways a reminiscence of the 'nekrophile Topographie' of Prague and its cemeteries, but the affinity, if any, is purely ideational, for the physical origins of the 'Klagelandschaft' lie clearly in Egypt. Certainly Prague is evoked in the eighth of the second group of the Sonnets to Orpheus, but only, as Politzer points out, to provide 'images of the unreality of reality, as well as of estrangement' (p. 59):

> Wagen umrollten uns fremd, vorübergezogen,
> Haüser umstanden uns stark, aber unwahr, – und keines
> kannte uns je. *Was* war wirklich im All? (SW, I, 756)

The early portrayals of Prague are a distinctive but unmomentous beginning for Rilke's landscapes. At worst they are little more than enumerations of 'sights' –

Demetz calls the *Larenopfer* 'ein poetischer Baedeker' (*Prager Jahre*, p. 118) and Politzer talks of Rilke's 'aesthetic tours through a scenic landscape' (p. 53) – whilst at best they provide a few pleasant sketches of various moments and places.[6] These poems gain their unity from their mood, an all-pervading, frequently cloying *Stimmung* of decay and lassitude that all too often threatens to submerge the poetic pretext on which it rests. For Blume the main fault of these works lies in the fact that the city rarely rises above the status of a pretext, not yet existing in its own right, but simply there for the sake of the poet: 'Kein Wunder, daß in diesen Versen Prag nicht zur "Landschaft" wird, sondern zur Kulisse, vor der Narziß sich in Szene setzt, ('Stadt', p. 69). He likens the preciosity of these early city-descriptions to some of Heine's work:

dieselbe intime Plauderhaftigkeit, dieselbe auf den Effekt bedachte farbige Angeregtheit, dieselbe Vermenschlichung des Unbelebten, mit der die geschilderte Landschaft gleichsam erst in Szene gesetzt wird. Wie Heine steht Rilke, als Conférencier seiner Empfindungen, dem Gegenstand, den er darstellt, im Wege, weder fähig, sich ganz an ihn zu verlieren noch ihn in sich hineinzunehmen und zu verwandeln.   (ibid., pp. 72f)

There is indeed much of the Self in these poems, but as yet the problem of its relationship to the Non-Self, the dominant concern in the later landscapes, has not arisen, for the two are not yet distinguished. This is, so to speak, the 'naive' young Rilke, unquestioningly and clumsily at one with a mood that emanates indistinguishably and unproblematically from himself and from his environment.

Bohemia

The Bohemian countryside, which mingles with the landscapes of Prague in much of Rilke's early poetry, seems to have inspired in him a much 'healthier' reaction than did the city. There is practically none of the atmosphere of decadence and oppressive lassitude that characterizes many of the Prague poems. Certainly the countryside is often imbued with a distinctive mood, but it is usually one of simple sentimental wonder and melancholy in the presence of what is seen as innocence and simplicity, and is far removed from the extravagant obsession with decay that marks some of the descriptions of the city. In the second part of the descriptive introduction to his essay on Emil Orlik Rilke turns from his description of Prague and lets his eye follow the river out into the open country:

Dann, an langen Alleen steilstämmiger Pappeln, beginnen rechts und links die wogenderen Ernten. Apfelbäume, krumm von den reichlichen Jahren, heben sich bunt aus dem Korn. Vorn, am Straßenrand, verstaubt ein Kartoffelfeld, und wie später Abendschatten dunkelt ein Dreieck Kohl, blau-violett, vor dem jungen Gehölz. Tannen dahinter beenden schweigsam das Land. Kleine hastige Winde hoch in der Luft. Alles andere – Himmel. So ist meine Heimat.   (SW, V, 469)

This description is fairly typical, both in technique and in content, of most of Rilke's portrayals of Bohemia. The language is more direct and purely descriptive, with fewer metaphors and personal reactions than in the Prague poems. The overall effect is much more that of a painting – even the 'enumerative' descriptions of Prague usually contain important abstract elements of a non-visual, exclusively poetic-linguistic nature that are largely absent in descriptions such as this. The most distinctive contrast probably lies in the vitality of these landscapes; they are, like this one, almost invariably summer scenes, in which the season is not the oppressive wilting summer of Prague, but a setting of light and clear-cut shapes, of growth and warmth. The whole landscape is much more alive and young than that of the city; in this passage there are indeed heavy old apple trees, a dusty potato field, a patch of cabbage 'wie später Abendschatten', but these only serve to temper and enrich the dominant sense of vitality, the 'steilstämmige Pappeln', the 'immer wogenderen Ernten', the 'junges Gehölz', the 'kleine, hastige Winde', whilst even the old apple trees 'heben sich bunt aus dem Korn'. The description is simple, perhaps almost banal, but it is unpretentious, and the features that Rilke notes reveal an attitude and reactions that differ markedly from those he evinced in Prague.

The patchwork pattern of fields and forests seems to have been for Rilke the most typical aspect of the Bohemian landscape, and it is one that he presents again in the poem 'Mittelböhmische Landschaft' – probably the best of these early verse descriptions:

> Fern dämmert wogender Wälder
> beschatteter Saum.
> Dann unterbricht
> nur hie und da ein Baum
> die falbe Fläche hoher Ährenfelder.
> Im hellsten Licht
> keimt die Kartoffel; dann
> ein wenig weiter Gerste, bis der Tann
> das Bild begrenzt.
> Hoch überm Jungwald glänzt
> so goldig-rot ein Kirchturmkreuz herüber,
> aus Fichten ragt der Hegerhütte Bau; –
> und drüber
> wölbt sich ein Himmel, blank und blau.   (SW, I, 68)

One could object to much in this poem – in a way it is little more than a list of objects, the elements of the landscape, many of them qualified by a rather stock epithet. The poet attempts to guide us through the scene by giving indications of the relative positions of these objects: 'Fern – Dann – hie – da – dann – ein wenig weiter – bis – das Bild begrenzt – überm – herüber – aus – drüber'. It demands much imaginative agility to follow the poet's eye as it leaps from object to object; indeed, he has described too many relationships: not only do they render an element of prosaicness, but their number leads to confusion. Such a wealth of prepositional detail arouses expectations at least of a fairly clear picture, but in fact by the end of the poem one has little more than a jumble of impressions; it is never clear whether the gaze is moving towards one or away, to left or right, and one cannot be sure to what extent, if any, the many woods – the 'wogende Wälder', the 'Tann', the 'Jungwald', and the 'Fichten' – are one and the same. But notwithstanding these many faults the poem is still vivid and fresh when compared with much of Rilke's early work. One has at the end of it a confused but composite impression of a landscape of woods and fields, and, as in the prose passage just quoted, the whole is held together, perhaps facilely but still quite effectively, by the image of the all-embracing vault of the sky. The unity is thus at least provided by an integral element of the landscape, whereas in many of the Prague poems it is the poet's subjective mood that imposes the common denominator, as in 'Ein Adelshaus', which finishes with the disastrous line: 'das nenn ich Stimmung, ja, das nenn ich – Zauber' (SW, I, 10). 'Mittelböhmische Landschaft' is to the Bohemian landscapes what 'Der Hradschin' is to those of Prague: it captures a picture of the place that, for all its faults, is distinctive in its independence, its freedom from too great a burden of mood and pretension. Demetz's description of 'Der Hradschin' as a kind of prototype 'Dinggedicht' is paralleled by Blume's comment on 'Mittelböhmische Landschaft': 'Hier redet der Dichter nicht dazwischen, hier fehlen auch die Gleichnisse völlig: es ist das gegenständlichste Gedicht des jungen Rilke.'[7]

Sometimes, but more rarely, Rilke's Bohemian landscapes are laden with mood, as in the description of an autumnal 'mittelböhmische Landstraße' that introduces the story 'Ihr Opfer', and concludes with the lines:

das ist ein Bild von unsäglicher, unbeschreiblicher, hilfloser Wehmut. – Wenn ich dies Bild denke, fühle ich einen großen Schmerz in der Nähe meines Herzens. Es zuckt dort etwas zusammen – und zerrt, zerrt bis mir die Tränen in den Augen brennen . . . (SW, IV, 474)

But the mood that usually, in varying degrees, accompanies his pictures of Bohemia, is one that springs from his attitude to the Czech peasants, who figure much more frequently in these poems than does the proletariat in those of Prague. As often as not these peasants are portrayed singing a folksong, and it is these songs that Rilke attaches a considerable sentimental significance to. His attitude to the peasants appears explicitly in the poem 'Volksweise', which begins with the lines:

Mich rührt so sehr
böhmischen Volkes Weise,
schleicht sie ins Herz sich leise,
macht sie es schwer   (SW, I, 39)

12

About this poem Politzer says;

... he approaches the Czech people as a civilized man faces a primitive one, or as an adult bends down to a child, surprised by the wonderful performance of somebody whom he has deemed to be far less developed than he is himself, and at the same time touched by the recollection of a state of innocence which he, the refined grown-up, has long since lost.[8]

From this comes the rather wistful, melancholy air that is often the hallmark of the Bohemian landscape poems, and the rather stereotyped images of the simple folk who inhabit them:

> Gott gab Hütten; voll von Schafen
> Ställe; und der Dirne klafft
> vor Gesundheit fast das Mieder.
>
> Gab den Burschen all, den braven,
> in die rauhe Faust die Kraft,
> in das Herz – die Heimatlieder.   (SW, I, 23; 'Land
> und Volk')

In this vision of the Czech peasants and their landscape there is already much of Rilke's sense of homelessness, and of the longing for a home, that becomes explicit in this connection in the 'Festspielszene' *Zur Einweihung der Kunsthalle* of 1902, where 'Der Künstler' talks of:

> ... das Land,
> darin die Kindheit mir vergangen ist;
> Das stand um mich und nahm an mir nicht teil
> und dennoch hab ich mich damit verwoben, –   (SW, III, 406)

In later years, when he revisited the country, Rilke's attitude to the Bohemian countryside was distinctly different from that with which he experienced Prague: whereas his view of the latter had developed into rejection, an almost complete failure to establish contact, he found the countryside and his reactions to it largely unchanged; it was still the old friendly landscape of woods and fields, and still, for Rilke at least, permeated with songs of the people:

Und das war Böhmen, das ich kannte, hügelig wie leichte Musik und auf einmal wieder eben hinter seinen Apfelbäumen, flach ohne viel Horizont und eingeteilt durch die Äcker und Baumreihen wie ein Volklied von Refrain zu Refrain.
(B, 211; 4 November 1907 to Clara)

... und da wie dort breitet sich hinter den Parkbäumen dasselbe böhmische Land in seiner einfachen, volkstümlichen und freundlichen Weise, die nichts von einem verlangt, und ich merke so nach und nach, daß es mir wohltut mit seiner Anspruchslosigkeit, seinem guten Herzen, das wie das Herz eines Haustiers ist –
(B 271; 7 September 1910 to Gräfin Lili Kanitz-Menar)

Thus he wrote of Bohemia in 1907 and 1910.

13

Many of the landscape poems of the early Rilke are not explicitly Bohemian in subject matter, but reminiscences of this countryside seem to play an important part in them. Bohemia provides him with an image of the 'tamed' landscape; with its woods and fields it is a landscape in which Man and Nature play an equal part and coexist in harmony. This landscape type from his native country remains with Rilke all his life as a constant element in his search for a home, and when he finally settles in the Valais it is remarkable how similar in some respects Rilke's reactions to the two environments are: in the Swiss Canton he finds again a countryside where rows of vines provide an echo of Bohemia's strips of fields and woods, where integrated peasants have cultivated and patterned the surface of the landscape, a landscape certainly more grandiose than that of Bohemia, but one that, in the *Quatrains Valaisans,* is often praised in terms very much like those used almost thirty years earlier in the *Larenopfer.*

Russia

The landscape of Russia made a deeper and more lasting impression on the young Rilke than that of any other country. He went there twice, accompanied each time by Lou Andreas-Salomé. The first visit lasted from April to June 1899 and involved mainly Moscow and St. Petersburg; during the second, covering nearly four months from May to August 1900, Rilke travelled extensively and came into close contact with rural Russia. The experiences that Rilke gained from these two journeys were recognised by him all his life as forming a momentous stage in his development: in a letter of 12 January 1922 to Robert Heinz Heygrodt he linked Russia and the Military Academy as 'die beiden bestimmendsten Epochen meines äußeren Lebens' (B, 730) and he described its significance in similar terms to all who enquired after the 'influences' on his life and work. Russia was one of the few places to become fused for Rilke with the idea of 'home': 'In Rußland nur ... habe ich Heimat gefühlt'[9] he wrote in 1903. In 1911 he talked of his long-standing 'Heimweh' for Moscow[10] and in 1920 he spoke of Russia as 'jenem, mir wahlheimatlichen Lande';[11] a year earlier he had written even more decisively:

was verdankt ich Rußland –, es hat mich zu *dem* gemacht, was ich bin, von dort ging ich innerlich aus, alle Heimat meines Instinktes, all mein innerer Ursprung ist *dort!*[12]

What impressed Rilke most in Russia was a sense of harmony, of a great unity of God, people and country, and it was during his second journey to Russia, in the countryside rather than in St Petersburg or Moscow, that he experienced this most forcefully. The sheer physical vastness of the landscape underlies all of Rilke's feelings about Russia, as this passage from the early diaries indicates:

Auf der Wolga, diesem ruhig rollenden Meer, Tage zu sein und Nächte, viele Tage und viele Nächte: ein breit-breiter Strom, hoher, hoher Wald an dem einen Ufer, an der anderen Seite tiefes Heideland, darin auch große Städte nur wie Hütten und Zelte stehen. – Man lernt alle Dimensionen um. Man erfährt: Land ist groß, Wasser ist etwas Großes, und groß vor allem ist der Himmel. Was ich bisher sah, war nur ein Bild von Land und Fluß und Welt. Hier aber ist alles selbst. – Mir ist, als hätte ich der Schöpfung zugesehen; wenige Worte für alles Sein, die Dinge in den Maßen Gottvaters . . .[13]

The style of this passage, with its almost ecstatic piling on of superlatives, makes it one of the most distinctive pieces of landscape description ever written by Rilke; only the letters describing Toledo reveal quite the same intensity of experience – and they reveal it in remarkably similar words, for in a letter of 13 November 1912 he describes the Castilian city as 'eine Stadt Himmels und der Erden' just as here he sees 'die Dinge in den Maßen Gottvaters'. The landscape around Toledo is also, like Russia, 'Schöpfung',[14] and just as in Toledo he saw a higher, more essential reality, so in Russia 'ist alles selbst' and no longer 'nur ein Bild' (B, 509f.; 27 October 1915 to Ellen Delp).

The religiosity of the Russian peasants is something frequently remarked upon by Rilke, and in the *Geschichten vom lieben Gott* he says of Russia: 'Der Einfluß Gottes ist sehr mächtig', and answers the question 'Ist denn Gott ein Land? ' with the words:

Ich glaube nicht, aber in den primitiven Sprachen haben viele Dinge denselben Namen. Es ist da wohl ein Reich, das heißt Gott, und der es beherrscht, heißt auch Gott. Einfache Völker können ihr Land und ihren Kaiser oft nicht unterscheiden; beide sind groß und gütig, furchtbar und groß.   (SW, IV, 310)

Here again, in the repetition of the word 'groß', it is the physical dimensions of Russia that, as in the description of the journey on the Volga, provide the attribute that joins the country indissolubly with its God, so that, two years later in the essay 'Russische Kunst', Rilke can call Russia 'Das weite Land im Osten, das einzige, durch welches Gott noch mit der Erde zusammenhängt' (SW, V, 494). The same theme – the wide, empty, open landscape and the brotherhood of its inhabitants in and with God – appears in one of the Russian poems that Rilke wrote for Lou in 1900 after his second journey:

Ich gehe, gehe, und immer noch ist ringsum deine Heimat, die windige Ferne, ich gehe, gehe und ich habe vergessen, daß ich früher andere Länder kannte. Und wie fern sind jetzt von mir die großen Tage am südlichen Meer, die süßen Nächte des Mai-Sonnenuntergangs; dort ist alles leer und heiter, und siehe da: es dunkelt Gott, . . . das leidende Volk kam zu ihm und nahm ihn wie einen Bruder auf. (SW, IV, 960f.)

In contrast with his experiences of the Russian countryside Rilke's impressions of the cities he visited appear to have been more disparate and to have affected him much less deeply. Moscow, St Petersburg and Kiev all figure in the letters and poems, but nothing like as forcefully and as frequently as does the open countryside, and when they do appear they are practically entities in their own right whose Russian-ness seems almost incidental. In the *Buch von der Pilgerschaft*, when he mentions the things that God will 'inherit' he talks of:

> die Troïtzka Lawra und das Monastir,
> das unter Kiews Gärten ein Gewirr
> von Gängen bildet, dunkel und verschlungen, —
> Moskau mit Glocken wie Erinnerungen, —   (SW, I, 314)

These lines are little more than a list of inconsequential memories, and, apart from the religious element, have little in common with the style or content of the descriptions of rural Russia. The only poem wholly concerned with Rilke's memories of a Russian city is 'Nächtliche Fahrt, Sankt Petersburg' (SW, I, 601), written in Paris in 1907, and very much in the style of the *Neue Gedichte*, to the second part of which it belongs. It presents a picture of a majestic city with its imposing palaces and streets in the strange light of a summer night. It is an eerie scene, and all in all the impression is, as Uyttersprot suggests (p. 97), that of a 'schwere Stadt' and one that has little organic connection with the rest of Rilke's Russia.

The experience of the Russian countryside, fused indissolubly with its inhabitants and, above all, with their God, found its finest and most extensive poetic expression in the first two books of the *Stunden-Buch*: *Das Buch vom mönchischen Leben* and *Das Buch von der Pilgerschaft*, written after the two Russian journeys respectively. In these poems Rilke captures something of the naive, quasi-pantheistic religiosity that he saw in the Russian peasants, and, although not identified as such, it is clearly the vastness of the Russian landscape that provides these poems with their settings, as Rilke suggests when he talks of the *Stunden-Buch* as 'das . . . Buch . . ., darin so viel von meiner Liebe für Rußland Zuflucht gefunden hat' (B, 04-07, 207; 10 December 1906 to Leonid Pasternak). One poem in particular is almost an autobiographical account of the homeless poet's journey, and presents in verse much that had been prefigured in the description of the journey on the Volga:

> Wer dich zum ersten Mal gewahrt,
> den stört der Nachbar und die Uhr,
> der geht, gebeugt zu deiner Spur,
> und wie beladen und bejahrt.
> Erst später naht er der Natur
> und fühlt die Winde und die Fernen,
> hört dich, geflüstert von der Flur,
> sieht dich, gesungen von den Sternen,
> und kann dich nirgends mehr verlernen,
> und alles ist dein Mantel nur.

Ihm bist du neu und nah und gut
und wunderschön wie eine Reise,
die er in stillen Schiffen leise
auf einem großen Flusse tut.
Das Land ist weit, in Winden, eben,
sehr großen Himmeln preisgegeben
und alten Wäldern untertan.
Die kleinen Dörfer, die sich nahn,
vergehen wieder wie Geläute
und wie ein Gestern und ein Heute
und so wie alles, was wir sahn.
Aber an dieses Stromes Lauf
stehn immer wieder Städte auf
und kommen wie auf Flügelschlägen
der feierlichen Fahrt entgegen.

Und manchmal lenkt das Schiff zu Stellen,
die einsam, sonder Dorf und Stadt,
auf etwas warten an den Wellen, –
auf den der keine Heimat hat . . .
Für solche stehn dort kleine Wagen
(ein jeder mit drei Pferden vor),
die atemlos nach Abend jagen
auf einem Weg, der sich verlor.   (SW, I, 322f.)

But in spite of the powerful impression that Russia clearly made on him, Rilke
never returned to this 'Wahlheimat', and after 1901, with such rare exceptions as
the St Petersburg poem of 1907 and the 'Schimmel' Sonnet of 1922,[15] neither of
which in any case belongs to the mainstream of the Russian experience, it
disappeared almost entirely as a manifest subject of his poetry. The reason
probably lies in the nature of the religious experience that Russia presented him
with. He undoubtedly saw the country with the eye of a pantheist as the above poem
makes clear: he hears God 'geflüstert von der Flur' and sees him synaesthetically
'gesungen von den Sternen', and sees that 'alles ist dein Mantel nur'. This makes of
the vast country something simple, something attractive to the man who is
disturbed by 'der Nachbar und die Uhr'. Indeed, in a letter to Clara in which he
contemplates a third journey to Russia in 1901 he says: 'Dort werden mir alle Züge
des Lebens klarer und seltsam vereinfacht' (B, 23; 18 October 1900). But the
pantheistic harmony, the monumental simplicity of Russia is experienced
essentially in a state of receptive passivity, and in the landscape itself the
individual elements are totally dominated by the overwhelming whole; everything
is 'sehr großen Himmeln preisgegeben / und alten Wäldern untertan', and the little
villages 'vergehen' in the sheer magnitude of their setting. Similarly in the
Geschichten vom lieben Gott he talks of the peasants in their cottages surrounded
by the empty spaces of the plain and says: 'Die Häuser selbst können nicht

17

beschützen vor dieser Unermeßlichkeit (SW, IV, 330). For Rilke the Russian's freedom sprang paradoxically from being an utterly passive subject – of his God, of his rulers, and, perhaps more than anything, of his landscape:

Der russische Mensch hat mir in so und so vielen Beispielen vorgestellt, wie selbst eine, alle Kräfte des Widerstandes dauernd überwältigende Knechtung und Heimsuchung nicht notwendig den Untergang der Seele bewirken muß. Es gibt da, für die slawische Seele wenigstens, einen Grad der Unterwerfung, der so vollkommen genannt zu werden verdient, daß es ihr, selbst unter dem aufliegendsten und beschwerendsten Drucke, etwas wie einen heimlichen Spielraum schafft, eine vierte Dimension ihres Dasein [sic], in der nun, mögen die Zustände noch so bedrängend werden, eine neue, endlose und wahrhaft unabhängige Freiheit für sie beginnt. (B, 646; 9 December 1920 to General-Major von Sedlakowitz).

The passivity of the Russian experience was, like the similar *fin-de-siècle* lassitude and decadence of the Prague years, only a phase, the phase of the young Rilke, and as such it was soon outgrown. Russia was not in itself a stimulus to new development, for what it did was simply to precipitate the expression of a mood that already underlay Rilke's attitude to life in his early years, thus clearing the way for his contact in the 'alien' atmosphere of France with a new, more active view of the world. In Russia Rilke found a unity far deeper than that provided by the affected *Stimmung* of Prague:

Ich fing mit den *Dingen* an, die die eigentlichen Vertrauten meiner einsamen Kindheit gewesen sind, und es war schon viel, daß ich es, ohne fremde Hilfe, bis zu den Tieren gebracht habe. . . . Dann aber tat sich mir Rußland auf und schenkte mir die Brüderlichkeit und das Dunkel Gottes, in dem allein Gemeinschaft ist. (B, 819; 22 February 1923 to Ilse Jahr)

Having found the unity that his youth had longed for he was now ready to turn to the parts, to the 'things', to an essentially active approach to the world. In a letter written nine months before his death Rilke points very clearly to the two attitudes – the passive one of 'Erleben' and 'Empfangen', and the active one of 'Gestalten' and 'Wollen' – and names the two places, Russia and Paris respectively, that enabled him to realize them:

Rußland (Sie erkennen das in Büchern, wie etwa dem Stundenbuch) wurde, in gewissem Sinne, die Grundlage meines Erlebens und Empfangens, ebenso wie, vom Jahre 1902 ab, Paris – das unvergleichliche – zur Basis für mein Gestaltenwollen geworden ist. (B, 929; 17 March 1926 to 'eine junge Freundin').

The development away from passive perception of unity towards active distinction of parts begins almost immediately the second Russian journey is over, and already by September 1900 Rilke is complaining of his 'immature eyes', his lamentable passivity and lack of selectivity in the face of the multiple impressions of the visit to Russia:

Die russische Reise mit ihren täglichen Verlusten ist mir ein so unendlich banger Beweis meiner unreifen Augen, die nicht zu empfangen, nicht zu halten und auch loszulassen nicht verstehen, die, mit quälenden Bildern beladen, an Schönheiten vorübergehen und zu Enttäuschungen hin. (T, 315)

The deeply regretful tone of this passage, in sharp contrast to the fervour of the earlier descriptions of Russia, marks the beginning of the Worpswede interlude – the important turning point that led Rilke on to the landscape of Paris, the total opposite of all that Russia had stood for.

Worpswede and Westerwede

Rilke's period in Worpswede and Westerwede, which stretched, with various interludes of absence, from the end of the second Russian journey through to his departure for Paris in 1902, united features of both his earlier and his later life. Here, on the open fens of North Germany, he found a landscape reminiscent of the Russian plain; but the people he found there were no longer the passive peasants of Russia, but a colony of artists, actively forming and delineating their experience of the environment about them. Much of his writing at this time is explicitly concerned with landscape – not only the landscape of Worpswede as he saw it, but also landscape through the eyes and the art of others, in particular of the five artists – Fritz Mackensen, Otto Modersohn, Fritz Overbeck, Hans am Ende, and Heinrich Vogeler – about whom Rilke wrote in the monograph *Worpswede* of early 1902. The importance of landscape for him in these years is testified not only in the constant recurrence in his work, with a frequency far above that of any other period, of the word 'Landschaft', but also in the fact that the introduction to the *Worpswede* monograph was originally to be an essay entitled 'Von der Landschaft'.[16] Rilke intended in this monograph 'von der Landschaft auszugehen, als von dem gemeinsamen Hintergrund der einzelnen Künstler, und mit besonderer Betonung bei ihr zu verweilen' (SW, VI, 1274 n.), and had intended initially to link the various sections with his own landscape sketches:

Darauf freue ich mich besonders, in einzelnen Kapiteln, welche wie Intermezzi zwischen die Monographien eingeschoben werden, Worpsweder Landschaft zu geben in kleinen abgetönten Stimmungen. (SW, VI, 1273 n.)

In the essay on Otto Modersohn he even goes so far as to declare quite emphatically that all the arts now originate in landscape:

Der Künstler von heute empfängt von der Landschaft die Sprach für seine Geständnisse und nicht der Maler allein. Es ließe sich genau nachweisen, daß alle Künste jetzt aus dem Landschaftlichen leben. (SW, V, 68)

Of the three diaries that Rilke wrote[17] the second two, the 'Schmargendorfer' and the 'Worpsweder' Tagebücher, are also in large part repositories of his impressions of the Worpswede countryside, the 'Worpsweder Tagebuch' being particularly rich in poems describing the open vistas of the 'Moor'.[18]

In a letter of 12 April 1922 to Gräfin Margot Sizzo-Norris-Crouy Rilke describes himself as 'im Innersten doch ein Anhänger der Ebene' (B, 782), and in the introduction to *Worpswede* he declares: ... wir leben im Zeichen der Ebene und des Himmels' (SW, V, 26). Clearly, for Rilke, two landscapes in particular stood 'im Zeichen der Ebene und des Himmels' — those of Russia and of Worpswede, and it is thus not surprising that, with the experience of Russia still fresh in his mind, Worpswede too impressed itself upon him almost at first sight as a 'home'. Very shortly after his first visit there he wrote to Clara from Berlin:

Eure Heimat war mir, vom ersten Augenblick, mehr als nur eine gütige Fremde. War eben Heimat, *die erste* Heimat, in der ich Menschen leben sah (sonst leben alle in der Fremde, alle Heimaten aber stehen leer . . .) (B, 21f.; 18 October 1900).

But the 'Heimat' of Worpswede is not quite the same as that of Russia; the 'Menschen' who inhabit it are no longer the simple naive peasants, but sophisticated, reflective artists. The peasants, the turf-cutters and farmers, certainly figure in Rilke's portrayals of Worpswede, but he no longer tries to mingle with them or to see the world exclusively through their eyes. Instead he turns for companionship and inspiration to the sculptors and painters, and begins in earnest the encounter with the visual arts that was to alter completely his vision of the world, and, not least, of the landscapes through which he progressed.

The following lines from a Westerwede poem, written in the autumn of 1901, reveal clearly something of the significance that the landscape experience of these years had for Rilke's development:

> Und du lernst, in Ebenen zu wohnen,
> weil du dort den Himmel größer siehst
> und weil dort der Strom beruhigt fließt
> zu den Andern, zu den Millionen.
> Ohne Berge wird die Erde weit,
> allen Wegen siehst du auf den Grund.
> Immer größer wird ein Haus, ein Hund
> welcher langsam sich von dir entfernt.
> Wer die Dinge um sich kennen lernt,
> muß sie einmal vor dem Himmel sehn
> wo sie wichtig und verlassen stehn,
> niemandem gehören, den
> du kränken könntest . . . (SW, III, 746f.)

The first few lines are a straightforward expression of Rilke the 'Anhänger der Ebene', and could refer just as easily to Russia as to Worpswede; indeed they are, if anything, more reminiscent of his descriptions of the former: the empty countryside with its vast sky, the calmly flowing river — possibly the Volga —, and the sense of fellowship, of a great unity in brotherhood among human beings. The final lines, however, bring in a distinctly new note that typifies the difference between Rilke's vision of the Worpswede landscape and his vision of the landscape of Russia. In Worpswede the word 'Dinge' begins to take on something of the significance that it ultimately assumed in Paris. Rilke now sees not only the harmony of the landscape, but, stimulated by the painters with whom he lived, he also begins to see and examine its parts. The image used in this poem of things 'vor dem Himmel', isolated, distinct and important against the background of the sky, of things standing out above the horizon, is a recurrent one in the poems and descriptive prose of the Worpswede period. The vastness of the whole no longer swamps the individuality of the parts: on the contrary, it enables them to appear more clearly in their own right. In the introduction to *Worpswede* Rilke says of the plain: 'da ist uns alles bedeutsam: der große Kreis des Horizontes und die wenigen Dinge, die einfach und wichtig vor dem Himmel stehen' (SW, V, 26), and similarly the fifth of the *Worpsweder Skizzen* 'Vom Tode' begins:

> Ganz in den Abend geht der Wasserlauf.
> Das Land liegt flach. Aber an seinem Saum
> steht immer wieder etwas auf,
> wird einfach, still und reimt sich in den Raum:
> ein Haus, ein Baum . . .   (SW, III, 690)

The fourth line here is particularly significant, for it shows Rilke using the painter's vision, seeing the landscape through the eyes of his new artist friends: the 'things' in Worpswede are not totally isolated; for all their individuality they are still part of a greater whole, of a meaningful harmony; each thing 'reimt sich in den Raum'. That it was in large part the painters who taught Rilke to see landscapes in this way is strongly suggested by the recurrence, in various formulations, throughout the *Worpswede* monograph of a theme that is summed up in what he sees as the object of Fritz Overbeck's art: 'Einzelheiten in ihrer ganzen Pracht hinzustellen, ohne dadurch den Gesamtwert aufzuheben' (SW, V, 93) — words that distinctly prefigure the concept of 'Bezug'. In Rilke's eyes the unity in Worpswede that provided the 'Gesamtwert' emanated from some peculiar quality of the light; he saw in the air something that enveloped and harmonized all the isolated parts of the landscape — again distinctly a painter's vision:

Man lernt aber tatsächlich ein Neues hier schauen. Neben Himmel und Landschaft steht ein Drittes mit gleichem Recht: die Luft. Immer schienen die Dinge mir wie Arme und Enden, zusammenhängend mit dem großen Körper der Erde; hier aber gibt es viele Dinge, welche inselhaft sind — allein, hell, allseitig umflossen von der immer bewegten Luft. Das macht ihre Formen so stark.   (T, 266f.)

So it is that, introducing the Worpswede painters, he describes 'wie sie den Bäumen gegenüberstehen und allen den Dingen, die umflutet von der feuchten, tonigen Luft,

wachsen und sich bewegen' (SW, V, 32). Rilke now sees the world through the
painters' eyes to such an extent that he even attributes colours to the air, talking
of 'die eigentümliche farbige Luft dieser hohen Himmel', and even after his
departure for Paris he writes in halting French to Don Ignacio Zuloaga:

C'était près de Brême, en nord de l'Allemagne, dans un territoire de tourbe, où l'air
est très coloré et plein de vie et de vent; il contourne et entoure les chose de toute
la grandeur des cieux énormes et (surtout le soir) il donne aux choses blanches des
nuances, des valeurs, toute une histoire des sentiments et des souvenirs blancs, il
remplit cette couleur de toutes ces richesses et la blancheur est telle, qu'on
dirait un sourire lointain qui se rapproche à travers les siècles.[19]

It was not only the colour of the air that Rilke became aware of in Worpswede;
he also grew more sensitive — though less extravagantly — to the colour properties of
the objects around him. He seems to have been particularly impressed by the way in
which things retained, and even intensified their colours when the sun had gone in.
Here again the training of the eye through his friends' paintings is manifest:

Zuerst sprach ich von den Stimmungen in Worpswede, wie schwer sie sind, wie voll
Traurigkeit; ich sagte, daß besonders eines mich so unheimlich berührte: die
starken Farben, die ohne Sonne, wenn nirgends mehr strahlendes Licht ist,
ausdauern. Das war an den Tagen mit grauem Himmel, der leise regnete: Aber deshalb
war nichts verblichen oder ungewiß geworden, im Gegenteil. Nur noch lauter
wurden alle Farben . . . (T, 249)

This experience found poetic expression in the poem beginning 'Die roten Rosen
waren nie so rot / als an dem Abend, der umregnet war . . . (SW, III, 688), which
immediately follows the above diary entry.

The sad and heavy 'Stimmungen' of Worpswede that Rilke mentions here
characterize most of his landscape descriptions of this period. The overall impression
is one of sombre brown expanses and of dark waterways stretching to the
horizon, and it is hardly surprising that the theme of death is again constantly in
his mind: 'Wenn irgendwo, so muß hier ein Totentanz entstehen (T, 253). But
death too has undergone something of a transformation; true to the rapid
development of his visual imagination Rilke now no longer writes of decay, of
mood-laden cellars and cemeteries as he had in Prague; he sees instead death
personified in the form of one of the strange silent peasants of the fenland:

Tod im Moor. Wie leicht muß es sein, ihm hier zu begegnen. Er muß nicht irgendwie
besonders sein in Kleidung und Gang. Es muß nur ein Mann kommen, dunkel wie
alle, groß, hart in den Schultern mit schweren hängenden Greifhänden. (T, 252)

This man is seen as someone who walks towards one on a narrow path or bridge
in the fen, and carries on even though the path is wide enough only for one
person. To express these ideas in poetry Rilke resorts to a series of *Worpswede
Skizzen* entitled 'Vom Tode' (SW, III, 688ff.) where he captures much of the

sombre *Stimmung* that typifies his impressions of Worpswede.

The importance of the Worpswede interlude in Rilke's development seems, on the whole, to have been underrated, and not least by Rilke himself. He mentions it comparatively rarely in later life, preferring to emphasize the importance of Russia and Paris, and ignoring the vital link between the two that Worpswede constituted. Two weeks after his arrival in Paris he wrote a poem of nostalgia and *Heimweh*, beginning 'Dunkelndes Moor, jetzt bist du tief und weit', and telling of his longing, in the depths of the stale city, for the open spaces again (SW, III, 757); but when he returns to Worpswede a year later he already finds it 'klein, deutsch und voll von Ansiedlungen',[20] and when he returns in 1907 to North Germany he writes:

Comment vous exprimer ce que je ressens, que je souffre et dont je me console depuis que je suis ici dans ce pays lourd; en face de cette plaine noire et verte, qui tristement s'en va dans des brumes. (B, 214; 7 December 1907 to Mimi Romanelli)

The dark marshy landscape practically disappears from Rilke's poetry the moment he leaves for Paris, and hardly ever occurs again in his work. An interesting exception is the trilogy 'Die Insel' of 1906, which, though not about Worpswede, is subtitled 'Nordsee' and describes one of the flat marshy islands of Theodor Storm's country — an unusual setting in Rilke, but possibly a reminiscence from the Worpswede days (see T, 247). What most distinctively links these poems with those of Worpswede is the closing lines of the second one:

Und draußen formt sich eines von den Schafen
ganz groß, fast drohend, auf dem Außendeich. (SW, I, 539)

Here there is a clear recurrence of the motif of the object standing out against the horizon. Indeed, at one point in the 'Schmargendorfer Tagebuch' Rilke describes almost the same scene:

Jeden Augenblick wird etwas in die tonige Luft gehalten, ein Baum, ein Haus, eine Mühle, die sich ganz langsam dreht, ein Mann mit schwarzen Schultern, eine große Kuh, oder eine hartkantige, zackige Ziege, die in den Himmel geht. (T, 242).

Such distinct reminiscences are, however, extremely uncommon after the departure for Paris. In fact Rilke soon dismissed the *Worpswede* monograph as hack-work, as 'Auftrag', merely an onerous publisher's commission, but he did at least acknowledge the importance of the landscape for him at this time: 'blieb nur das Land und was an Größe von ihm ausgeht', and also concluded that even the 'Auftrag' was at least a pretext that enabled him to clarify and organize his environment:

Und dann half mir auch noch, daß der gegebene Vorwand mich zwang, vieler

Dinge Klang zu sein und es kam vieles herbei und ging in den Zeilen mit, was von verwirrten Tagen zurückgedrängt worden war in das Nichtsein des Ungeformten. (B Lou, 76; 1 August 1903)

Rilke's deep interest in the visual arts had already been stimulated in Italy before he came to Worpswede, but it was only when he arrived among the artists of the North German colony that he was able to watch and discuss the creative process itself, and, above all, it was only in Worpswede that he was able to experience for himself both the landscape and its aesthetic transformation. In Florence the landscape of Tuscany had borne little relevance to the long completed paintings that Rilke saw, but here in Germany he learnt to see the world about him through the eyes and the work of the living artists whom he frequented. Certainly there is much of Rilke and often comparatively little of the painters themselves in the *Worpswede* monograph, but undoubtedly he did learn from this contact. The 'Auftrag' was a salutary imposition and a distinctive turning point in his career.

In a sense, the 'home' that Rilke was looking for was, if anywhere, already available in Worpswede, for it was there that he found harmony, the balance of whole and part in the landscape, and an incipient ability to perceive 'Einzelheiten in ihrer ganzen Pracht . . . ohne dadurch den Gesamtwert aufzuheben' — in short the 'Bezug' that he did not again attain until his last years in the Valais. But the swing away from the extreme of Russia towards that of Paris carried him out beyond the integrated mid-point to which he only later returned. In the Worpswede works there is still much of the young Rilke, still an excessive concern with mood; the atmosphere is still rather too strong for the integrity of the objects that it contains, and the movement away from this, coupled with the failure of his marriage, his natural restlessness and the opportunity to visit Rodin and thus further his rapidly developing interest in art all helped to lead him on to Paris and the landscape of 'things'.

Italy

Rilke first visited Italy in the spring of 1897, and his last visit there was in the summer of 1920, when he went back for the first, and only, time after the outbreak of the First World War. Before the War he visited Italy at least fifteen times; some of these visits, which became almost annual after 1906, were little more than interludes on a longer journey, but others were examples of the typical Rilkean attempt at staying in one place and coming to terms with the environment it presented. His encounters with Italy were very varied, both in time and place, for he visited, and usually revisited, most of the important towns and regions of the country during widely differing periods of his development, at different seasons, for different reasons and in the company of different people. It is accordingly more practical to examine individually the influence on him

24

of some of the more important landscapes before considering the role that Italy as a whole played in Rilke's life. Four places were particularly important for him; in roughly chronological order they are: Rome, Capri, Venice, and Duino.[21]

Rome

Rilke made four visits to Rome. The first, which lasted from September 1903 to June 1904, was by far the longest; he passed through the city in 1907, and stayed there briefly again in 1908 and 1910. His impressions of Rome as revealed in the letters written at the time are, in general, notably different from those that the poems on Roman subjects, mostly written somewhat later, appear to suggest. The letters that Rilke wrote during his 1903–4 stay in Rome are, on the whole, despondent and irritated in tone, and reveal this as a singularly unsuccessful encounter with a new environment, surpassed in this respect only by the enforced restriction to Munich during the War years. The poems that the city directly inspired are few in number, and concerned with individual objects rather than with the landscape as a whole, but they are free of the unpleasant aspects of Rome that the letters describe.

When Rilke first arrived in Rome he was immediately uneasy – so much so, in fact, that he spoke of it in terms that, for him, were the ultimate indictment of any new surroundings: it was, he said, a place where 'die Fremde mit der Last der Heimatlosigkeit auf uns lag',[22] a place, in other words, that seemed to offer no points of contact, no hope of communion for the new settler. His complaints amount basically to the fact that he found Rome 'exaggerated' in all possible respects; he saw it as a noisy, showy, overrated place with an intolerable climate. When he arrived it was still summer – 'zu einer Zeit, da es noch das leere, das heiße, das fieberverrufene Rom war' – and he looked forward to withdrawing into the peaceful seclusion of the Villa Strohl-Fern. But even here he could not escape the violence of the Southern climate, for, after a rainy winter, the early spring came in with a force and a luxuriance that he found almost overwhelming:

Auch diese Wiesen voll Anemonen und Gänseblümchen sind zu dicht, zu schwer, zu engmaschig, und es giebt an den Himmeln jene grauen Tage nicht hinter noch leeren Bäumen, jene weiten, verwandelnden Winde und die weich fallenden Regen, die für mich alles Frühlings Tiefe sind. Es ist, ach, ein Frühling für Fremde, die nur wenig Zeit haben, augenfällig und laut und übertrieben.[23]

The weather epitomised the whole city for Rilke, for its exaggeration and vulgarization seemed to exist for the sake of the hard-pressed tourists, and so it was, in his eyes, with the whole of Rome: he talked of

die unlebendige und trübe Museumsstimmung, die es ausatmet . . . die Fülle seiner hervorgeholten und mühsam aufrechterhaltenen Vergangenheiten (von denen eine kleine Gegenwart sich ernährt) . . . die namenlose, von Gelehrten und Philologen unterstützte und von den gewohnheitsmäßigen Italienreisenden nachgeahmte Überschätzung aller dieser entstellten und verdorbenen Dinge, die doch im Grunde nicht mehr sind als zufällige Reste einer anderen Zeit und eines Lebens, das nicht unseres ist und unseres nicht sein soll. (B. j. Dichter, 19; 29 October 1903)

It was thus modern Rome — 'cette ville qui avec la banalité de ses mouvements modernes déforme les contours de son ancienne gloire' (Gebser, *Spanien*, pp. 63f.) — that Rilke found most displeasing, and consequently he turned his attention to those remnants of former ages that he could extract from the tourist-orientated 'Museumsstimmung' that so oppressed him. Here he found and portrayed 'things', individual items in the Roman landscape, and, ever eager to establish organic links with the past, he took a particulat delight in those ancient objects that were still used by the people of Rome: the fountains, the aqueducts, and the water-bearing sarcophagi. In those aspects of Rome that Rilke found pleasant it is notable how important a part is played by water; in its eternal movement and its life-bringing significance it must have been for him a kind of bridge drawing the modern and the ancient city together across the gap in time that he so regretted:

aber es ist viel Schönheit hier, weil überall viel Schönheit ist. Unendlich lebensvolle Wasser gehen über die alten Aquädukte in die große Stadt und tanzen auf den vielen Plätzen über steinernen weißen Schalen und breiten sich aus in weiten, geräumigen Becken und rauschen bei Tag und erheben ihr Rauschen zur Nacht . . . (B, 62f.; 29 October 1903 to Franz Xaver Kappus)

And so it was that he saw even the steps of Rome like cascades of water: 'Treppen, die nach dem Vorbild abwärts gleitender Wasser erbaut sind, — breit im Gefäll Stufe aus Stufe gebärend wie Welle aus Welle' (ibid.).

Rilke was by now well under the influence of Rodin and had developed an eye for 'things'. This alone appears to have saved these ten months in Rome from disaster, for while he found the city as a whole confusing and largely unpleasant, he was able to take refuge among the durable and richly significant objects that he found scattered within it:

man . . . gewinnt sich zurück aus dem anspruchsvollen Vielen, das da spricht und schwätzt (und wie gesprächig ist es!), und lernt langsam die sehr wenigen Dinge erkennen, in denen Ewiges dauert, das man lieben, und Einsames, daran man leise teilnehmen kann. (ibid.)

'Die sehr wenigen Dinge' is very apt, for Rilke wrote very little during his ten-month stay in Rome, and only five poems in later years reveal much trace of the city: three of them — 'Römische Sarkophage', 'Römische Fontäne' and 'Römische Campagna' — are in the *Neue Gedichte*, and two — the 'Sarkophage' sonnet (I/10) and the 'Brunnen-Mund' sonnet (II/15) — are in the *Sonette an Orpheus*. The subject matter is similar in all of them: the ancient monuments — the Appian Way, the sarcophagi and the fountains, fed by the Roman aqueducts — objects that, still very much in

26

use, were not merely 'zufällige Reste einer anderen Zeit', but the scarce evidence of organic continuity and living tradition that Rilke was able to find during a disappointing ten months.

Capri

Rilke stayed twice on Capri: his first visit was during the winter and spring of 1906–7 and the second, shorter, visit was in the spring of 1908. On both occasions, but especially the first, he was deeply impressed by the landscape of the island, and wrote a number of poems that vividly testify to this fact. Rilke's attraction to Capri was by no means immediate, however. It was one of the places that he only gradually came to like, being deterred at first by his characteristic horror of all that smacked of Tourism, especially when it involved German tourists. Even in later years, notwithstanding his affection for the island, he could still talk of the 'capreser Stimmung, geprägt durch die taktlose deutsche Bewunderung und dieses gewisse Weichwerden des deutschen Gemüts unter dem Einfluß landschaftlicher "Schönheit", wie Semmeln im Wasser' (B Lou, 433; 16 January 1920). This totally false appreciation of a place by tourists was something Rilke had also found in Rome and Venice, and he was careful to distinguish it from the 'real' place that he was looking for. Thus he said of the Tessin, where he sensed a similar touristic falsification: 'Es ist überhaupt reichlich "deutsch" da unten, im Sinne des deutschen "Capri" und des deutschen "Rom", so unverschämt epanouiert, wie der Deutsche in gewissen Klimaten sich zu geben wußte, wo er "genoß" ' (B. Nölke, 19; 3 November,1919). At first he found Capri rather 'überfüllt' – spoilt by an excess of both tourist dwellings and mountains[24] and he described it with an arrogant and sarcastic humour paralleled only in his similar rejections of the 'over-beautiful' Swiss Alps:[25]

Ich werde jedesmal recht traurig in solchen Landschaftsausstellungen, vor dieser deutlichen, preisgekrönten, unanfechtbaren Schönheit . . . was soll man in solchen Schönheitskonzerten, wo alles Programmnummer ist und erprobt und beabsichtigt und ausgewählt? Es kann sein, daß man mit diesen Schönheitsbilderbogen anfangen könnte, sehen und lieben zu lernen, aber ich bin ein klein wenig zu fortgeschritten, um davor A und O zu sagen. Das Entzücken-Buchstabieren ist lange hinter mir.

Capri, he concluded, was an 'Unding' (B, 04-07, 209f.; 11 December 1906 to Elizabeth and Karl von der Heydt).

Capri's superabundance of facile 'beauty' was not entirely akin, however, to that which Rilke later found in Switzerland, for it was basically a human creation – 'Nein, was die Menschen hier aus einer schönen Insel gemacht haben, ist nah am Abscheulichen' (ibid.), he complained, – and once his initial antipathy had subsided he was able to discover a Capri very different from that of the 'tourists'. He saw it as a landscape that more than made up for his failure to visit Greece, a landscape more ancient even than that of Greece,[26] and certainly one where there was nothing of the flabby atmosphere of 'Semmeln im Wasser'. The fact that he visited the island in winter and early spring doubtless helped him to avoid seeing too much of the German 'Capri', and what he portrays is in fact a rainy, windy, rugged landscape whose main characteristic is one of hardness, as the first lines of the 'Improvisationen aus dem Capreser Winter' clearly show:

> Täglich stehst du mir steil vor dem Herzen,
> Gebirge, Gestein,
> Wildnis, Un-weg: Gott, in dem ich allein
> steige und falle und irre . . .   (SW, II, 11)

When he writes a description of the vineyards of Capri he does not describe them in the warm sunshine, but begins:

Sprich von den Weinbergen zur Zeit, da an einem windigen Tag (der früh mit Sonne begann, dann aber in einem dünnen Grau sich auflöste) die ersten Arbeiten an ihnen beginnen   (SW, VI, 988)

and goes on to describe the subtle gradations of grey that colour the vineyards in winter. This sombre colouring typifies the Capri poems; they are nearly all concerned with a bleak exposed landscape, and some of the most impressive descriptions are of nocturnal scenes, for Rilke frequently walked at night on the island.[27]

Capri in these poems appears as a particularly grandiose landscape, as an overwhelming environment in which the individual struggles to maintain his identity, to find some sort of meaning for himself amid the threatening magnificence of the world outside. This is the theme of the first of the 'Improvisationen aus dem Capreser Winter', and the second takes it up again in the form of the search for a home, for roots with which the dizzy individual can fasten himself to the monumental indifference of this unified world. Again it is the hard rocks that characterize Rilke's Capri:

> Und hielte es [scil.: mein Herz], soweit ich kann, hinein
> in Wind und Stille; wenn ich nicht mehr kann,
> nimmst du es dann?
> Oh nimm es, pflanz es ein!
> Nein, wirf es nur auf Felsen, auf Granit,
> wohin es fällt; sobald es dir entfallen,
> wird es schon treiben und wird Wurzelkrallen
> einschlagen in das härteste von allen
> Gebirgen, welches sich dem Jahr entzieht.   (SW, II, 14)

Hardly anywhere in Rilke's poetry is the struggle between Self and Non-Self so frequently and so vividly evoked as in these Capri poems. This was at the heart of his experience of the island's winter hillsides and coast, and the image in which it is most frequently expressed is that of the wind — the wind in the form of the force

that links and unites, the 'ewige Strömung' of the First Elegy with its implicit
challenge to Man, who seems excluded from the circuit, the wind that expresses
an ideal of circular self-sufficiency that we fail to attain:

> Von irgendwo bringt dieser neue Wind,
> schwankend vom Tragen namenloser Dinge,
> über das Meer her *was wir sind.*
>
> . . . Wären wirs doch. So wären wir zuhaus.
> (Die Himmel stiegen in uns auf und nieder.)
> Aber mit diesem Wind geht immer wieder
> das Schicksal riesig über uns hinaus.   (SW, II, 16; 'Ein
> Frühlingswind')

The wind is also seen as that which impinges, the force from outside, the Non-Self
against which the Self must fight to maintain its integrity. The wind with this and
all its other significance is the subject of the best-known of these Capri poems,
the 'Lied vom Meer', a work that sums up much that Rilke saw in the island: the
bleak winter night with the eternal wind in concert with the eternal rock in a
totality of being from which Man is excluded, threatening his very existence, and
the fig tree thrashing in the gale — a symbol both of the ecstasy of union and of
the fight for individual survival against this threat from outside:

> Uraltes Wehn vom Meer,
> Meerwind bei Nacht:
> du kommst zu keinem her;
> wenn einer wacht,
> so muß er sehn, wie er
> dich übersteht:
> uraltes Wehn vom Meer,
> welches weht
> nur wie für Ur-Gestein,
> lauter Raum
> reißend von weit herein . . .
> O wie fühlt dich ein
> treibender Feigenbaum
> oben im Mondschein.[28]

The problem of the relation between Self and Non-Self is also examined more
explicitly in the second of the two prose passages entitled 'Erlebnis', which,
although not written down until 1913, describes an experience Rilke had in a
garden on Capri, where, for a moment, the contour of his body no longer seemed to
form a barrier between himself and the outside world; he heard the cry of a bird
both outside and within, 'und es ging das Unendliche von allen Seiten so
vertraulich in ihn über, daß er glauben durfte, das leichte Aufruhn der inzwischen
eingetretenen Sterne in seiner Brust zu fühlen' (SW, VI, 1040–42). The human
figure in a landscape who becomes a kind of symbol for this type of experience is

for Rilke the shepherd, and it is hardly surprising, in view of his preoccupations at the time, that he pictured in similar terms a shepherd whom he saw on Capri:

Dem fließt
der Tag hinein und fließt ihm wieder aus . . .   (SW, II, 19)

Rilke's experiences of Capri left traces that may be discerned in a number of later poems. Although Capri itself is rarely mentioned as such, the basic elements of Rilke's experience of its landscape appear again; the hard and rocky hillsides described in the Capri poems have much in common with the 'Bergen des Herzens' (SW, II, 94), and the alien rocky landscape certainly becomes a more frequent motif after the winter in Capri. The wind, already present in Rilke's poetry, takes on added significance after the experience on Capri of the 'Meerwind bei Nacht' — possibly even the lines: 'O und die Nacht, die Nacht, wenn der Wind voller Weltraum/ uns am Angesicht zehrt' from the First Elegy hark back to the nights on Capri. This was also one of the comparatively few occasions on which Rilke came into daily contact with the sea, and here, as at Viareggio, the poet's experience foreshadows certain elements of Valéry's poetry, with which he later became closely involved. The poems, such as 'Lied vom Meer', that describe meditations on the absolute and individuation in a setting of a windy night above a rocky shore have much immediate resemblance to 'La Jeune Parque', and an even more notable echo of the Capri experience occurs in the lines:

Das weht vom Meer, und in dem Wehen enthalten
ist meine Seele . . .   (Valéry Gedichte, p. 22)

— Rilke's translation, written in 1921, of Valéry's: 'Une fraîcheur, de la mer exhalée, / Me rend mon âme . . . (Valéry p. 151).

Capri certainly supplied Rilke with landscape motifs that he later used, but it was probably more important in his development as a place where, in clear and concrete terms, in the landscape imagery of a real environment, he became more deeply aware of the central importance of the relationship between the Self and the outside world.

Venice

Only one of Rilke's visits to Venice — that of 1912, when he stayed from May to September — lasted more than a month, but the frequency of his stays there (there were ten in all) is considerably higher than that of visits he made to any other place in Italy. Venice was both the first and the last city Rilke ever went to in Italy, for he spent a few days there in 1897, a year before the Tuscan journey, and when, in 1920, he made his single postwar trip to Italy, Venice was the only place he visited.

The experiences that the twenty-one-year-old Rilke had in Venice found poetic expression in the 'Fahrten' section of *Advent*, where four short poems deal with the city (SW, I, 116-18), as do three poems of the same period in the 'Nachlaß' (SW, III, 563f.), and the same setting is given to one of the 'Christus-Visionen' (SW, III, 153-56), also written early in 1897. These poems all reveal a place that for the young Rilke was clearly the decadent environment *par excellence*, for Venice appears here as a city heavy-laden with the atmosphere of a great but decayed past, a silent place of dark canals and drifting gondolas, above all a place steeped in the presence of death. One of the *Advent* poems, describing a gondola journey, has the lines:

> traun: ich bin ein toter Kaiser,
> und sie lenken mich zur Gruft.[29]

— an idea that is repeated in the 'Christus-Vision', where it is closely followed by the sound of a gondolier singing 'Vorrei morir . . .' (SW, III, 153). Venice was obviously an 'easy' city for the decadent young Prague aesthete with his morbid obsession with death, and he certainly seems to have succumbed fully to the temptation to sit back in his gondola and let the superficial *Stimmung* of a *fin-de-siècle* environment drift around him. The remark from the *Florenzer Tagebuch* in which he says 'Florenz erschließt sich nicht wie Venedig dem Vorübergehenden' (T, 25) is an indication of Rilke's totally passive and uninquisitive attitude to the city in these early years, and it is a remark that, in his later descriptions of Venice, he was to disavow totally.

In the later poems and letters dealing with Venice the sense of decay is still sometimes present, but it has been radically refined, the air is no longer heavy with the sweet mood of death, but instead the city appears more as a brilliant exemplification of the containment of transcience, a symbol of what later becomes the joyfully affirmed 'Verwandlung' of the *Sonette an Orpheus*. Venice is thus seen no longer in the heavy-handed images of the first poems, but as a city of intangible subtlety, a place to be approached only with the utmost delicacy:

man nimmt hier nicht wie mit Gefäßen und Händen auf, sondern wie mit Spiegeln, man 'faßt' nichts, man wird nur einbezogen ins Vertrauen seines Entgehens. (B, 622f.; 26 June 1920 to Gräfin M.)

These later Venice poems are concerned almost entirely with visual effects, with the play of light on the buildings and, above all, with the reflections on the constantly changing surface of the water. The city is portrayed as a beautiful woman, bedizened with glittering jewels (SW, I, 526; 'Die Kurtisane'), as an alluring world of nuance that, like the reflections in the waves, is in a perpetual state of dissolution and recreation, a place that every day must come into being anew, yet one that, in its stolidly magnificent palaces and churches, with their knowledge of a deep and glorious past, is assured of eternal existence:

31

Fürstlich verwöhnte Fenster sehen immer,
was manchesmal uns zu bemühen geruht:
die Stadt, die immer wieder, wo ein Schimmer
von Himmel trifft auf ein Gefühl von Flut,

sich bildet ohne irgendwann zu sein.
Ein jeder Morgen muß ihr die Opale
erst zeigen, die sie gestern trug, und Reihn
von Spiegelbildern ziehn aus dem Kanale
und sie erinnern an die andern Male:
dann giebt sie sich erst zu und fällt sich ein

wie eine Nymphe, die den Zeus empfing.
Das Ohrgehäng erklingt an ihrem Ohre;
sie aber hebt San Giorgio Maggiore
und lächelt lässig in das schöne Ding.   (SW, I, 609; 'Venezianischer
                                            Morgen').

This poem shows one side of the mature Rilke's Venice, the female city, glittering and beautiful, a permanent embodiment of fickle transience: this is essentially the summer Venice. In 1907, however, Rilke visited Venice in the late autumn, and the result was a distinctively new vision of the place, which was supremely expressed in the much-analysed poem 'Spätherbst in Venedig':

Nun treibt die Stadt schon nicht mehr wie ein Köder,
der alle aufgetauchten Tage fängt.
Die gläsernen Paläste klingen spröder
an deinen Blick. Und aus den Gärten hängt

der Sommer wie ein Haufen Marionetten
kopfüber, müde, umgebracht.
Aber vom Grund aus alten Waldskeletten
steigt Willen auf: als sollte über Nacht

der General des Meeres die Galeeren
verdoppeln in dem wachen Arsenal,
um schon die nächste Morgenluft zu teeren

mit einer Flotte, welche ruderschlagend
sich drängt und jäh, mit allen Flaggen tagend,
den großen Wind hat, strahlend und fatal.[30]

The autumn Venice now comes to be seen as the 'real' one, and once again, as on Capri, it is the departure of the summer visitors, the tourists, that enables this more genuine manifestation to emerge. Malte Laurids Brigge talks of the tourists in terms that make it clear that Rilke in 1897 had himself been very much a 'tourist', making it all the more likely that Rilke's excessive antipathy to this type of visitor was linked in no small measure to his general embarrassment at, and rejection of, all things appertaining to his youth:

Wie sie, ganz unvorbereitet, keine Gefahr begreifend, von den fast tödlichen

Geständnissen der Musik sich anreizen lassen wie von körperlichen Indiskretionen, so überliefern sie sich, ohne die Existenz Venedigs im geringsten zu bewältigen, der lohnenden Ohnmacht der Gondeln. (SW, VI, 932)

Malte Laurids looks round in despair among a gathering of 'tourists' in Venice, searching for someone who has seen through this false Venice — 'Ein junger Mensch, der es sofort begriff, daß hier nicht ein Genuß aufgeschlagen war, sondern ein Beispiel des Willens, wie es nirgends anfordernder und strenger sich finden ließ' (SW, VI, 933). This hard, active, male Venice is the one he has seen, and the one Rilke portrays in the 'Spätherbst' poem:

Das weiche, opiatische Venedig ihrer Vorurteile und Bedürfnisse verschwindet mit diesen somnolenten Ausländern, und eines Morgens ist das andere da, das wirkliche, wache, bis zum Zerpringen spröde, durchaus nicht erträumte: das mitten im Nichts auf versenkten Wäldern gewollte, erzwungene und endlich so durch und durch vorhandene Venedig. (SW, VI, 932)

Again, there can be little doubt about the relevance of the words 'das weiche, opiatische Venedig ihrer Voruteile und Bedürfnisse' to the experience and poems of the young Rilke. The new autumn Venice is, as in its poem, brittle, 'spröd', in contrast to the soft abandon of the tourists' vision; it is characterized by a distinctively active *will*, the sheer will to *be* with which it has lifted itself up from the sea 'aus alten Waldskeletten', on the 'versenkten Wäldern' of its past, its foundations and its ships 'mitten im Nichts'. The image is, as it were, the masculine equivalent of that in the poem 'Venezianischer Morgen' (quoted above) — the city that every morning recreates itself perpetually from the waters on which it stands. Perhaps the most important attributes of this autumn Venice are contained in Malte's epithets 'wirklich' and 'durch und durch vorhanden', for these are terms that Rilke reserves for the highest stages of existence, for the heightened *Sein* and ultimate reality exemplified in the 'Kunstding'. So it is that from now on he refers to Venice as an 'inkommensurables Wesen',[31] as 'die einzigste (Erscheinung), die alle meine Reisen mir gezeigt haben',[32] he talks of its 'besonders und nicht zu steigernde Existenz',[33] and he compares Venice with a 'Sternbild' (Blume, 'Spätherbst', p. 353) — thus putting the city on a par with Toledo and the Valais, the 'higher' environments, the most intensely experienced and the most meaningful landscapes of his life.

Blume, in his excellent analysis of 'Spätherbst in Venedig', suggests that Rilke saw in Venice, as a result of the 1907 autumn visit, a kind of symbol, an external equivalent for his own life, and this in two main aspects of its existence: on the one hand he was fascinated by its 'Leistung aus dem puren Nichts', the 'Umschlag' by which it created itself out of the lagoons — a parallel to Rilke's own development out of very inauspicious beginnings by means of a determined act of will, the application of Rodin's principle of 'toujours travailler'; and on the other hand he saw

Venice floating precariously on the sea, on the 'Nichts' from which it had emerged
– a symbol of death, of the constant threat of collapse into the horrors of Malte
Laurids Brigge, or even back into the world of Prague (Blume, 'Spätherbst', pp. 353f.).
Blume quotes an unpublished letter of November 1907 that prefigures and
elucidates the ideas underlying 'Spätherbst in Venedig', and that, more than
anything, emphasizes Rilke's concern with the wilful activeness, the hardness and
conquering vitality of Venice, with all that the 'tourists', and he in his youth, had
failed to see – the true Venice:

Es scheint mir seltsam, daß man auf den Einfall kam, diese Stadt zu träumerischen
Stimmungen auszunützen; sie war vollendet und verlassen, und so ließ sie es mit sich
geschehen. Wenn man aber in diesem harten Meerwind durch ihre klingenden Gassen
geht, wenn man das Wasser mit scharfen Rändern die Paläste berühren sieht, die
ganz aus Willen sind, aus Widerstand, aus Erfolg, und wenn man über der Pracht des
Platzes das Arsenal nicht übersieht, das Wälder in Flotten verwandelt hat und die
Last der Flotten in die Flügel eines Siegs; wenn man bedenkt, daß aus dem Mangel
an Blumen Spitzen entstanden sind und aus dem Fehlen von Bergwerken Dinge aus
edelsteingleichem Glas, daß die ganze Welt diesen köstlichen Betrug annahm und ihr
Gold hingab dafür – und daß zur Verwirklichung von alledem nicht einmal die Stelle
vorhanden war, daß der Kontinent für diesen Staat erst gezimmert werden mußte:
dann erschrickt man vor der Fülle von Aktion, die hier zusammengekommen ist, und
man fühlt sie immer noch dasein, auffordernd und beruhigend, immens
verpflichtend . . . [34]

Throughout this passage it is the idea of hardness and activeness that recurs as the
distinctive feature of Venice in such words as 'hart', 'scharf', 'Willen', 'Widerstand',
'Fülle von Aktion', and the activity of Venice, its very existence, is described in
terms that are, significantly, those that Rilke often uses to express the creative
'Arbeit' of the artist, terms such as 'verwandelt' and 'Verwirklichung', and the last
words of the passage show how he sees Venice partly as a consolation, as a
confirmation – 'beruhigend' –, but mainly as a stimulation, an exemplary challenge
– 'auffordernd' and 'immens verpflichtend'. This is the Venice that Rilke had
described in a letter of 11 October 1907 to Clara even before his autumn visit, a
Venice that he saw there as past, the noble state best expressed in the name 'Venezia'
(B, 183). His visit was like a confirmation of all that this past stood for, for he saw
it resurrected in the autumn air, past and present triumphantly fused as Venezia rose
again from the waves.

The 'summer' Venice, the real summer Venice as opposed to that of the 'tourists'
– 'Venise', as Rilke called it in the same letter to Clara –, has, for all the superficial
difference, much in common with that of the winter months. It too seems to
express a paradox, but whereas the paradox of the winter Venice is basically spatial
– the perfect balance of being above and amongst non-being – that of the summer,
the 'female', Venice has more to do with time, with the victorious embodiment of
transience, the balance of permanence and temporality. In a letter of June 1920,

which Mason cites as an admirable example of Rilke's 'way of finding symbols for his own states of feeling in the external world' (*Rilke, Europe*, p. 121), Rilke says of a garden on the Giudecca: 'niemals hab ich das Gefühl des Abschieds so restlos in räumliche Erscheinung umgesetzt gesehen'[35]— words that, though not describing the actual city of Venice, still illustrate very explicitly the mood and the thoughts that occupied him there, the elusive and subtle balance between presence and absence constantly re-enacted in the glittering waves of the 'Venezianischer Morgen', in the contrast of the dark interiors and the gleaming exteriors of Venice's buildings (see SW, I, 610f.; 'San Marco'): in these features of the Venetian landscape Rilke saw transience transmuted, time perfectly captured and expressed in space.

Rilke's many returns to Venice testify to his fascination with the place, as do poems and letters throughout his life. He writes to Clara on 11 October 1907 to tell her how he hears the name 'Venise' wherever he goes in Paris (B, 183); in 1924 he writes in a poem to Pia di Valmarana of his 'cœur *vénitien*' (SW, II, 653) and a few days later, in a letter of 26 February to Alfred Schaer, he talks proudly of his familiarity with Venice that enabled him to direct strangers even among the maze of the 'Calli' (B,860). Rilke's relationship with Venice could almost be described as an obsession; certainly, in terms of landscape, it was the most rewarding and the most meaningful of the places that he visited in Italy. He found in it expressions of ideas that fascinated him all his life, and it was the only major landscape experience that, in its variety of significance, transcended the various stages of his development. In his youth he found there an embodiment of his lassitudinous aestheticism and obsession with death; later, in 'Venezia', he found sturdy, manly proof of the value and meaning of 'Arbeit', whilst at the same time 'Venise' seemed to embody all the concern with evanescence, with nuance and subtle states of being that the *Sonette an Orpheus* ultimately expressed, and in the coexistence of 'Venezia' and 'Venise' he found brilliant evidence of that conquering by the human spirit of the decaying effects of time and place with which the later Elegies are concerned.

Duino

The environment in which the *Duineser Elegien* were conceived apparently made comparatively little impression on Rilke. He stayed in the clifftop castle on the rocky coast overlooking the Gulf of Trieste three times in all: he made a brief visit in 1910 and another in 1914, but his principal stay lasted for over six months during the winter and spring of 1911–12, and it was on this occasion that the first two Elegies, together with fragments of the later ones, were written. The Duino landscape however, does not appear in any poems written during Rilke's stay, nor does it find explicit expression in any later works.

The basic feature of the Duino environment as Rilke portrays it in his letters is the contrast between the inner and the outer worlds, between the enclosure and containment of the castle, and the exposure and emptiness of the sea, the sky and the barren Karst outside. Initially Rilke sees something positive, something inspiring in this situation:

es liegt etwas Endgültiges in dieser Einrichtung, die Nähe sehr nah heranzuziehen, damit die Weite mit sich allein sei. Das Enge bedeutet viel, und das Unendliche wird dadurch eigentümlich rein, frei von Bedeutung, eine pure Tiefe, ein unerschöpflicher Vorrat von seelisch verwendbarem Zwischenraum. (B, 268; 30 August 1910 to Fürstin Marie)

In his early days at Duino he saw the castle as 'ein Vorgebirg menschlichen Daseins' (B294; 25 October 1911 to Hedwig Fischer), as a thick-shelled fruit that contained 'verhältnismäßig viel Fruchtfleisch, in dem es sich ziemlich saftig wohnt', though he qualified his approval with the words: 'wenngleich nicht ohne einige Anpassung und Müh' (B,296; 14 December 1911 to Elsa Bruckmann). The idea of containment, of snugness, of a human fortress underlies all of these early descriptions, and the castle is even described in terms reminiscent of those he had applied to Rodin's sculptures — just as these were their own centres of gravity, so that no line radiated from them without returning, so at Duino

selbst die später vor den steinernen Burgkern vorgerückten Balkone halten mehr zurück als daß sie austreten, die Anziehung der ungeheueren Schloßmasse zieht alle Vorsprünge ein . . .[36]

But Duino was one of the landscapes that Rilke came to like less and less, and by January 1912 the castle was no longer cosy, no longer a fruit, its gravitational force had become oppressive, and the outside world was harsh and barren:

Das Schloß ist ein immenser Körper ohne viel Seele; besessen von der Idee seiner Festigkeit, hält es einen mit seiner nach innen gekehrten Schwerkraft wie einen Gefangenen; es ist eher ein strenger Aufenthalt. An dem steilen Felsen, vom Meer her, klettert ein immergrüner Garten zu ihm hinauf, sonst ist Grünes rar, wir sind im Karst, und die abgehärteten Berge verzichten auf die Verweichlichung einer Vegetation. (B,315; 14 January 1912 to Emil Freiherr von Gebsattel)

Still, however, the solitude, the absolute concentration without the impingement of any outside world, was seen by Rilke as a positive advantage, and his main complaint concerned not the setting, but the climate; the winds, the constantly alternating Scirocco and Bora, which caused him much discomfort (B, 314f.; ibid.). Isolation could certainly foster poetic production, but in general Rilke could not exist happily for long in so negative and indifferent a setting, he needed a situation like that of Muzot, where he could both be alone and at the same time in contact with a sympathetic landscape. He wrote of his failure to feel at home in Duino in a letter to Lou in January 1912, where Duino's political status combines with the landscape to increase his feeling of exclusion:

Schade nur, daß mir die Natur hier fast nichts entgegenbringt, sogar das Meer läßt mich gleichgültig; als ob diese dumme österreichische Mehrsprachigkeit sogar der Landschaft ihren einigen eindeutigen Ausdruck nähme. Es ist kaum zu sagen, wie sehr mir alles Österreichische zuwider ist.[37]

What had originally been seen as an advantage in Duino, the, in Rilke's eyes, unprepossessing landscape, turned out to be its major fault.

This failure to find anything meaningful in the environment of Duino explains largely why the castle and its grounds are not to be found in Rilke's poetry. He saw Duino as something empty, a vacuum waiting to be filled:

Es war eine Einsamkeit von unendlichem Umfang, da auch eigentlich keine Natur da war, auch der Raum über der sehr wenig bewegten Bucht was nur eine negative Form, in der die Winde sich ausgossen, für einen Moment dastehend in der Gestalt ihres Andrangs. (B, 352; 5 June 1912 to Helene von Nostitz)

Yet it is probable that the setting of the writing of the first *Duineser Elegien* is not entirely incidental, especially as Rilke gave the cycle that name despite the fact the the bulk of these poems was written later, mainly at Muzot. Rilke told Marie von Thurn und Taxis how he felt he heard the opening lines of the First Elegy — 'Wer, wenn ich schriee, hörte mich denn aus der Engel Ordnungen?' — in the wind and storm on the cliffs at Duino,[38] and certainly the setting, precisely in its negative features, is appropriate to the anguished sense of isolation and abandonment in an apparently meaningless universe expressed in these early Elegies. The vast and empty setting was a challenge; Rilke saw it in terms of the need to assert the Self and establish a counterweight in his castle walls to the mighty, totally alien Non-Self outside — a conception reminiscent of his attitude to the somewhat similar landscape of winter Capri:

Nun bin ich wirklich seit vorgestern ganz allein in dem alten Gemäuer, draußen das Meer, draußen der Karst, draußen der Regen, vielleicht morgen der Sturm — : nun soll sichs zeigen, was innen ist als Gegengewicht so großer und gründlicher Dinge. (B, 296; 14 December 1911 to Elsa Bruckmann)

His concentration, his withdrawal into himself and the resulting Elegies were the answer to that challenge, but the theme of these poems bears very much the stamp of the challenge, of the inhospitable environment, of Man's need to assert and justify himself in the face of an apparently alien outside world. Rilke did not write the Elegies simply because of the isolation at Duino, he wrote them also about that isolation.

Nearly all the landscapes that Rilke experienced found at least some direct expression in his poetry, they are nearly all described in identifiable terms somewhere in his work. Not so, however, the landscape at Duino. Any assessment of the importance for him of this setting must rest, initially at least, entirely on the letters, for only there is Duino explicitly described. What Duino seems to have done for Rilke was to supply him with a definite experience of certain aspects of the

Self / Non-Self theme; it embodied for him the idea of the Self's total existential isolation — the initial theme of the Elegies; it provided an experience of the 'tamed' environment, of what, in landscape terms, the garden and the park signify, in the form of the Castle, the 'Vorgebirg menschlichen Daseins', the little fortress of human containment and control in the midst of a-human exposure; furthermore this feeling of containment, of being very distinctly 'inside' was undoubtedly both an expression of and a stimulus to the womb-motif that culminates in the Eighth Elegy and its assertion 'denn Schooß ist alles'. These ideas, already present in Rilke, were clarified and intensified by the experience of Duino, but their expression takes on forms other than that of the Duino landscape.

Italy — Conclusion

Rilke's visits to Italy naturally took him to places other than the four centres already discussed, even if only in transit. The most important of these was Tuscany, which he visited four times between 1898 and 1908. His first stay there, in the spring of 1898, which he spent in Florence and Viareggio, is reflected in the prose and verse of the first of his diaries, the *Florenzer Tagebuch*. This was the first major visit that Rilke made to a non German-speaking country, and he was still very much the young neo-Romantic aesthete of the Prague years, a 'Schönheitssucher' (T, 12; Introduction) who turned his attention almost exclusively to the artistic treasures of Florence, and largely ignored the landscape of the city itself. The importance of Florence in Rilke's development lay in the fact that here he came into contact with vast collections of the visual arts; his latent interest was enormously stimulated, and the way was opened for his later, more fruitful encounters with the Worpswede school, with Rodin and Cézanne. The other location of Rilke's visits to Tuscany — Viareggio — was by contrast experienced almost entirely as a landscape, but it had little discernible effect on him. It appears only in the few minor early poems that have the, for Rilke, unusual setting of pinewoods by the sea, and it was a major inspiration for *Die weiße Fürstin* and the *Lieder der Mädchen* (both of these minor works were written during his first stay there), but little else shows evidence of this setting. Viareggio was essentially a retreat, an easy, relaxing environment, and certainly not one of Rilke's major landscapes.

In effect, only two other areas of Italy are discernible in Rilke's poetry: South Tyrol, especially the district around Arco, which Rilke visited on a number of occasions in his youth, and which is described in four of the *Advent* poems of 1897,[39] and which also provides the setting for a few early stories — all quite insignificant early works; and Naples. That no mention is made in the poetry of the imposing site of Naples is surprising, for Rilke's visits to the city were second in frequency only to those he made to Venice. One can only assume that its significance was overshadowed by that of Capri, to which it served as port of

38

embarcation. Certainly Rilke was not averse to Naples: he described enthusiastically its vivid and subtle colours in a letter to Clara of 2 December 1906 (B 04-07, 198ff.), whilst on 10 January 1912 he wrote from Duino: 'Ich sehne mich nach Neapel' (B, 311; to Lou Andreas-Salomé); the *Neue Gedichte* too contain poems evoking brilliantly the vitality and bustle of the streets, the wealth of 'things' in the shops and stalls,[41] but these do not amount to an overall impression, a consolidated landscape experience.

Looked at as a whole Rilke's encounters with the various landscapes of Italy do not seem to have a great deal in common, nor are their effects on his work, either individually or in sum, anything like as demonstrably important as were those of some other countries — in particular France, Spain and Switzerland. His first visits to Italy were subjective to such an extent that the setting was almost incidental — 'ses poèmes d'Italie . . . ne se distinguent en rien des autres, tant le poète a cessé d'individualiser les choses pour ne voir rien en elles que le reflet de sa nostalgie', as Angelloz says of the early work (p. 75). The young Rilke saw Florence and Venice in very much the terms in which he saw Prague, and in a way this was the pattern that his later visions of Italy were to follow. Certainly he soon became more realistic, more active in his experience and much more objective, but still the landscapes of Italy did not provide him with anything radically new; instead they tended more to confirm — and sometimes disappoint — him in ideas, feelings, attitudes that he already possessed. The basic theme of his life and work, the problem of Self and Non-Self, was experienced, and perhaps clarified, on Capri and at Duino, but it had arisen much earlier; in Rome and in Naples he looked at 'things', but in fact found very few, and this too was an attitude he had already learnt in Paris. Only Venice, the most outstanding of his Italian landscape experiences, showed him things that he already vaguely knew in so striking a manner that what he gained there could really be called 'original'.

Rilke was aware of the great variety in landscape and experience that Italy had offered him, and he rarely mentioned the country as such, preferring to talk separately of its constituent parts. Thus when, on 17 March 1926, he wrote about the influences on his life, he said of Italy that it had become for him almost a symbol of the many-sidedness of his wandering life: 'es war in seiner deutlichen Vielfalt und Formfülle, sozusagen, die Fibel meines beweglichen Daseins (B, 929; to 'eine junge Freundin'). When he does mention Italy, it is usually in very elementary sensuous terms of light and warmth — he was particularly fond of the idea of placing his hands on a warm garden wall, an action that he frequently mentioned in order to describe the attraction that Italy had for him.[42] Or alternatively and much more rarely, he would unjustly judge the whole country by what was manifestly a local experience, as during the unfortunate Rome months of 1903 to 1904 when he complained of the harshness and forcefulness of outlines in Italy:

jedenfalls, haben nördlichere und ernstere Länder meine Sinne seither zu Leisem und Einfachem erzogen, so daß sie jetzt das Grelle und Starke, Schematische und Unabgewandelte italienischer Dinge wie einen Rückfall in den Bilderbogen-Unterricht empfinden . . . Und die Himmel, in denen so billige Farbenspiele vor sich gehen, sind seicht und wie versandet; sie sind nicht überall, sie spielen nicht, wie die Himmel des Moores, des Meeres und der Ebenen, um die Dinge, sind nicht unendlicher Anfang von Weiten, sind Abschluß, Vorhang, Ende, – und hinter den letzten Bäumen, die flach wie Kulissen auf diesem gleichgültigen Fotografen-Hintergrund stehen, – hört alles auf.

And then, after further complaints at the excesses and extravagances of Italy and its climate, he comes to the peremptory conclusion:

Es ist gut, daß ich das alles so langsam und leibhaft erfahren habe; denn Italien war immer noch ein Ruf für mich gewesen und eine unabgeschlossene Episode. Nun aber kann ich es getrost verlassen, denn der Abschluß ist da.   (B Lou, 153ff.; 12 May 1904)

Sentiments such as these are clearly more the result of Rilke's temporary inability to adjust himself to the environment of Rome, and are belied by his experience on later visits to Italy. Nonetheless there is perhaps an indication here of something that, even at the best of times, prevented him from establishing a full, sympathetic and rewarding contact with the Italian landscapes. Underlying nearly all Rilke's contacts with Italy there seems to be a certain antipathy; usually it is hidden, but at times, as in this letter, it breaks through and becomes manifest, revealing itself as a dislike of what he sees as a characteristically Italian extravagance, a tendency to extremes, to gaudiness and vulgar show unsympathetic to his sensitive and introverted nature. In later years he no longer yearned so much for 'die Himmel des Moores, des Meeres und der Ebenen', and became more appreciative of harsher Southern landscapes, but the antipathy seems to have survived in vestigial form at least, dogging him like the intolerable heat and the tourists – expressions of all that he disliked in Italy – that both crop up time and again in his letters from that country. Rilke never rejected Italy – far from it, he was obviously deeply and sincerely attached to it, but in the Italian landscapes he never found a 'Heimat', nor did he find quite the uniquely significant experiences that other countries supplied.

Paris
    Inasmuch as it was the place to which he repeatedly returned, and where he deposited what little he had in the way of property, Paris was, in the years from 1902 to 1914, Rilke's 'home'. A better word would probably be 'base', for his five stays there during the pre-War years were repeatedly interrupted by lengthy journeys not only to other parts of France, but also to Germany, Italy, Austria (i.e. Czechoslovakia), North Africa and Egypt. The War prevented Rilke's return to

France, and he did not visit Paris again until 1920, when he stayed very briefly, making his last visit to the city from January to August in 1925, by which time Switzerland had become not only his 'base', but also quite decidedly his 'home'.

Rilke's experience of Paris was of immense significance to him, and the greater part of his work is inconceivable without it. This experience had two main aspects: his initial encounter with Paris was primarily a landscape experience in which Paris became the archetypal big-city with all its horror and misery, a setting with which he came to grips in *Malte Laurids Brigge*; this landscape aspect continued to play an important part in Rilke's experience of Paris, with the horrors tending to give way to a more appreciative vision, but it was soon to be joined, and in many ways superseded, by the second aspect of his encounter with the city — by the fact that Paris was the place where Rilke came into contact with French culture. It was here that he mastered the French language and began to study French literature; it was here that he encountered the paintings of Cézanne; above all, it was in Paris that he became acquainted with Rodin and his work. This encounter with French culture does not immediately concern us here, but its importance must be stressed from the outset. It is the aspect of Rilke's experience of Paris that has been most widely documented and commented on, and it has often been noted that Paris and France were to Rilke what Italy had been to many Germans before. Wocke, for instance, notes in his study 'Rilke und Italien':

was anderen Deutschen . . . der Süden und Rom für ein Leben wurden, das waren und blieben für Rilke Paris und die französische Kultur. In seiner Beziehung zu Frankreich offenbart sich die seiner Art gemäße Auseinandersetzung mit der lateinischen Welt. (p. 70)

The two aspects of the Paris experience, the landscape and the cultural, are obviously not neatly separable — Rilke's developing vision of Paris as a city was very much tied up with the outlook he gained from his contact with French culture —, but there are still many occasions on which he talks quite explicitly about the physical environment as such.

Rilke's attitude to the landscape of Paris varied enormously, for the overall development from dislike to approval was by no means even, and violent fluctuations are sometimes discernible almost from day to day. There is a certain amount of truth in Blume's contention ('Stadt', pp. 138f.) that these alternations of repulsion and attraction often corresponded respectively with Rilke's presence in or absence from Paris, but only to the extent that it is the case with nearly all of Rilke's landscape experiences that he tended to think more positively of a place when he was not actually there. He rarely complained about Paris when he was away from it, whereas he often did so when he was in the city, but it still remains true that his letters from Paris more often than not speak positively of his environment.

Rilke's first visit to Paris was marked by expressions of horror and claustrophobia – hardly surprising for one who had come straight from the lonely fens of Worpswede, the 'Moor' that he remembered with longing from the depths of the city:

> Da denk ich dich inmitten dieser Stadt
> und atme Atem; denn nur Atem steht
> in ihren Gassen, und der Himmel hat
> die Luft zu sich genommen: wehe weht
> sie um die ersten Sterne, schrecklich fern.
> Wohin ist diese volle Stadt gefallen?
> Abgrund ist hier, nie ausgetaucht und tiefer
> als Meeresgrund; da lieg ich nun mit Allen,
> lastend wie sie, ein Stück von ihrer Schwere.   (SW, III, 757)

The stale, crowded streets, the feeling of having fallen through to the very bottom of existence, confusion and desperate hopelessness, combined with memories of an open Northern landscape – these elements of this poem already prefigure the themes of *Malte Laurids Brigge*, which Rilke began writing one and a half years later in Rome. The first main result of this visit to Paris was, however, the third section of the *Stunden-Buch*, the *Buch von der Armut und vom Tode*, which portrays the miserable existence of the poor people of Paris. The subject-matter of these poems is not entirely new in Rilke, for they have a certain amount in common with the 'Naturalistic' poems of the Prague years, the descriptions of the working-class suburbs in such works as 'Hinter Smichov' (SW, I, 46f.), but the feeling in the Paris poems has become much more intense, the sympathy much more genuine. A new theme also appears in the Paris poems, one that had not been associated with Prague – the theme of inauthenticity, of falseness and superficiality:

> Die großen Städte sind nicht wahr; sie täuschen
> den Tag, die Nacht, die Tiere und das Kind;
> ihr Schweigen lügt, sie lügen mit Geräuschen
> und mit den Dingen, welche willig sind.   (SW, I, 352)

This idea is not only taken up again in *Malte Laurids Brigge*, but it remains with Rilke for the rest of his life as a basic lament at the state of the modern world. This image of the city as the epitome of all that is wrong with the present day occurs again in the *Duineser Elegien* in the form of the falsely bedizened 'Platz in Paris' of the Fifth (SW, I, 704), and, most prominently, in the vulgar 'Leidstadt' and 'Jahrmarkt' of the Tenth. Later, after Rilke had come to like Paris, the blame, as in the Hulewicz-Brief (postmarked 13 November 1925; B, 898f.) with its complaints about 'Schein-Dinge' and 'Lebens-Attrappen', was transferred to America, and on 30 December 1913 he wrote: 'Je n'aime plus Paris . . . parce qu'il se déforme, s'américanise' (to Contesse Pia de Valmarana; B428). The complaint occurs again in 1925, when the blame is placed even more clearly on America, and Paris is seen as possessing sufficient individuality to resist in some measure the anonymising forces of superficiality and falsity:

selbst Paris . . . tut so vieles, wenn auch nur äußerlich, den Amerikanern zulieb, daß es eben schon Paris sein muß, um nicht irgendeine riesige Stadt zu werden, aus der man sich fortwünscht. (B Sizzo, 73; 12 November 1925)

Superficiality and falsity are accusations of a fairly generalized nature. Rilke's more immediate and personal complaints are those of heaviness and confusion. Paris was not so obviously unified and harmonious as the plains of Russia or Worpswede; it presented instead an overwhelming chaotic man-made jungle of streets, buildings, people and noise; a mass, in other words, of essentially disparate impressions, a place where things had fallen apart and no longer maintained a meaningful relationship with one another, but instead, like the self-assertive, ill-fitting tin lid of *Malte Laurids Brigge* (SW, VI, 871ff.) existed in a state of disintegrated 'Zerstreuung'. This is the essence of Malte's Paris, and these were still the features that finally disturbed the latter part of Rilke's 1925 visit; his indisposition, as he suggests, was doubtless partly responsible for the confused impressions, but the description is too much like the complaints of the earlier years to be fully attributable to this cause:

Jedenfalls wars dieser dumme unzuverläßige Zustand meiner sonst so leicht freudigen und zustimmigen Natur, der mir Paris mehr zu einer Konfusion, zu einem Zuviel hat anwachsen lassen; und ich blieb am Ende nur, um's doch noch zu einiger Beherrschung der ungeordneten Überfülle zu bringen, zu einer Übersicht. Umsonst am Ende: was ich mitgebracht habe, ist ein dicker Erinnerungsknäuel, der sich, sooft ich ihn bei einem Fadenende zur Rede stelle, nur noch wirrer und trotziger zusammenzieht. (B Taxis, 836f.; 18 September 1925)

This was the Paris that, in 1913,[43] Rilke had called 'ein Ort der Verdammnis', and, even more significantly, quite simply 'schwer'.

The idea of the 'schwere Stadt' is fundamental to Malte / Rilke's Paris. The city was 'schwer' both in the sense of 'heavy', of debilitating oppressiveness, and in the sense of 'difficult'. In this latter sense the importance for Rilke of the unpleasant aspects of the Paris environment becomes apparent. Paris was the first landscape that he conceived of as a 'task', as the 'Auftrag' of the First Elegy, and this because it was 'difficult'. In Paris the unpleasant aspects of the environment were so prominent that they could not be ignored: 'Die Stadt war wider mich, aufgelehnt gegen mein Leben und wie eine Prüfung, die ich nicht bestand' (B Lou, 46; 30 June 1903). This was for the first time in Rilke's life a challenging landscape, an alien setting that, by no stretch of the imagination, could be seen to conform comfortably to the poet's vision in the manner of Prague, Russia and Worpswede, or of the first encounters with Venice and Florence. Rilke could no longer maintain a passive attitude to his surroundings, he had to learn to control them, and to do this he had to change himself. This was why Paris was 'schwer', it demanded 'Beherrschung der ungeordneten Überfülle', it demanded that the poet's vision change from passive subjectivity to a more active objectivity.

It was from Rodin that Rilke learnt the new, and alien, attitude demanded by Paris, and he acknowledged the importance of this vital acquaintanceship all his life:

daß ich mir diese aus Vollzähligkeit unzugängliche Multiplizität, diesen summenden Schwarm, nirgends hätte zuwenden können, wenn ich ihn nicht erst über Rodin ganz vergessen hätte. An ihm, an seinem lebhaften Werk, draußen auf dem ländlich freien Hügel oberhalb Sèvres wohnend, gewöhnte ich mich an das inkommensurable Wesen, mit dem er so verschieden zusammengekommen war; er brachte es, teilweise gezähmt, dicht an mich heran.　(B336; 13 February 1912 to Norbert von Hellingrath)

'Taming', ordering the chaos of the environment, giving meaning to the otherwise meaningless multiplicity of objects: this is the lesson that Rilke learnt from Rodin and his heightened, essentialized 'Dinge', the lesson that Rilke applied in the *Neue Gedichte*, the 'Dinggedichte' that epitomize the poetry of the main Paris years. Many of them have as their subject scenes — people, places and animals — observed by Rilke in Paris, and are subtitled 'Paris'. They represent attempts at approaching the environment objectively, actively delineating and depicting a single phenomenon, creating eternal 'Kunstdinge' out of the manifold unstable confusion of objects in the Paris landscape, something that is 'von allem Zufall fortgenommen, jeder Unklarheit entrückt',[44] an 'Insel, überall abgelöst von dem Kontinent des Ungewissen' (SW, V, 217). Thus Rilke sought to 'tame' Paris in the *Neue Gedichte* in portrayals of its crowds ('Die Gruppe'), its traffic ('Der Marmor-Karren'), its mysterious and sinister old women ('Eine von den Alten'), its old and infirm ('Der Blinde', 'Pont du Carrousel'), its noisy fairs ('Das Karussell'), its zoological gardens ('Papageien-Park', 'Die Flamingos', 'Der Panther', 'Die Gazelle').

These attempts at coming to terms with an initially hostile world, at finding something positive in the outwardly negative, represent the beginnings of what was to become a dominating theme in later years: the 'Umwertung' by which, in the Elegies, conventionally negative aspects of existence such as transience, sorrow, death, unrequited love are affirmed as being in fact the most genuine, the most positive assets we possess. Thus in 1903 he was already noting the strange affinities between beauty and ugliness in Paris: 'in Paris . . . griff alles Häßliche und Schwere mich wie Schönes an' (B02-06, 52; 17 October, 1902 to Arthur Holitscher). This attitude to the world was one that Rilke observed in Rodin, formulating it in the words: 'Der Schaffende aber hat nicht das Recht, zu wählen' in the 1907 Rodin monograph (SW, V, 217), but the artist who brought home to Rilke most forcefully the hidden beauties of the 'ugly' face of the Parisian landscape was undoubtedly Baudelaire.[45] Rilke was intrigued by the significance of the poem 'Une Charogne',[46] in which Baudelaire creates a strange new beauty out of the unpromising subject of a putrefying corpse, and there are clearly many points of contact between the

Parisian scenes of *Les Fleurs du Mal* and those of the *Neue Gedichte* and *Malte Laurids Brigge*. One passage in particular in the latter work — the famous description of the wall of a demolished house (SW, VI, 749ff.) — is a perfect example of the approach that Rilke associated with Baudelaire and 'Une Charogne'.

Rilke learned to see, to tame and to capture Paris not only with the help of the sculptor Rodin and the poet Baudelaire, but also through the paintings of Cézanne, which he studied with intense and perspicacious enthusiasm day after day during their exhibition at the Salon d'Automne in October 1907. Rilke linked Cézanne in many ways with Baudelaire — that the painter knew by heart the poem 'Une Charogne' impressed him deeply[47] — but the visits to the exhibition were, as the 'Cézanne-Briefe' of the period indicate, an important element in their own right in Rilke's development; indeed, in a letter of 26 February 1924 he talked of the artist's work as 'das stärkste Vorbild' (B, 860; to Alfred Schaer). In Cézanne Rilke found not only confirmation of Rodin's doctrine 'toujours travailler' and of Baudelaire's 'Bewältigung des Häßlichen', but he also learnt to see more clearly the colours and forms in the Parisian landscape, and, above all, their relation to one another. It was a visual schooling akin to that which he received among the Worpswede painters, but its nature was distinctly different, for now Rilke had learnt from Rodin to see the parts, the 'things' in all their isolated individuality, and the harmony of the scene was no longer there in the all-embracing brown Worpswede air, but instead it was a harmony of relationships, of 'Zusammenhänge', of the pure balance of the integral parts. This vision of Cézanne's must have helped Rilke immensely in his appreciation of the Spanish landscape, but meanwhile he was already applying it to Paris, as is revealed by the following passage from a letter of 12 October to Clara, written during the 1907 Exhibition, and later incorporated in a slightly revised form in *Malte Laurids Brigge*:

Da sind die Tage, wo alles um einen ist, licht, leicht, kaum angedeutet in der hellen Luft und doch deutlich; das Nächste schon hat die Töne der Ferne, ist weggenommen und nur *gezeigt*, nicht wie sonst hingestellt, und was Beziehung zur Weite hat: der Fluß, die Brücken, die langen Straßen und die verschwenderischen Plätze, das hat diese Weite zu sich genommen, hält sie an sich, ist auf ihr gemalt, wie auf Seide. Du fühlst, was dann ein lichtgrüner Wagen sein kann auf dem Pont Neuf oder irgendein Rot, das sich nicht halten kann, oder ein Plakat einfach an der Feuermauer einer perlgrauen Häusergruppe. Alles ist vereinfacht, auf einige richtige helle Plans gebracht, wie das Gesicht in einem Manetschen Bildnis. Und nichts ist gering und überflüssig. Die Bouquinisten am Kai tun ihre Kästen auf, und das frische oder welke Gelb der Bücher, das violette Braun der Bände, das Grün einer Mappe: alles stimmt, gilt, nimmt teil und tönt in der Einheit der hellen Zusammenhänge.   (B, 184f. Cf. SW, VI, 722f.)

In the *Malte Laurids Brigge* version this passage finished with the words 'alles stimmt, gilt, nimmt teil und bildet eine Vollzähligkeit, in der nichts fehlt' — similar in meaning to the original, but significant in the word 'Vollzähligkeit', for this is the term Rilke uses to describe the unity in multiplicity of the 'tamed' Paris; 'Vollzähligkeit' is the result of the artist's 'Beherrschung der ungeordneten Überfülle', an ideal in which nothing of the variety of the Paris landscape is lost, but in which a new harmonious whole is established out of the disparate chaos of superficial impressions. Thus in a letter of 31 December 1920 Rilke describes his joy at reestablishing contact with an unchanged Paris after the War, and twice it is the word 'Vollzähligkeit', the ideal he had learnt from Cézanne, that he uses to express his delight:

Und diese Straßen: oh sie waren nicht weniger geworden, nichts war unterdrückt, vermindert, entstellt oder auswählig geordnet –: sie besaßen ihre alte Vollzähligkeit, ihr Strömen, ihr ununterbrochenes Geschehen, ihre an allen Stellen spielende nirgends versagende Erfindung . . . es war das maltesche Paris in seiner ganzen Vollzähligkeit.   (B Lou, 440f.)

Apart from the more 'difficult' aspects of Paris – those that had to be transformed by an act of will on the part of the artist – there were others that Rilke found more immediately amenable and already pleasant. These features of the landscape are nearly always connected with the idea of openness, of wide, free vistas in boulevards, squares and parks, and represent the opposite of the constricting and oppressive environments described in some of the earlier poems and in *Malte Laurids Brigge*. in 1922 he even compares the light and atmosphere of Paris to that of the Valais, and continues: 'Entferntere Flächen, – wie oft bewunderte ich das in Paris, mitten in der Stadt, in der rue de Varenne, wie oft!' (B, Sizzo, 28; 15 July 1922). In these later years he often saw Paris as a remarkably rural landscape, a 'längst Natur gewordene Stadt',[48] and talked of it as 'dieser einzigen Stadt, die den Frühling nicht unterdrückt, sondern ihn wie in lauter lichten Spielgeln auffängt und vertausendfältigt';[49] above all it was the great wide Parisian sky that was responsible for this:

selbst das innerste Paris ist Landschaft und hat nicht einen Stadthimmel über sich (einen Himmel-Ersatz) sondern die herrlichen Himmel der Welt, die freiesten, offensten Himmel, die Himmel des Heiligen Ludwig und der Jeanne d'Arc, lebhaft, teilnehmend und süß im Licht, wach im Wind, inspirierte Himmel, Himmel des Ruhms und der Erinnerung, Sieges-Himmel, auf die sich keine andere Stadt berufen kann.   (B, 893f.; 12 November 1925 to Gräfin Margot Sizzo-Noris-Crouy).

This delight in the skies of Paris had stayed with Rilke most of his life, for eighteen years earlier he had declared similarly in a letter of 13 June 1906 to Clara: 'wie weit sie sind, wie viele Himmel da sind über dieser Stadt (alle, möchte man sagen)' (B, 162). One feature in particular in the Parisian landscape found a special place in Rilke's affection, and that was the Luxembourg Gardens. He talked of the 'unversehens stattlich gewordenen Bäumen meines vertrauten und immer noch und immer wieder wunderbaren Luxembourg' (B Verleger, 483; 7 May 1925); he called them 'unerschöpflich' (B, 894; 12 November 1925 to Gräfin Margot Sizzo-Noris-Crouy), and delighted in their 'rhythmic landscape' (von Salis, p. 203).
    These affirmative references to the open spaces of Paris and the skies above them

indicate that Rilke's distinctive love-hate attitude to the city was in no small measure tied to geographical factors: he reacted differently to different features of the landscape rather than to Paris as a whole. Rilke never came to appreciate the confined spaces of Paris,[50] the scenes of his earlier 'Ängste', in the way that he did the wide *Avenues*, the *Places*, and, above all, the parks — those features that, in other words, were least oppressively urban. Paris remained a city of two distinct faces, a city that intensified both good and bad:

Paris, das die Sichtbarkeit alles Erlebbaren steigert und Himmel und Höllen beschwört, wo ein anderes Milieu nur eben Annehmliches und Lästiges zu bieten hat; (B, 658f.; 3 February 1921 to Rudolf Zimmermann)

but this very intensification made of Paris that ideal of Rilke's, the meeting place of life and death: 'die einzige Stadt, die eine Landschaft des Lebens und Todes werden konnte unter der unerschöpflichen Zustimmung ihrer großmütigen und leichten Himmel[51] — a distinction that Paris thus shared with the ecstatically experienced 'Stadt Himmels und der Erden' Toledo.

But the Paris of death, Malte's Paris, the 'ugly', 'difficult' Paris demanded an active response; it had to be dominated, accepted, affirmed and transformed into art, just as death itself had to be accepted and affirmed:

Und über das gründliche Miterlebnis des Todes: verhält es sich damit nicht, wie mit dem Häßlichen in der Kunst, das eben durch die Bewältigung zur Kunst schuldlos wird? (B, 505; 11 September 1915 to Ilse Erdmann)

The home that Rilke sought after the War was a landscape that did not demand such an active response, but his search bore very distinctly the marks of the Paris experience; the attitude of passive surrender to the environment was no longer possible, instead he looked for, and in the Valais found, a place where the tension and balance, the sharp outlines and distinctive patterns of his vision of Paris were present, but where they did not have to be maintained in a constant struggle against the ever-present forces of 'Angst', somewhere he could relax in the assurance that the 'Bezug' of the landscape did not depend on his own alertness. It is not surprising that when Rilke did return to Paris in the 'twenties he delighted more than at any other time in the landscape of the Luxembourg Gardens.

Paris taught Rilke the active vision; it was, as he observed in the last year of his life, the 'Basis für mein Gestaltenwollen',[52] the place where he learnt delineation — 'Gestalten', and self-assertive activeness — 'Wollen'. Its essentially alien and hostile landscape threatened him to the extent that he was forced to master it in order to survive, and from Rodin, together with Baudelaire and Cézanne, he learnt the technique of mastery, of 'Beherrschung der ungeordneten Überfülle', of aesthetic transformation, to such an extent that 'seeing' in Paris became for him virtually a creative act: 'wie sehr ist anderswo Sehen und Arbeiten verschieden; Du siehst und denkst: später —. Hier ist es fast dasselbe' (B04-07, 322;

3 June 1907 to Clara). He learnt to see and 'say' the 'things' in his environment, the parts that demanded affirmation if the whole were to become meaningful, and thus from the ugliness of the landscape he learnt to affirm rather than reject the superficially negative aspects of experience — death, sorrow, transience, unrequited love. At the same time, in the works of Rodin, and even more in those of Cézanne he came to appreciate the importance of that balance of part and part, and of part and whole, that he later called 'Bezug'.

Spain

Rilke's single visit to Spain was during the winter of 1912/13. The two main stations on this journey were Toledo, which he visited first, remaining there for a month, and Ronda, where he stayed for just over two months. He also stayed a few days in Cordoba, Seville and Madrid. His experience of the Spanish landscape, and in particular of Toledo, was in many ways the most vivid and the most ecstatic of his life. He described Spain in a letter of 17 March 1926 as the 'bedeutendstes Ereignis nach Rußland und dem unerschöpflichen Paris' (B, 930; to 'eine junge Freundin'), comparing it thus with the two landscapes that, over a much longer period, had expressed and formed the first two major stages in his development. The depth of the Spanish impressions is all the more noteworthy for the fact that Rilke was at this time suffering from a bout of his peculiar nervous indisposition that, apart from causing him headaches, also seemed to dull his receptivity to impressions from without, and that he accordingly described as 'Stumpfheit' (B, 386; 19 December 1912 to Lou Andreas-Salomé).

Rilke arrived in Toledo on 2 November 1912, and his enthusiasm was immediate. No other landscape, with the exception of the Valais, seems to have inspired in Rilke such an affirmative response from the very first moment. He wrote that same day to the Fürstin Marie von Thurn und Taxis-Hohenlohe:

Sagen können, wie es hier ist, werd ich ja nie, liebe Freundin (da ist Sprache der Engel, wie sie sich unter den Menschen helfen), aber daß es ist, daß es *ist*, das müssen Sie mir aufs Geratewohl glauben. Man kann es niemandem beschreiben, es ist voll Gesetz, ja, ich begreife augenblicklich die Legende, daß Gott, da er am vierten Schöpfungstag die Sonne nahm und stellte, sie genau über Toledo einrichtete: so sehr sternisch ist die Art dieses ungemeinen Anwesens gemeint, so hinaus, so in den Raum —, ich bin schon überall herumgekommen, hab mir alles eingeprägt, als sollt ichs morgen für immer wissen, die Brücken, beide Brücken, diesen Fluß und, über ihn hinüber verlegt, diese offene Menge der Landschaft, übersehbar wie etwas, woran noch gearbeitet wird.   (B, 365)

Toledo was clearly seen by Rilke as existing in some higher state — the emphatic '*ist*' in this letter is already an indication of this fact, for it is a term that he reserves for the higher, intensified, more genuine being of the ideal realm, the realm of the angels, the realm that is attained through aesthetic transformation, through the

artist's 'sagen', 'preisen' and 'rühmen'. It is a term that becomes increasingly a part
of Rilke's vocabulary — it occurs several times in the Elegies —, but he had already
formulated it in 1903 after his first encounter with Rodin when he used the
emphatic form of 'sein' to define the 'Kunst-Ding':

Das Ding ist bestimmt, das Kunst-Ding muß noch bestimmter sein; von allem
Zufall fortgenommen, jeder Unklarheit entrückt, der Zeit enthoben und dem Raum
gegeben, ist es dauernd geworden, fähig zur Ewigkeit. Das Modell *scheint*, das
Kunst-Ding *ist*. So ist das eine der namenlose Fortschritt über das andere hinaus, die
stille und steigende Verwirklichung des Wunsches, zu sein, der von allem in der
Natur ausgeht. (B, 58; 8 August 1903 to Lou Andreas-Salomé)

This heightened, more genuine being is, then, the state of Toledo; it is
'überlebensgroß', 'außerordentlich', 'unvergleichlich', it is 'eine Stadt Himmels und
der Erden', a place that achieves the Rilkean ideal not only of the union of life and
death, but even links these with the realm of the Angels, for it is 'in gleichem
Maße für die Augen der Verstorbenen, der Lebenden und der Engel da' (B, 368f.; 13
November 1912 to Fürstin Marie). The adjectives 'pur' (ibid.) and 'rein' (B, 380; 17
December 1912 to the same) with which Rilke describes the Spanish mountains are
equally attributes of the higher realm of '*sein*'. He saw Toledo also as an elemental
landscape, a moving landscape in the process of creation:

Diese unvergleichliche Stadt hat Mühe, die aride, unverminderte, ununterworfene
Landschaft, den Berg, den puren Berg, den Berg der Erscheinung, in ihren Mauern
zu halten, — ungeheuer tritt die Erde aus ihr aus und wird unmittelbar vor den
Toren: Welt, Schöpfung, Gebirg und Schlucht, Genesis. (B, 369; 13 November
1912 to Fürstin Marie)

Thus it is later described as a landscape the measure of which can be found only in
the Old Testament[53], a place where he would have read aloud the *Messias* in the
wilderness (B Kippenberg, 47; 9 April 1913).

A recurrent element in the Toledo letters is the statement that this experience
came to him as if it were the culmination of something, as if it were an experience
for which he had been somehow prepared and that he was half expecting: 'ich sah
gleich am ersten Tag, daß hier vieles ist, was ich seit lange brauchte', he wrote on
17 November 1912 to 'N.N.' (B, 372), and similarly a few days later on 25
November: 'Was mich angeht, so ists jedenfalls merkwürdig, wie stark ich meine
bisherigen Reisen als Vorbereitung auf diese (lang gewünschte) empfinde, fast wie
Wörterbücher dienen sie mir jetzt, um hiesige Dinge nachzuschlagen' (B, 377; to
Alexander Fürst von Thurn und Taxis). Toledo was somehow the realization, the
becoming real, of what before had been only vaguely perceived: 'ich lebte in lauter
Vorgefühl, und nun erst ists wieder das Fühlen selbst' (B, 367; 4 November 1912 to
Anton Kippenberg). Partly no doubt this feeling of Rilke's was engendered by the
fact that he had already seen and admired El Greco's paintings of Toledo, and had

indeed been inspired to visit the city as a result of this, and in order to see more of El Greco's work.[54] His vision of the real Toledo bears distinct traces of Greco's portrayal, and to this extent his Spanish journey brought the culmination of an interest that had long been present, but in most of the descriptions of the Toledo landscape El Greco is not mentioned, and when he is, then it is stated that the reality of Toledo surpasses his artistic portrayal of it: 'bisher, wo man ihn sah, bedeutete er alles dies, für die Hierseienden geht er zunächst im Vorhandenen unter' (B370; 13 November 1912 to Fürstin Marie); 'Denken Sie, daß ich wochenlang zuerst Greco-Bilder nicht nötig hatte, so stark waren sie da, drin, auf dem Grunde von allem' (B07-14, 283; 20 December 1912 to Leo von König). This is the fact that seems to have impressed Rilke most in Toledo – that here was a city, a real landscape, that was equal to, if not greater than, art; a 'Modell' that had elevated itself from the everyday world of 'scheinen' into the ideal of the 'Kunst-Ding' the realm of 'sein'. A few years later Rilke wrote a letter from Munich in which he described the significance of the Spanish landscape for him:

Die 'Arbeit nach der Natur' hat mir das Seiende in so hohem Grade zur *Aufgabe* gemacht, daß mich nur selten noch, wie aus Versehen, ein Ding gewährend und gebend anspricht, ohne die Anforderung, in mir gleichwertig und bedeutend hervorgebracht zu sein. Die spanische Landschaft (die letzte, die ich grenzenlos erlebt habe), Toledo, hat diese meine Verfassung zum Äußersten getrieben: indem dort das äußere Ding selbst: Turm, Berg, Brücke zugleich schon die unerhörte, unübertreffliche Intensität der inneren Äquivalente besaß, durch die man es hätte darstellen mögen. Erscheinung und Vision kamen gleichsam überall im Gegenstand zusammen, es war in jedem eine ganze Innenwelt herausgestellt. (B, 509f. 27 October 1915 to Ellen Delp)

Toledo was then a landscape that could not be transformed, that could not be 'said', as it was already in the heightened state – this had been Rilke's first reaction in his first letter from Toledo: 'Sagen können, wie es hier ist, werd ich ja nie' (see above, page 48), and the truth of this exclamation is borne out by the fact that there are indeed no poems by Rilke on Toledo. It was in this way that Toledo came to Rilke as the natural climax of a stage in his development; not quite a turning point, but a crystallization, an exemplification in concrete terms of much that he already felt, a confirmation of the ideas he had been developing in Paris.

The only other place in Spain that impressed Rilke was Ronda: he described it in terms similar to those he had used for Toledo, but in a less emphatic tone, talking of it as 'die unvergleichliche Erscheinung dieser auf zwei steile Felsmassen, die die enge tiefe Flußschlucht trennt, hinaufgehäuften Stadt . . . es ist unbeschreiblich, um das Ganze herum ein geräumiges Tal, beschäftigt mit seinen Feldflächen, Steineichen und Ölbäumen, und drüben entsteigt ihm wieder, wie ausgeruht, das reine Gebirg, Berg hinter Berg, und bildet die vornehmste Ferne' (B, 380; 17 December 1912 to Fürstin Marie). Here again he found a town built above a river gorge and surrounded by the open Spanish countryside. Ronda, like Toledo, was 'unbeschreiblich'. Gebser offers an interesting suggestion to explain why Toledo and Ronda should have been particularly attractive to Rilke:

Es war kein Zufall, daß es vor allen anderen Städten Toledo und Ronda waren, die auf Rilke den entscheidenden Eindruck machten und ihn länger verweilen ließen. Abgesehen von allem, was man über seine Beziehung zu Toledo weiß –, beide Städte sind über dem Abgrund erbaut und überstehen die Ängste ihrer Geburt, verwandeln sie in ein Hinauf, einem Himmel zu, der, was Toledo anbetrifft, so einzigartig ist, daß er fast wie eine Schöpfung dieser Stadt erscheint, durch ihre Kraft und Leidenschaft entstanden und auf eine ergänzende und wirkende Weise einen Teil von ihr bildend. (Gebser, *Spanien*, p. 22)

Although Gebser adduces no direct evidence for this suggestion, it seems reasonable enough in view of Rilke's explicit search for external equivalents for his inner state to see in Toledo a symbol almost of his whole life built above the 'Abgrund' of his youth and the constant threat of collapse into 'Ängste', a life reaching up to an ideal of its own laborious and passionate making. The idea is remarkably similar to the explanation that Blume gives of Rilke's liking for the constantly threatened but artistically perfect city of Venice poised above the depths of the sea – again a symbol of his own situation.

Rilke seems not to have noticed the landscape of the other places in Spain that he visited; no doubt his 'malaise' had something to do with this – certainly he ascribed his dislike of Seville, which he found 'kleinstädtisch' to this cause[55] –, but he presumably also found these places uninspiring in themselves, as his 'Stumpfeit' had after all been overcome by Toledo.

For all the forcefulness of its impact, the Spanish landscape appears explicitly in only one work, the 'Spanische Trilogie', which Rilke wrote at Ronda. These three poems are reminiscent in many ways of the 'Aufzeichnungen aus dem Capreser Winter'. Their theme is again that of Self and Non-Self, of unity and individuation, and the subject matter takes the form of meditations in the landscape around Ronda, where, as on Capri, Rilke finds and portrays the figure of a shepherd. The mystical experience of the bird-call heard on Capri is again evoked, as is the subsequent one of the tree at Duino (both described in detail in the two parts of the prose passage 'Erlebnis' (SW, VI, 1036ff.), which was also written at Ronda). That Rilke was grappling again in the Spanish landscape with the problems of Self and Non-Self is revealed not only in these references, but also in the fact that here too he had a similar experience. He mentions it in a letter of 14 January 1919, comparing it with the bird-call experience on Capri: it was the

Moment . . . da mir (ich stand nachts auf der wunderbaren Brücke von Toledo) ein in gespanntem langsamen Bogen durch den Weltraum fallender Stern zugleich (wie soll ich das sagen?) durch den Innen-Raum fiel: der trennende Kontur des Körpers war nicht mehr da.   (B, 571; to Adelheid von der Marwitz)

This was the experience that provided the cryptic ending to the poem 'Der Tod' of 1915:

O Sternenfall,
von einer Brücke einmal eingesehn –:
Dich nicht vergessen. Stehn!   (SW, II, 104)

The only other distinct references to Spain in Rilke's poems are 'Corrida' (SW, I, 615), written five years before he visited the country, and Sonnet I/21, which, as Rilke explains in his notes, was inspired by a song he had heard children singing in Ronda (SW, I, 772).

The effect that Spain had on Rilke is not, then, measurable in terms of explicit references in the poetry. But the language with which he describes Toledo does provide several clues as to the significance of these Spanish experiences. The tone of these letters is distinctive and almost unique in Rilke's correspondence, but it does recur once in later years in the letters with which he announces the completion of the *Duineser Elegien*. These letters also are ecstatic in tone, but their content as well is often remarkably reminiscent of the Toledo letters; they too are concerned with a climactic event for which there have been many years of unconscious preparation, and the letter addressed to the Fürstin on 11 February 1922 contains the words:

'Aber nun *ists*. Ist. Ist.
Amen'   (B, 742)

Here Rilke is employing not only the same tone, but the same expression he had used to the same addressee over nine years earlier in announcing his discovery of Toledo: '*daß* es ist, daß es *ist*, das müssen Sie mir aufs Geratewohl glauben' (B, 365; 2 November 1912). A comparison along these lines of the two sets of letters makes it seem not unreasonable to suggest that the two experiences – that of Toledo and that of the completion of the Elegies – had much in common for Rilke. The vision of the Spanish city *showed* him that which '*ist*', but it was as yet beyond his powers to express it; he could only stand and stare in astonished ecstasy. When he wrote to the Fürstin in 1922 it was to tell her that he himself had *created* that which '*ist*': what had seemed beyond him in Toledo he had now achieved. The Elegies and the Sonnets attempt to define and to create that higher realm that Rilke had seen manifested in the Toledo landscape: the realm that is 'in gleichem Maße für die Augen der Verstorbenen, der Lebenden und der Engel da'. It was thus that he could say of the Toledo landscape that it had 'diese meine Verfassung zum Äußersten getrieben'; the 'Verfassung' by which he needed to reproduce, to heighten through artistic transformation the things around him, had been immensely encouraged and stimulated by the sight of this reality that was a living example of the ideal he was striving for, of 'die unerhörte, unübertreffliche Intensität' of the 'Innenwelt'. The years before Toledo had seemed merely a premonition, a 'Vorgefühl', spent amidst ordinary, untransformed environments; Toledo, the world of *Sein*, was 'das Fühlen selbst', a whole world existing in the state of a 'Kunst-Ding'.

In more concrete terms, the Spanish landscape seems, like Capri, to have supplied Rilke with more images of a hard, rocky landscape, a setting that, virtually absent in the early years, becomes noticeably more frequent in the poems of the middle period. It also undoubtedly provided a further schooling in the idea of 'Bezug'. Buddeberg's remark: 'Die Raummetaphern häufen sich in den spanischen Briefen' (*Biographie*, p. 235) is certainly apt, although this is by no means a unique characteristic of these letters alone — that Rilke was always intrigued by spatial relationships is revealed by his considerable exploitation of the German language's ability subtly to describe these with prefixes, suffixes, particles and compound prepositions, all of which abound in both his poetry and his letters of all periods. The Worpswede painters and, above all, Cézanne taught him to see more clearly the spatial relationships in landscape, as the 'Cézanne-Briefe' abundantly illustrate, and the influence of Cézanne is apparent in the Spanish experience. The vision of Cézanne is essentially a static one, of solid blocks of form and colour, whereas that of El Greco, with which Rilke approached Toledo, is one of movement, of flux and surge:

L'orage s'est déchiré et tombe brusquement derrière une ville qui, sur la pente d'une colline, monte en hâte vers sa cathédrale et plus haut vers son château-fort, carré et massif. Une lumière en loques laboure la terre, la remue, la déchire et fait ressortir ça et là les prés, verts-pâles, derrière les arbres, comme des insomnies. Un fleuve étroit sort sans mouvement de l'amas de collines et menace terriblement de son bleu-noir et nocturne les flammes vertes des buissons. La ville épouvantée et en sursaut se dresse dans un dernier effort comme pour percer l'angoisse de l'atmosphère.   (B07-14, 58; 16 October 1908 to Rodin)

This was how Rilke described Greco's 'Toledo' in 1908, and it is worth noting to what extent Rilke's descriptions of the real Toledo conform with this passage. The ever-present emphasis on spatial relationships is retained, but the violent, elemental movement of this terrifying, almost Expressionistic, vision has considerably subsided. There is indeed movement in the descriptions of the real Toledo, but nothing like the movement which dominates in the painting; the vision of Cézanne is clearly more congenial to Rilke, and it has reasserted itself in the descriptions of Spain: Rilke seems to have found the Spanish landscape to be more solid, sharper, clearer and firmer than he had envisaged it through El Greco.

The rugged, barren countryside with its gorges and rocks, the dry, empty plain and the bare mountains were something practically unique in Rilke's experience; certainly it would be difficult to imagine a natural setting further removed from the fens of Worpswede or the plains and forests of Russia, and, as far as natural landscapes are concerned, Spain is without doubt one of the extremes of Rilke's experience. Here he found a harshness of outline and an isolation of elements, but at the same time an overall unity almost unprecedented in his journeys so far. Gebser describes its effect as follows:

Jene Stellung der Dinge zueinander, die er in Spanien wahrnahm (dessen übermächtiges Licht isolierend auf die Dinge wirkt, sehr im Gegensatz etwa zu jenem unheimlich verbindenden Licht von Paris), findet man in den 'Elegien' wieder: jene Beziehung der Dinge zueinander, welche der gleicht, die zwischen einzelnen Sternen herrscht. (Gebser, *Spanien*, p. 50)

This effect of the Spanish light and of the harsh elements in the Spanish landscape is, of course, another instance of that ideal relationship of part and whole that comes to be called 'Bezug'. It is, as Gebser points out, an essentially a-perspective vision,[56] and it is what Rilke means when, in 1912, he writes in letters to the Fürstin Marie of the landscape of Toledo as being 'voll Gesetz' and 'sternisch' (B, 365; 2 November) 'ganz ins Geschehen einbezogen' (B, 370; 13 November); it is what he means when he describes the mountains in this landscape as being 'pur' (B, 369; 13 November) and 'rein' (B, 380; 17 December).

The main effect of the Spanish landscape on Rilke was more subtle and at the same time more fundamental than the more immediately obvious provision of imagery: it provided him in immense landscape terms with a vision of what he had before glimpsed in the individual 'Kunst-Werk', in Rodin's 'Dinge' — the vision of the higher realm of 'Bezug', a vision that, encouraged by his memories of Toledo, he preserved through the barren years of the War until he could express it himself in the Elegies.

Switzerland

For the greater part of his life Rilke's attitude to the Swiss landscape was, to the extent that it existed at all, an entirely negative one. His frequent journeys across Europe must inevitably have taken him through Switzerland many times, but his letters bear no trace of this until he went to settle there after the War, when he remembered how he had been in the habit of drawing down the blinds in his compartment when his train crossed Switzerland (B, 607f.; 12 November 1919 to Gertrud Ouckama Knoop). He had made only one journey to a destination in Switzerland, and that was when, very briefly, he visited Zurich in 1914. He found there a setting that was unbearably tame, an environment that, for all its distinctions, had been stiflingly humanised — a place that, in the later parlance of the Elegies, had been 'gedeutet' rather than 'gesagt'. It was, he said, 'eine zwar gesteigerte, aber unsäglich bürgerliche Landschaft . . . eine menschlich-nüchterne Natur', and he concluded: 'ich kann mir nichts vorstellen, was mir fremder wäre, gleichgültiger, außenseitiger als diese Umgebung' (B, Kippenberg, 105; 23 March 1914).

When he first revisited Switzerland after the War his reaction was again disapproving, but for a very different reason. If the city of Zurich had been too constrictingly tame — and indeed still was, for in 1919 he talked of it as 'diese politisch trübe Stadt'[57]— , the alpine countryside on the other hand was too incommensurably wild. The meaninglessness of this totally alien landscape had been the cause of the blind-drawing incidents on earlier train journeys, but now the mountains did at least evoke some description in a number of letters written mainly in 1919. He found this countryside exaggerated, both by itself and, inevitably, by the 'tourists', and he responded to it at times in a manner reminiscent of his response to Rome in 1903—04, where he had also found a setting of exaggeration and tourists; he summed up both experiences in the word 'Bilderbogen'.[58] His reaction was unusual, for he described central Switzerland in a very distinctive tone of irony, an attitude that rarely appears in someone who must have been one of the most un-ironic major writers in the twentieth century, and certainly an attitude that is almost unique in his landscape portrayals:

Schade, daß (die Natur) mir in der Schweiz nur in Übertreibungen vorzukommen scheint; was für Ansprüche machen diese Seen and Berge, wie ist immer etwas zu viel an ihnen, die einfachen Augenblicke hat man ihnen abgewöhnt. Die Bewunderung unserer Groß- und Urgroßeltern scheint an diesen Gegenden mitgearbeitet zu haben; die kamen das [sic; = da?] aus ihren Ländern hergereist, wo es sozusagen 'nichts' gab, und hier gab es dann 'Alles', in Pracht-Ausgaben. Lieber Himmel: eine Salon-Tisch-Natur, eine Natur mit Auf und Ab, voller Überfluß, voller Verdoppelung, voll unterstrichener Gegenstände. Ein Berg? bewahre, ein Dutzend auf jeder Seite, einer hinter dem anderen; ein See: gewiß, aber dann auch gleich ein feiner See, bester Qualität, mit Spiegelbildern, und der liebe Gott, als Kustos, eines nach dem anderen erklärend; wenn er nicht gerade als Regisseur beschäftigt ist, die Scheinwerfer des Abendrots nach den Bergen zu richten, von wo den ganzen Tag der Schnee in den Sommer hineinhängt, damit man doch so recht alle 'Schönheiten' beisammen habe. Denn der Winter hat doch die seine, und so ists das Volkommenste, ihn nicht zu entbehren, während man mitten in den gewärmten Genüssen des Gegenteils sich geborgen fühlt . . . (B, 607; 12 September 1919 to Gertrud Ouckama Knoop)

The ironic tone of this passage may well be the result of a certain unease that Rilke felt in the face of the gradiosity of the Swiss Alps — a semi-humorous dismissal was the only way he could defend himself against what he had earlier literally closed his eyes to. These mountains, in containing 'Alles', represented one of the most imposing and most threatening landscapes of his life; they presented a situation in which the Self was in distinct danger of being overwhelmed by the Non-Self, and Rilke's attitude wavered unsteadily between awe and a sense of the ludicrousness of it all. Ultimately, though, he could establish no contact with this gigantic scenery; its vastness was so totally disproportionate to all human references that its threat became meaningless, it could offer no external correlative whatsoever to the internal scale of human existence: 'es fehlt mir . . .

das Gleichnis, die innere fühlbare Parallele dazu, die erst den Eindruck zum Erlebnis macht.' There were too many mountains in Switzerland with the result that 'Ihre Formen heben sich gegenseitig auf',[59] and he compared them unfavourably with the hills of Bohemia:

Die böhmischen Gebirge haben eben ein Maß, an das uns vergleichender Anschluß möchte verstattet sein; hier handelt es sich um ein unaufhaltsames Übersteigen und Übertrumpfen des Menschlichen, die Natur spielt sich aus, und es wäre ein trübes Wunder, wenn sie nicht gewänne. Aber was geht uns das an, die wir doch nur leben auf Grund der Deutbarkeit aller Dinge, vollends erst dessen, was unsere Maße nicht einhält.   (B Kippenberg, 356f.; 3 August 1919)

Rilke developed these thoughts to reach a conclusion that, apart from explaining his failure to portray the Swiss Alps in his poems, also brings his opinion of them more closely into line with what he had earlier said about Zurich; both of these Swiss landscapes were 'heightened', 'gesteigert', but, unlike the equally untractable Spanish landscape, they were false, their 'higher state' was empty and vulgar:

Ist nicht, letzten Sinnes, dieses Auswahlhaft-Schöne der schweizerischen Natur der Grund, der sie verhindert, ein Gegenstand wirklicher Kunst zu sein,   (ibid.)

he asked in August 1919, and a few days later in the same month he came to the rather hasty conclusion: 'die Schweiz, gewiß kein Land für mich' (B14-21, 262; 14 August 1919 to Elisabeth von Schmidt-Pauli).

As it happened, of course, his discovery of the Valais soon proved him totally wrong in this initial estimation of the country's potentiality as a 'home', and even in these earlier months his attitude to Switzerland was far from being entirely one of disapproval. He retained his dislike of the central Alps for the rest of his life – in 1923 he wrote of the Vierwaldstättersee: 'welcher unglückselige See, . . . *un lac en lambeaux*, wie vier Taschentücher, die nach verschiedenen Seiten Abschied winken' (B Taxis, 770; 24 August 1923) –, but other areas nearer the borders found favour from the beginning. Possibly one may see in Rilke's attitude to Switzerland yet another manifestation of his recurrent dislike of things German and Austrian, for the landscapes that he appreciated most were nearly all in the Italian- and French-speaking Cantons. The few exceptions included Bern, the city through which he felt, writing on 12 September 1919 to Gertrud Ouckama Knoop, that Switzerland was finally beginning 'mir begreiflich zu werden' (B, 608); but even here it was social factors, particularly his 'glückliche Beziehung zu einer der Berner Familien',[60] as much as the landscape of the city that brought him to appreciate its tradition-steeped solidity, with its 'schönen, altangestammten Häusern',[61] and a year later he found he had almost come to dislike the place for its very bourgeois air, especially when he compared it with French-speaking Geneva (von Salis, pp. 74f.). More successful was his stay at Schloß Berg, which lasted from November 1920 to May 1921, and where he was able to say: 'So faß ich meine gegenwärtige Lage am besten zusammen wenn ich sage, daß sie allen meinen Neigungen entspricht' (B, 650; 21 December 1920 to Carl Burckhardt). But at Berg Rilke's attention rarely strayed beyond the confines of the garden; this, with its fountain and Rilke's rooms in the Schloß, are described in detail in the letters of the period, but the wider landscape setting is hardly mentioned. One minor favourable mention of a landscape in German-speaking Switzerland concerns Pratteln, in the Baselland, where he spent some three months in the spring of 1920: here he liked the open, rolling countryside; it was 'das erste Mal in der Schweiz, daß ich wieder ein rechtes Gefühl der Weite aufbringe' (B Nölke, 44; 6 March 1920). But even here a month later he was complaining of an excess of openness, in particular: 'Was mir hier sehr fehlt, ist der Garten' – the Baselland had gone too far to the opposite extreme from the rest of Switzerland; things became lost 'im zu Weiten, Offenen', things that a well-ordered garden landscape would have held in place (B Nölke, 48; 20 April 1920).

With French and Italian Switzerland things were much more satisfactory, though it is not always clear just to what extent Rilke looked upon these areas as being actually Swiss. The Ticino was, if anything, a kind of *Ersatz*-Italy where he was able to enjoy again 'die lang entbehrte Südlichkeit'[62] and to lay his hands once more on a warm stone wall;[63] it was even a place where the German tourists were behaving as if they were in Capri or Rome.[64] In the French-speaking areas he was especially fond of Geneva, but here again his attachment was based very much on the city's non-Swiss attributes – he found it resembled Paris:

Es ist nicht Genf allein, es ist alles das, was hier Paris heraufruft und beinah verwirklicht, das graue spielende Licht, darin helle Kleider und die Flächen eines Gesichts dieselbe süße Duftigkeit bekommen, die manche Pariser Jahreszeit so vergänglich-verführend macht . . . (B, 623; 19 August 1920 to Fürstin Marie)

and when, for a while, he found himself preferring Lausanne to Geneva, calling it 'reizend', 'malerisch' and 'lebendig', he found that it too was full of 'französischem Gefühl' (B, 610f.; 26 September 1919 to Gräfin M.). Only one landscape feature that pleased him in these cities struck him as being typically Swiss, and that was the tree-lined square around their cathedrals (B, 611; ibid.). This same unwillingness to admit to liking a specifically *Swiss* landscape even appears in Rilke's attitude to his final, and in many ways his only, home – the Valais, for in nearly all the letters written during his first months there he compared it with Spain and Provence, repeatedly pointing out that it was linked with these Mediterranean areas by the Rhône, and he was delighted to discover that certain plants and butterflies were peculiar to these three regions (B, 677; 25 July 1921 to Fürstin Marie). Soon, however, he decided that he had been mistaken in making these comparisons, and had neglected the qualities that the Valais possessed in its own right; but still he saw its Swissness as something incidental – indeed, he even found it remarkable that such a magnificent landscape was part of Switzerland, talking of it as 'dieses Tal, von dem man kaum glauben will, daß es noch zur Schweiz gehöre',[65] and calling it 'diesen großartigen (dem Begriffe nach schon fast nicht mehr schweizerischen) Kanton',[66] just as he had earlier remarked: 'soviel die Schweiz auch enthält, diese Gegenden, die die Provence und Spanien heraufrufen, würde ich ihr nicht zugetraut haben' (B, 636; 23 November 1920 to Inga Junghanns). One thing, though, remains certain about these first years in Switzerland: whatever Rilke's attitude to the phenomenon 'Switzerland' as a whole, these journeys brought with them a remarkable reawakening of his interest in the landscapes about him; the letters he wrote during the War years contain virtually no landscape descriptions, but the letters from Switzerland, from the very beginning, abound in them, and contain the most lengthy travelogues since his visit to Spain.

Rilke's first trip to the Valais took place in October 1920, when he spent a few days in Sion and Sierre. He was immediately deeply impressed, and felt from the outset a close affinity with this area that reminded him so much of Spain and Provence — two of the most meaningful landscapes of his pre-War journeys (B, 677; 25 July 1921 to Fürstin Marie). His real encounter with the Valais began in July of the next year, when he settled in the tower of the little Château de Muzot, where he was to remain until his death, and almost immediately he began writing a series of letters that describe at length and with great enthusiasm the landscape around him. Time and again the idea that recurs in these descriptions is that of balance, of proportion, of an ideal harmony of part and whole in which the elements of the scenery are contained 'im Rahmen der großen Randgebirge', set into their background 'wie die Bilder einer Tapisserie' (B, 678; ibid.). The following passage, from a letter of 17 August 1921 is typical of many that he wrote at the time. He begins by comparing the Rhône valley to Spain and Provence, and continues:

En fin de compte könnt ich nicht beschreiben, was mich hier hält, ich müßte denn eine Beschreibung des Valais überhaupt aufbringen, dieses vielleicht größesten Tals in Europa, in dessen Umgrenzung ein Spiel schön bestellter und bewachsener Hügel die reichsten Verwandlungen des Ausblicks vollzieht, es bilden sich Länder vor einem als schüfen sie sich erst — und was an Dingen (: Häusern und Bäumen) innerhalb dieser Perspektiven vorkommt, hat die Distanzen und Spannungen, die wir aus dem Aufgang der Sternbilder kennen: als ginge aus diesem großartigen Entfaltet- und Aufeinanderbezogensein der Einzelheiten Raum hervor, — eine Erscheinung, die nicht so überzeugend könnte erfahren werden, wäre die Luft nicht von einer unbeschreiblichen Teilnehmung an allem Gegenstand, umschauerte sie ihn nicht so und machte sie nicht jeden Zwischenraum, bis in die Hintergründe hinein, zu ihrem Glück, zum Schauplatz so und so vieler gefühlter (dächte man!) Übergänge . . . (B, 688; to Nora Purtscher-Wydenbruck)

In descriptions such as this there are echoes of all that Rilke had found ideal in different landscapes throughout his life, and it soon becomes clear that this is the culmination of them all, the 'home' that he had constantly sought. The all-enveloping and unifying light had been a characteristic of Worpswede, and later of Paris and Geneva, but whereas initially it had tended to swamp the individuality of the parts it linked, here in the Valais it effected that ideal of integration plus integrity that Rilke called 'Bezug' and that he illustrated with the image of the constellation, the 'Sternbild'. In the Valais there was full existence for both part and whole — 'diese vollkommene Gegenwart des Einzelnen und wie es doch zum nächsten und übrigen und fernsten in die Tiefe führt' (B, 701; 26 November 1921 to Gertrud Ouckama Knoop). That this vision was that of an artist, a visual artist, becomes apparent not only in the image of the tapestry, but also when Rilke talks of this landscape's

Modelé — hervorgerufen durch das unbeschreiblich mitwirkende Licht, das in allen Zwischenräumen Ereignisse schafft und die Distanz von einem Ding zum anderen mit so eigenthümlichen Spannungen erfüllt, daß sie (Bäume, Häuser, Kreuze, Kapellen und Thürme) zueinander mit der gleichen reinen Bezogenheit konstelliert erscheinen, die, für unser Anschaun, die einzelnen Sterne zum Sternbild zusammennimmt.   (B Lou, 451; 10 September 1921)

It is a vision that goes back to the painters of Worpswede, about whom Rilke had said in 1902:

Gesundheit ist Gleichgewicht. Und hier, in diesem Bilde [scil. by Fritz Mackensen] ist Gleichgewicht. Gleichgewicht in der Raumverteilung, in Form und Farbe. (SW, V, 50)

But also, and more distinctly, it harks back to the experience of Cézanne and the distinctive descriptions of Paris that Rilke wrote under his influence. The following passage written on 26 November 1921 reveals exactly those ideas of the startlingly distinct individual element integrated perfectly — 'richtig' — into the picture that the 'Cézanne-Erlebnis' had inspired:

Kapellen, Missionskreuze an allen Scheidewegen, Hänge, gestreift von den Reihen des Weins und später reichlich gekräuselt von seinem Laub, Obstbäume, jeder mit seinem zärtlichen Schatten, und (richtig, ach so richtig!) einzelne erwachsene Pappeln hingestellt, Rufzeichen des Raums, die sagen: Hier! — und keine Gestalt, keine — natürlich landestümlich gekleidete — Bauernfrau, die nicht Figur wäre in alledem, Akzent wäre oder Maß, kein Karren, kein Maultier, keine Katze, durch deren Gegenwart nicht alles wieder weiter, offener, luftiger würde weithin —; und diese Luft von Ding zu Ding, dieses Nirgends-leer-sein der Welt.   (B, 701; to Gertrud Ouckama Knoop)

Indeed, so magnificently did the Valais exemplify for Rilke all that he had learnt to appreciate in great art, that he added sculpture to the paintings and saw in the mountains around Muzot clear evocations of the works of Rodin:

wie eine Rodinsche Skulptur eine eigene Geräumigkeit in sich mitbringt und um sich herum ausgibt: so benehmen sich — für meinen Blick — die Berge und Hügel in diesen Gegenden des Valais. (B21-26, 109; 2 March 1922 to Xaver von Moos)

Reminiscences of Spain are also present, not only in Rilke's explicit comparisons (which he never actually illustrates), but in the idea that the landscape is in motion and indeed in creation: 'es bilden sich Länder vor einem als schüfen sie sich erst', that it is a 'beinah biblische . . . Landschaft' (Nevar, p. 179) where one 'den Akt der Schöpfung immer noch in ihrer Gestaltung zu erkennen meint' (Albert-Lasard, pp. 172f.) — descriptions that all suggest very immediate connections with the 'Genesis' landscape of Toledo.

As well as possessing the ideal qualities of many past landscapes, the Valais was also conspicuous in not possessing their faults. Thus it differed from 'Switzerland', of which Rilke had complained in 1919 that it was 'ein *enges* Land',[67] by being 'welthaft weit' (Nevar, p. 179); this had been one of his first impressions of the Valais, for he wrote in 1920 (to a Swiss correspondent — a fact that may explain the unusually glowing terms of the first phrase):

Ich sah unter den schönen Talschaften der Schweiz noch keine, die geräumiger gewesen wäre: das Valais ist eine Ebene, die es weit hat bis zu den Bergen; und diese selbst sind nichts als Hintergrund, keine Schwere hereinwirkend und von einer solchen Duftigkeit der Abhänge, daß sie zu Zeiten imaginär wirken, wie die Bergbilder in einer Spiegelung. (B14-21, 321; 12 October 1920 to Hans v.d. Mühll)

Thus even Rilke's nature as an 'Anhänger der Ebene' could be satisfied in what Valéry, after his visit to Rilke in April 1924, described in the words:

Un très petit château terriblement seul dans un vaste site de montagnes assez triste; des chambres antiques et pensives, aux meubles sombres, aux jours étroits; cela me serrait le coeur. (B Gide, 169n.)

Valéry's description makes much clearer Rilke's distinctive appreciation of landscape: even allowing for any fundamental difference in outlook between the two men, Rilke's attitude was still remarkably opposed to one that could see in Muzot something sad, let alone 'terriblement seul', for such a view completely disregarded the connections, the 'Bezug', that Rilke saw in this landscape and that meant that nothing could really be alone.

In this fact more than in any other the faults of all previous landscapes seemed corrected, for here Self and Non-Self existed in a harmonious balance, and not only did this balance exist within the landscape, but it also existed between the observer and the observed environment. There was no longer an overwhelming of Self by Non-Self as there had been in the early neo-Romantic landscapes, nor was there the overwhelming of Non-Self by Self that he had regretted in the poem 'Wendung' of 1914, nor was there that feeling of exclusion, of being nothing but an external observer, that he had expressed in the

60

'Aufzeichnungen aus dem Capreser Winter' and the 'Spanische Trilogie', in which the only 'insider' had been the shepherd, his individuality totally drowned by the sun and the clouds that drifted through his almost immaterial being. All of this had been surpassed in the Valais where 'man plötzlich *im* Bilde wohnte, zugehörig, statt ihm aufnehmend gegenüber zu sein' (B Lou, 450; 10 September 1921); here the fate lamented in the Eighth Elegy, that of 'gegenüber sein', had ceased to apply, and with it the penultimate stanza of that Elegy, which describes the various unhappy relationships between Self and Non-Self:

> Und wir: Zuschauer, immer, überall,
> dem allen zugewandt und nie hinaus!
> Uns überfüllts. Wir ordnens. Es zerfällt.
> Wir ordnens wieder und zerfallen selbst.   (SW, I, 716)

The castle of Muzot was neither 'seul' nor 'gegenüber': it was 'eine der gleichsam eingeborenen Stellen in der Landschaft, von der aus man wunderbar eingeführt wird in die große Konstellation ihrer Betonungen',[68] an integral part of the 'Sternbild' of the Valais landscape. Here Rilke could feel that he had finally arrived at a 'home', and such an ideal one at that, that he said of Muzot: 'Auch dieses wäre ein Ort, das *Paradiso* zu lesen.'[69]

The reference to the *Paradiso* indicates not only Rilke's view of the Valais as a heightened, perfected, and, above all, welcoming landscape, but it also shows how he looked upon this valley as the culmination and conclusion of his life-long wanderings, as the goal finally attained. Not only had the Valais re-established the continuity that the War had broken, but it represented also the fulfilment of childhood dreams of the ideal landscape, of those

Abende, wo man als Kind vor gebundenen Zeitschriften saß, darin Reisen beschrieben waren, vielleicht nicht gut, aber von versprecherischen Bildern begleitet, in die man die ganze Bedeutung dessen legte, was einmal erfahrbar sein würde, zugleich mit der fast wehmütigen Ungeduld, durch so viel Jahre des Aufwachsens davon getrennt zu sein. Ja, vielleicht wirkte in diesem hingegebenen Anschauen etwas noch viel Inningeres mit, die unaussprechliche Furcht wegzusterben, ehe dies alles würde erfaßlich und erfüllbar sein: diese, genau diese Landschaften mit allem gewissermaßen, was man in sie hineinlegte, diese Landschaften der Sonntagsnachmittage und der Winterabende, die gehen hier in Erfüllung, denken Sie!   (B, 700; 26 November 1921 to Gertrud Ouckama Knoop)

Ensconced in his tower Rilke felt that he was now fully settled: 'ich . . . "wohne" wahrhaftig', he wrote on 20 February 1923 to Regina Ullmann (B, 817). The situation had some similarities with Duino, where he had begun the Elegies, for he talked of the 'Rüstung' of the castle walls about him,[70] and felt himself a prisoner, but by no means in a negative sense, for he was 'ein Gefangener meiner selbst in meinem alten Turm' (ibid.). But there the similarity with Duino ended, for at Muzot, where the

Elegies were triumphantly completed with the finding of a place for Man in the Universe, the landscape outside was far from empty and meaningless, it too had a place for Man, and the castle, far from holding at bay the vast outside, brought it closer in the rich pattern of the constellation.

Things were not always so perfect with the Valais landscape, however. There were occasions when Rilke found it difficult to maintain his initial high enthusiasm. On 21 June 1922 he wrote to Merline:

quelquefois il me semble que je suis bien fatigué de ce pays,

but even then he reverted to his old tone a few lines later:

Quelle splendeur, la douceur des ombres, la pureté des 'traits' de ce paysage —, vraiment à certains moments il semble posséder tout ce qui fait le charme et l'esprit d'une figure aimée.   (B Merline, 406f.)

This particular regression seems to have lasted, on and off, for about a year, for on 13 January 1923 he wrote to Lou:

Seltsam abgestumpft bin ich . . . gegen die Landschaft selbst, deren so tief erfahrene Großartigkeit ich mir angestrengt und absichtlich vorhalten muß, um noch an ihr teil zu haben,   (B, 809)

and in April he was complaining about the weather, the strong sun and drought that tended to remove any semblance of a real spring (B, 836; 23 April 1923 to Clara), and after some storms he came to the conclusion: 'A la fin je dirai, je crains, du Valais:"jolie fille, mais mauvais caractère . . ." ' (B Merline, 428; 21 April 1923). The complaints are familiar — all his life Rilke had been subject to these attacks of 'Stumpfheit', and now more than ever they could be ascribed to a pathological condition. He was always sensitive to the weather, and had talked in very similar terms in 1904 in Rome about the regrettable tendency of the Southern climate to overlook his beloved Northern spring. Even apart from these peculiarly Rilkean factors it is hardly surprising that anyone should have occasional lapses of enthusiasm for his daily surroundings, however fervently he may have received them initially. What is really remarkable is that Rilke should have gone on praising the Valais right up to the end, for these intervals of unease were very temporary, and in December 1925 he was still able to talk of 'das Ereignis der großgearteten Landschaft des Wallis, an die ich mich tiefer angeschlossen habe von Jahr zu Jahr'[71] — an attitude that continued to be echoed in the letters of his last year.

Rilke's continuing affection for the Valais is manifested in the many poems he wrote there, for, more than at any time since his departure from Prague, he wrote in these last years poems that had as their explicit subjects the landscape about him. Initially the Valais had helped him complete the Elegies and write the Sonnets, for it had offered him 'Maße und Gleichnisse für die inneren

Erscheinungen',[72] but even more obviously it had inspired the French poems, the *Quatrains Valaisans*, of which he said:

Abgesehen von jenen früheren jugendlichen Versuchen, in denen die Einflüsse meiner Prager Heimat sich durchsetzen wollten, hatte ich mich nie mehr hingerissen gefühlt, eine erlebte Umgebung unmittelbar im Gedicht zu rühmen, sie zu 'singen'.   (B, 932; 20 March 1926 to Eduard Korrodi)

These French poems are the most serene and constantly affirmative that Rilke ever wrote, and they represent not only a token of gratitude to French culture as a whole for its 'eindringliche und rettende Gastlichkeit',[73] but their publication was prompted more specifically by 'der Wunsch, vor allem, dem Canton du Valais den Beweis einer mehr als nur privaten Dankbarkeit für soviel (aus Land und Leuten) Empfangenes wiederzugeben' (B, 933; to Korrodi). Their calm and assured tone is a clear indication of the 'Geborgensein' that Rilke had come to feel in this sympathetic valley; they were products neither of the strenuous 'Arbeit' of earlier years, nor of the violent inspiration of the Elegies, but were, Rilke insisted, 'nebensächlich',[74] products of 'Nebenstunden: in denen gleichwohl ein Hauptgefühl sich geltend machte' (B, 932; to Korrodi). This period of release, of 'free time' once the Elegies had been completed, was the fulfilment of a wish Rilke had expressed as long before as 1899:

> Ich möchte *einmal* nur tüchtig sein
> und eine *wirkliche* Arbeit tun!
> Nicht, um hernach zu ruhen, –
> nein;
> um dir zu sagen mit seligen Sinnen:
> Jetzt laß mich beginnen.
> Jetzt ist getan, was man tuen muß,
> und was jetzt kommt, ist der Überfluß.
> Mit dem Andern hab ich mich freigeschafft,
> jetzt bin ich allein mit meiner Kraft.   (SW, III, 669)

— words that prefigure remarkably closely the situation from which the French poems sprang.

The *Quatrains Valaisans* are poems about a landscape that already exists in a heightened state, a landscape that the poet does not need to form or to tame in any way, but simply to accept as it is. It is a landscape where Man and Nature coexist in a perfect balance — a balance that is expressed in the recurring theme of the vineyards and in the mention of the towers and paths, the integrated human elements in a setting of light and warmth, of wind and sky, clouds, streams, poplars and flowers: of what the second poem calls a 'beau pays achevé' (SW, II, 557). It is impossible to select any one poem that is 'typical' of them all, but the twenty-seventh can serve, as well as any other, as an example of their tone and content. It portrays a landscape that human and natural elements have conspired

63

harmoniously together to create, a place where all extremes are reconciled in a fertile, heightened unity of 'choses comblées':

> Les tours, les chaumières, les murs,
> même ce sol qu'on désigne
> au bonheur de la vigne,
> ont le caractère dur.
>
> Mais la lumière qui prêche
> douceur à cette austérité
> fait une surface de pêche
> à toutes ces choses comblées.   (SW, II, 567)

The tone of serenity and the theme of balance run through all these French poems; the titles of the collections are in themselves an indication of Rilke's mood and preoccupations during these years: *Vergers*, the symbolic landscape of reconciliation between Man and Nature, where, in the fruit, life and death are united — the word itself was one for which Rilke felt the German language had no equivalent:

> ce nom rustique dont l'unique empire
> me tourmentait depuis toujours: Verger.   (SW, II, 531)

Les Roses, the flower that Man and Nature have created together, with all its rich evocations for Rilke of plenitude and fulfilment; *Les Fenêtres*, the human frame that perfectly rounds off and lifts into a more meaningful realm the world outside.

In his integration into the landscape of the Valais Rilke had finally found a 'home', and from his descriptions of this landscape one learns what it was that he was looking for, what were the ideals of his life and art. Here he found balance, a perfect mid-point in a countryside that Man and Nature had produced in concert, a place that was neither too tame nor too wild, where the lines and patterns were those of a great painting in which part and whole, observer and observed existed in a mutually heightened harmony; this was a landscape where northern and southern Europe met, in a country that was the epitome of Rilke's own supra-nationality, holding together in a stable balance, devoid of all their extremes, the three great cultures of his mature years — the French, the German, and the Italian. Undoubtedly, as Fülleborn points out (p. 261), his vision was selective, he avoided the themes of 'montagne, neige, glace', he did not see the terrifying harshness that Valéry did, but the very fact that these elements were there and Rilke chose to ignore them makes his peculiar vision all the more significant for an understanding of his life and work.

1. This situation has been well documented by Demetz; see also Politzer.
2. Politzer attributes the cultivation of 'decadence' more to the social than to the physical environment: 'If the German writers of Prague seemed to be stricken more violently and for a much longer time by a-vitality (a malaise that had been a literary fashion around the turn of the century), it was because their unique position in an alien environment tended to aggravate and to perennialize their disturbances' (pp.50f.).
3. See especially SW, IV, 124ff., 193ff., and 197ff.
4. See SW, IV, 984, where it is pointed out that this was the site of the Rilke family grave.
5. B Kippenberg, 14; 22 August 1910.
6. Demetz distinguishes five recurrent types of poem in the *Larenopfer:* 'Das deskriptive Gedicht; der neuromantische Gefühlserguß; die impressionistische Momentaufnahme; das naturalistische Tendenzgedicht, und eine mißglückte Mischform, die naturalistische Themen vergebens mit der Technik der Neuromantik zu fassen versucht' *(Prager Jahre,* p.119).
7. Blume, 'Stadt', p. 73. Gunert, on the other hand, objects to this poem's 'schon an Naturalismus grenzenden Realistik'. He prefers the heavier 'Stimmung' of the earlier poems: 'Aus freien Rhythmen erwachsen, ist es mit seiner Aufzählung kaum mehr als ein Schaubericht, eine Bildbeschreibung ohne den Zauber, der schon von so vielen Verszeilen seiner anderen, in dieser Zeit entstandenen Gedichten ausgeht' (p. 275).
8. Politzer, p. 53. Rilke's attitude to the Czechs is also discussed at length in both of the works by Demetz. Rilke's attitude was dominated by the image of the Czechs as an immature people beside the 'mature' Germans (see for instance SW, IV, 182f.).
9. B 92-04, 336; 3 April 1903 to Ellen Key.
10. B, 285; 16 June 1911 to Rudolf Kassner.
11. B, 646; 9 December 1920 to General-Major von Sedlakowitz.
12. B, 617; 21 January 1920 to Leopold von Schlözer. See also B 92-04, 107; 18 October 1900 to Paula Becker: 'Mir ist ja Rußland doch das geworden, was Ihnen Ihre Landschaft bedeutet: Heimat und Himmel.'
13. T, 231f. ('Aus einem Brief. St. Petersburg, am 31. Juli'). Brutzer's little book *Rilkes russische Reisen* talks of the 'großer Dreiklang ... – russisches Land, russisches Volk, russischer Gott' (p. 101) as the heart of Rilke's experience of Russia. Brutzer is, however, almost exclusively concerned with Rilke's experience of Russian culture.
14. B, 369; to Fürstin Marie von Thurn und Taxis-Hohenlohe (referred to hereafter as: Fürstin Marie).
15. SW, I, 743f. See also B 743f.; 11 February 1922 to Lou Andreas-Salomé, where Rilke mentions this experience.
16. Now published separately in SW, V, 516ff.
17. Collected in T.
18. There is really no adequate translation for this word, just as the English 'moor' – a uniquely British landscape feature – has no German equivalent. For lack of anything better, I have resorted to the word 'fen'.
19. Published in Gebser, *Spanien,* p. 62.
20. B Lou, 76; 1 August 1903.
21. Politically Duino belonged to Austria at the time of Rilke's visits, and accordingly most of his letters of the time give its location as 'Österreichisches Küstenland'. Geographically and linguistically, however, it was part of Italy, and all three of Rilke's stays there were combined with visits to that country. In view of these facts, and of the fact that Duino today is also politically within Italy, it seems appropriate to deal with it under this heading.
22. B. j. Dichter, 28f.; 29 October 1903.
23. B Lou, 145; 15 April 1904. Stahl mentions Rilke's preference for the Northern spring as an example of his attachment to all experiences of 'das Leise' (p. 64).
24. B 04-07, 203f.; 6 December 1906 to Clara.
25. See B, 607; 12 October 1919 to Gertrud Ouckama Knoop.
26. B, 160; 4 March 1907 to Clara. See also SW, II, 208f.
27. See B, 151ff.; 1 January 1907 to Clara; SW, II, 30f.; and B 04-07, 239f.; 5 January 1907 to Gudrun Baronin Uexküll.
28. SW, I, 600f. Fülleborn (pp. 85ff.) suggests that this poem, in its 'passive' attitude, is essentially different from the other *Neue Gedichte.* The demand for active self-

assertion is nonetheless a central theme (see especially lines 5 and 6).

29.   SW, I, 116. A similar idea was of course later expressed by Thomas Mann in *Der Tod in Venedig.*
30.   SW, I, 609f. See critical studies by Rose, Blume, and Schwarz.
31.   B, 860; 26 February 1924 to Alfred Schaer.
32.   Letter to Julie Freifrau von Nordeck zu Rabenau, 'am Dienstag nach Ostern 1912', published in Blume, 'Spätherbst', p. 346n.
33.   B, 352; 5 June 1912 to Helene von Nostitz.
34.   Letter to Sidonie Nadherny, Freiin von Borutin, 24 November 1907, in Houghton Library, Harvard, published in Blume, 'Spätherbst', p. 348.
35.   B, 622; 26 June 1920 to Gräfin M.
36.   B Kippenberg, 32; 31 October 1911. Reference to Rodin in SW, V, 158f.
37.   B, 311; 10 January 1912 to Lou Andreas-Salomé. See also Rilke's similar complaints, three months later, about Duino's unstable 'österreichisches Klima' in B 07-14, 237; 11 April 1912 to Elsa Bruckmann.
38.   Holthusen, *Selbstzeugnissen*, p. 108.
39.   'Tenno', 'Casabianca', 'Arco', 'I Mulini'; SW, I, 119f.
40.   E.g. 'Ein Morgen', 'Der Grabgärtner'; SW, IV, 609ff.
41.   E.g. 'Vor-Ostern', 'Der Balkon', and 'Auswanderer-Schiff'; SW, I, 595ff. See also 'Die Auslage des Fischhändlers'; SW, VI, 1131ff.
42.   E.g. B, 337; 13 February 1912 to Norbert von Hellingrath; B Nölke, 14; 22 October 1919; and SW, II, 215.
43.   B, 421f.; 27 December 1913 to Fürstin Marie; and B, 410; 21 October 1913 to Lou Andreas-Salomé.
44.   B, 58; 8 August 1903 to Lou Andreas-Salomé.
45.   See Batterby, pp. 105ff., and de Sugar, passim.
46.   B, 195, 19 October 1907 to Clara.
47.   Ibid.
48.   B Lou, 439; 31 December 1920.
49.   B Verleger, 44f.; 8 April 1908.
50.   His enthusiastic account of the Ile St-Louis is an exception − here he was impressed by the old, homely atmosphere lacking in the anonymous slums and suburbs (B Taxis, 356f.; 2 February 1914).
51.   B, 887; 12 February 1925 to Anton Kippenberg.
52.   B, 929; 17 March 1926 to 'eine junge Freundin'.
53.   B, 378; 28 November 1912 to Elsa Bruckmann.
54.   B 07-14, 58; 16 October 1908 to Rodin; and B Verleger, 178ff.; 2 October 1912.
55.   B Taxis, 240; 4 December 1912; and B, 379; 17 December 1912 to Fürstin Marie.
56.   Gebser, *Spanien*, pp. 91f. Gebser, in fact, goes much further than this: he suggests that the perspective vision had tyrannized the post-Renaissance European intellect, and is the root cause of our insatiable Faustian outlook on life. Rilke and the late Hölderlin, he contends, were two of the few who have surmounted this tyranny.
57.   B, 593; 6 August 1919 to Gräfin Aline Dietrichstein.
58.   B Lou, 153; 12 May 1904; and B 14-21, 263; 14 August 1919 to Elisabeth von Schmidt-Pauli.
59.   B, 592; 6 August 1919 to Gräfin Aline Dietrichstein.
60.   B Verleger, 343; 7 July 1919.
61.   B, 593; 6 August 1919 to Gräfin Aline Dietrichstein.
62.   B 14-21, 281; 28 December 1919 to Emmy von Egidy.
63.   B Nölke, 14; 22 October 1919.
64.   B Nölke, 19; 3 November 1919.
65.   B Lou, 450f.; 10 September 1921.
66.   B 716; 27 December 1921 to Lisa Heise.
67.   B 14-21, 283; 12 January 1920 to Prinz Schönburg.
68.   B 21-26, 201; 28 May 1923 to Hugo von Hofmannsthal.
69.   B Taxis, 686; 8 September 1921. Compare his similar wish to read the *Messias* in the countryside around Toledo (B Kippenberg, 47; 9 April 1913).
70.   B, 679; 25 July 1921 to Fürstin Marie.
71.   B, 914; 18 December 1925 to Arthur Fischer-Colbrie.
72.   B, 925f.; 1 March 1926 to Veronika Erdmann.
73.   B, 916; 18 December 1925 to Arthur Fischer-Colbrie.
74.   Ibid.

PART TWO : FEATURES

Although Rilke's letters and diaries contain numerous, and sometimes lengthy, descriptions and discussions of various landscapes, there are few comparable passages in his poetry. He is thus not, in the conventional sense of the term, a 'landscape poet', for — with the exception of the very early and very late periods of his life — it is only rarely that his poems set out to describe in any detail a particular location. What Rilke's poetry (and, for that matter, much of his 'creative' prose) does offer is a large number of recurrent *pieces* of landscape: he uses certain landscape *features* as images in his poetry rather than taking whole places as his subject matter.

As was seen in Part One, Rilke's preference in *life* lay with settings in which Nature and Man had come to co-exist in mutual respect, and he shied away from places in which either Nature or Man were unduly dominant. This same attitude is discernible in the landscape feature motifs of Rilke's *work*, and the first three chapters of this second Part accordingly group together respectively those features that are mainly products of Nature, those that have been fashioned by Man, and those that have resulted from a fruitful interaction of both Nature and Man. The axis that may be established by examining these features from the point of view of their 'tamedness' runs from the mountain at one end to the city at the other, with, at the peak of Rilke's preference, the park in the middle. These three features are thus the most definitive members of their respective groups.

The park's deep significance for Rilke lay in the fact that here he found a landscape feature that had not only been literally physically 'tamed', but one that was also filled with figurative associations that fascinated him all his life. For all its naturalness, however, the park is in the last analysis evidence of the ordering hand of Man, and, as the landscape metaphors investigated in Chapter Five show, Man was always Rilke's central concern: landscape was of little interest to him in itself; he saw it rather from the point of view of its potentiality as both a literal and a figurative 'home' for humanity.

2

NATURAL LANDSCAPE FEATURES

a) *LAND*

Mountain (and Valley)

The mountain is a frequent image in Rilke's work, particularly in the later years, and more especially after his personal experience of the imposing landscapes of the Pyrenees and the Atlas Mountains. It is normally the rugged, barren tops with which he is concerned, and this is the setting he portrays in the poem 'Ausgesetzt auf den Bergen des Herzens' of 1914, one of the most vivid of all his landscape poems, and one that provides the key to the significance this image held for him:

> Ausgesetzt auf den Bergen des Herzens. Siehe, wie klein dort,
> siehe: die letzte Ortschaft der Worte, und höher,
> aber wie klein auch, noch ein letztes
> Gehöft von Gefühl. Erkennst du's?
> Ausgesetzt auf den Bergen des Herzens. Steingrund
> unter den Händen. Hier blüht wohl
> einiges auf; aus stummen Absturz
> blüht ein unwissendes Kraut singend hervor.
> Aber der Wissende? Ach, der zu wissen begann
> und schweigt nun, ausgesetzt auf den Bergen des Herzens.
> Da geht wohl heilen Bewußtseins,
> manches umher, manches gesicherte Bergtier,
> wechselt und weilt. Und der große geborgene Vogel
> kreist um der Gipfel reine Verweigerung. — Aber
> ungeborgen, hier auf den Bergen des Herzens ....   (SW, II, 94f.)

The mountain here appears as the ultimate 'untamed' landscape: it is the totally inhospitable and uninhabited realm beyond that world that Man has marked out for himself with his words ('Ortschaft der Worte') and his feelings ('Gehöft von Gefühl' — feelings, being more subtle and natural, are able to reach further into the 'untamed' realm than clumsy words; this little settlement is thus higher up the mountain than the 'letzte Ortschaft der Worte'. It is also a farmstead, i.e. more integrated with Nature than the town — the symbol of fragmentation — lower down the mountainside, with its divisive words.). The wordlessness of the high mountain regions is one of their most frequent and important features in Rilke, and as early as 1898 he had written of this in imagery that is an astonishingly close prefiguration of the 1914 poem:

Frage jeder sich selbst, ob auf den Höhepunkten seines Lebens Worte stehen? Ist es mit den Worten nicht vielmehr wie mit der Vegetation, die hinter der großen Pracht des Tals immer ernster, schlichter und feierlicher wird, je höher man steigt, bis das zaghafte Zwergholz zurückbleibt, das die reinen festlichen Firnen nicht zu betreten wagt?   (SW, V, 440)

Silence is equally a feature of the mountains in the *Duineser Elegien*, as in the Ninth:

> Bringt doch der Wanderer auch vom Hange des Bergrands
> nicht eine Hand voll Erde ins Tal, die Allen unsägliche . . .   (SW, I, 718)

and as too in the Tenth, in which verbal communication between the 'Jüngling' and the 'Klage' gradually diminishes as they move further and further from the human world, until finally:

> Einsam steigt er dahin, in die Berge des Ur-Leids.
> Und nicht einmal sein Schritt klingt aus dem tonlosen Los.   (SW, I, 725)

Similarly, a fragment written during the War consists of the lines:

> Nur das Geräusch, indem er das nächste Stück Stummsein
> abbricht vom Schweigengebirg   (SW, II, 432)

whilst a letter of 18 November 1920 points again to the inapplicability of all words in this silent realm: 'Moi, "chasseur d'images", je monte dans mes montagnes, sauvage, taciturne . . . là où je vais aucun nom n'est valable' (B Merline 91).

The hardness of the mountaintops, the 'Steingrund / unter den Händen' of 'Ausgesetzt . . .', is another of their most frequent attributes in Rilke's descriptions, and it too is an image of their intractability, of the fact that they are untamed and untamable. This aspect of the mountain was one that struck Rilke forcefully in his stay on Capri, as in the letter to Clara in which he described how at night the 'Berghänge sahen so mondhaft verfallen aus und ragten aus den Häusern empor wie Unbewältigtes' (B, 152; 1 January 1907); he talks in similar terms in the opening lines of the 'Improvisationen aus dem Capreser Winter':

> Täglich stehst du mir steil vor dem Herzen,
> Gebirge, Gestein,
> Wildnis, Un-weg . . .   (SW, II, 11)

This supreme indomitability of the mountain had already been the subject of 'Der Berg', in the second group of *Neue Gedichte*, in which Rilke described Hokusai's

many vain attempts to capture Fujiyama on paper (SW, I, 638f.), and it must have
played an important part in his difficulty in coming to terms with the Swiss Alps,
and his statement, in a letter of 6 August 1919, that 'Gebirge sind mir von
vornherein nicht leicht zu begreifen' (B, 592; to Gräfin Aline Dietrichstein).

The mountain, then, represents for Man an intractable, harsh and hostile realm.
It does, however, have its inhabitants: in 'Ausgesetzt . . .' these are above all the
animals, and it is stressed that they are fully at home here — they are 'heilen
Bewußtseins', 'gesichert', 'geborgen', and their situation contrasts sharply with that
of Man, who is 'ausgesetzt', 'ungeborgen'. These are the integrated creatures, the
'Kreatur' of the Eighth Elegy, and thus it is not surprising to find those other ideal
beings of the Elegies, the Angels, sharing this world with the animals; so
integrated are the Angels, in fact, that they are identified with the mountaintops
in the Second Elegy's imagery:

> Höhenzüge, morgenrötliche Grate
> aller Erschaffung . . .   (SW, I, 689)

The fact that the animals and the angels are associated with the high mountains
helps considerably in elucidating this image in Rilke; as Allemann points out:

Es ist vermutlich mehr als eine zufällige Bildverwandtschaft, wenn die Engel der
Elegien unter anderem als 'Höhenzüge, morgenrötliche Grate / aller Erschaffung'
erscheinen . . . Von der Landschaft des Fragmentes 'Ausgesetzt auf den Bergen des
Herzens' her gesehen, sind sie damit als das auf der bisherigen Grundlage von Rilkes
Dichtung gar nicht mehr Besprechbare bezeichnet, als Phänomene, die resolut
jenseits jeder möglichen Wortlandschaft angesiedelt sind. Dem entspricht
tatsächlich ihre Funktion innerhalb der *Elegien*. [1]

Other mountain-dwellers in Rilke's imagery follow this pattern of being superior
beings, like the now almost extinct race of the 'Klagen', whose 'Väter trieben den
Bergbau dort in dem großen Gebirg' (SW, I, 723), or like Christ, of whom Mary, in
Das Marien-Leben, says:

> Heilande muß man in den Bergen schürfen,
> wo man das Harte aus dem Harten bricht.   (SW, I, 676)

Rilke's mountain imagery is linked consistently to his use of the valley. Their
polar relationship is paralleled by the masculine associations of the mountain and
the feminine associations of the valley; associations based in part on the mountain's
fundamental attribute of hardness. In the Third Elegy he talks of

> . . . die Väter, die wie Trümmer Gebirgs
> uns im Grunde beruhn . . .   (SW, I, 696)

and Mary, in the *Marien-Leben* poem already quoted, goes on to talk of herself as
a 'valley':

Tut dirs nicht selber leid, dein liebes Tal
so zu verwüsten?   (SW, I, 676)

The 'female' valley in one particular form has distinctively erotic connotations –
this is the gorge, the 'Schlucht' of the Sixth Elegy (SW, I, 707) and of the poem
'Immer wieder, ob wir der Liebe Landschaft auch kennen',[2] written shortly after
'Ausgesetzt . . .'. A further instance of the female associations of the valley occurs
in a poem dedicated to Lulu Albert-Lazard, a pendant to 'Ausgesetzt . . .' in which
the beloved's soothing effect on the 'Ausgesetzten' is described in terms of a sweet
breath of wind blowing up from the valleys:

> Einmal noch kam zu dem Ausgesetzten,
> der auf seines Herzens Bergen ringt,
> Duft der Täler.[3]

A poem of 1923, with its reference to 'das Weiche der Täler' (SW, II, 141),
emphasizes again the contrast between the harsh mountains and the gentler
hospitable valleys, and this is also the theme of a fragmentary draft for a
continuation of 'Ausgesetzt . . .', in which Rilke completes this landscape with an
actual mention of the 'valleys of the heart':

> Lächeln Lächeln du hast es gekonnt; mehrmals
> haben es dir geneigte
> Augen vom Antlitz gepflückt.
> Aber das war in den Tälern des Herzens. Dort auch
> weintest du oft. Wie war es dort zärtlich zu weinen.   (SW, II, 424)

All these various associations of the mountain are present to a greater or lesser
extent in the poem 'Ausgesetzt . . .'. That Rilke should have used the mountain to
symbolize a wild realm beyond human control is not in itself particularly remarkable;
the image is a natural and obvious one, and one that Rilke had dealt with in his 1902
essay 'Von der Landscahft', where he talked of the Ancients' vision of landscape:
they were, he said, concerned only with landscape as habitation, and the mountain
was thus totally alien to them – the idea is close to Rilke's own concern with
landscape as potential 'home' and with Man's 'taming' activities in the world:

Aber der Berg war fremd, auf dem nicht menschengestaltige Götter wohnten, das
Vorgebirge, auf dem sich kein weithinsichtbares Standbild erhob, die Hänge, die
kein Hirte gefunden hatte, – sie waren keines Wortes wert. Alles war Bühne und leer,
solange der Mensch nicht auftrat und mit seines Leibes heiterer oder tragischer
Handlung die Szene erfüllte. Ihn erwartete alles und wo er kam, trat alles zurück und
gab ihm Raum.   (SW, V, 517)

More specifically Rilkean, however, is the distinctive 'internal' nature of these
'Bergen des Herzens'.[4] 'Ausgesetzt . . .' is one of the most remarkable of these
'inner landscapes', but there are other instances involving the same image, as in the

71

closing lines of the trilogy 'Vor Weihnachten 1914' with their reference to 'Herzgebirge' (SW, II, 98), and it also appears in one of Rilke's last poems, written in the clinic at Val-Mont in 1926:

> . . . ces monts
> qui forment une chaîne dans le coeur
> en sa partie abrupte et sauvage . . .   (SW, II, 623)

Taken as a personal document — it was written at a time when Rilke's depression was at its greatest — 'Ausgesetzt . . .' represents a cry of despair. As Bollnow puts it in his Existentialist study of Rilke: 'Hier ist es, wo er einsam der nackten Wirklichkeit seiner schmerzhaften Existenz gegenübersteht' (p. 35), comparing this setting with the conclusion of the Tenth Elegy. Most revealing, however, in the context of Rilke's landscape imagery as a whole is the explicitness with which this setting is portrayed and explained. This is achieved in the first two sentences by the three genitive metaphors: 'Bergen des Herzens', 'Ortschaft der Worte', and 'Gehöft von Gefühl'. These serve to indicate the allegorical nature of this landscape and to provide a key to its significance, and the poem then proceeds with a description of the landscape in which there are no more of these metaphors until the reversed one at the end — 'der Gipfel reine Verweigerung', which sums up the theme of total alienation that underlies the whole poem. It is this explicitness that makes this poem so outstanding as a key to Rilke's vision not only of the mountain, but of Man's place and role in the world as a whole: here, in vivid landscape terms, he shows how words and feelings are the tools with which Man 'tames' the 'untamed' world about him, and he thus prepares the way for the later Elegies and their exhortations to 'sagen' and 'verwandeln' — Man's duty to save the world by fervent naming and feeling.

One further aspect of these 'Bergen des Herzens' remains to be mentioned, and that is the distinct ambiguity of this landscape: on the one hand it presents a terrifying and hostile environment; on the other hand it has a certain almost paradisiacal quality about it — it is a place of integrated plants and animals, and the Garden of Eden parallel is strengthened by the fact that Man, unlike the 'unwissendes Kraut', has been expelled from this integration because he is 'der Wissende . . . der zu wissen begann'. This ambiguity becomes more comprehensible when one considers the identification of the Angels with these mountaintops: they too are ambiguous, for they are, like this landscape, beautiful, serene and monumentally integrated, but also they are fatal to Man, and terrifying — 'schrecklich' (SW, I, 685 and 689). As the Elegies proceed Rilke slowly comes to terms with this situation; he learns that it is not for us to attempt to emulate the Angels, that their supreme realm is closed to us mortals with our words — like the realm of the stars it is *besser* unsäglich' — (SW, I, 718); our place, he concludes, is not in this realm of supreme silence, but down below in the world of words: '*Hier* ist des *Säglichen* Zeit, *hier* seine Heimat' (ibid). It is not for us to go venturing into the alien heights, but to seek instead

> . . . ein reines, verhaltenes, schmales
> Menschliches, einen unseren Streifen Fruchtlands
> zwischen Strom und Gestein. Denn das eigene Herz übersteigt uns.
>
> (SW, I, 692)

In other words, in the imagery of 'Ausgesetzt . . .', we should not aspire beyond the 'sayable', 'tamed', or at least 'tameable', world that ends with 'die letzte Ortschaft der Worte' and the 'letztes / Gehöft von Gefühl'. Certainly our ambitions will be pointed in the *direction* of the Angels' mountaintops, for it is in these upper reaches of mortal experience, in the magnificent setting of the highest villages and farmsteads — to use again the imagery of 'Ausgesetzt . . .' — that the realm of earthly beauty lies; but to overreach ourselves by venturing beyond these limits would be to expose ourselves to the silent and unsayable realm of terrifying perfection:

> . . . Denn das Schöne ist nichts
> als des Schrecklichen Anfang.   (SW, I, 685)

Only in death may we proceed beyond the sayable world, like the youth of the Tenth Elegy, whom we lose as he climbs on into the peace beyond words of the mountains:

> Einsam steigt er dahin, in die Berge des Ur-Leids.
> Und nicht einmal sein Schritt klingt aus dem tonlosen Los.   (SW,I,725)

This is that realm of death that Rilke felt he had been thrust into prematurely in 1914, a silent and monumental world of 'Ur-Leid' for which he, alive, was totally unsuited. His depression had cast him beyond words and feeling into a world that words and feeling could not control, and thus he expressed his poetic and emotional barrenness of the time as a state of being 'Ausgesetzt auf den Bergen des Herzens', thus, in a typical Rilkean paradox akin to his concretizations of transience, capturing in a brilliant verbal image the very impossibility of all creative communication. As in the lament for Linos at the end of the First Elegy, where 'wagende erste Musik dürre Erstarrung durchdrang', so in this poem the apparently negative experience has kindled the positive song 'die uns jetzt hinreißt und tröstet und hilft' (SW, I, 688).

Plain (including Heath and Meadow)

It has already been noted how Rilke was from an early age attracted to flat, open countryside — such as he found in Russia and at Worpswede —, and that this attitude remained with him throughout his life is indicated by such statements as that of 12 April 1922, when, in Muzot, he described himself as 'im Innersten doch ein Anhänger der Ebene' (B, 782; to Gräfin Margot Sizzo-Noris-Crouy). The

73

origins of this *penchant* are somewhat obscure, but Rilke himself, in a dedicatory poem of 1904, suggests that he first encountered the open plain in his childhood readings of Liliencron:

> Ein Stadtkind war ich damals, dem der Hang
> sich abzusondern viele Tränen brachte,
> ein Noch-nicht-Lebender und stubenkrank,
> bis daß ich meine ersten Reisen machte:—
> wohin? — In Deinen wehenden Gesang.
> Der war für mich das Land, an das ich dachte;
> wenn Stadt und Stube lieblos schien und leer,
> dann war er Ebene und Wind vom Meer.   (SW, III, 777)

For the early Rilke the plain was more or less synonymous with the heath, and this too was a landscape feature that was, at least in part, first brought to his notice by Liliencron:

> Du, der die Heide kennt zu einer Zeit
> da meilenweit kein Mensch ist, weit und breit.   (Ibid.)

At the age of eighteen Rilke, inevitably, wrote a poem entitled 'Auf der Heide' (SW, III, 428f.) describing a dreamy, lassitudinous evening landscape strongly reminiscent of Theodor Storm — although the last stanza surprisingly introduces a sudden note of stark barrenness:

> Halbverdorrte Sträucher ragen
> aus dem Boden kahl und leer,
> und er wiegt mit leisem Klagen
> dürre Disteln hin und her . . .

As this stanza shows, the heath had unfriendly as well as friendly potentialities. The heaths of the juvenilia were, however, predominantly sympathetic, and in 1895 he wrote:

> die Heide sprach wie eine Schwester
> zu mir so manches milde Wort.   (SW, III, 429)

The heath disappears from Rilke's landscape repertoire after these early works, and one may assume that it was not a very important landscape feature for him — one can deduce very little of the poet's true attitude from these early references, as all of them fail to convince with their trite descriptions and conventional reactions.

A much more frequent and clearly genuinely enjoyed open landscape feature is represented by the meadow. This is the most consistently gentle landscape feature in Rilke — his meadows always evoke a mood of softness and peace, as in 'Orpheus. Eurydike. Hermes', with its 'Wiesen, sanft und voller Langmut' (SW, I, 542), or 'Die Liebende', who is 'duftend wie eine Wiese' (SW, I, 622). In a letter of 29 July 1904 Rilke wrote to Clara of his stay at Borgeby-Gård, and described the meadows in the summer evening: 'ich ging und blieb erst am Rande des Parkes stehen vor den dunklen Weidewiesen, von denen durch die große Stille knirschendes Kauen und warmes verhaltenes Malmen kommt . . .' (B, 04-07, 42). Possibly this experience lay behind the cryptic enthusiasm with which, in the Seventh Elegy, he talks of 'die Wiesen im Abend' (SW, I, 710); but in any case it is worth noting that earlier in the 1904 letter from Sweden Rilke had quite explicitly used the evening meadow as a symbol of life itself:

> Ach und das wirkliche Leben ist wie die wirkliche Welt.
> Und liegt wie eine Weidewiese da, von der abends warmes
> Atmen kommt und Duft und Menschenlosigkeit.   (B 04-07, 43)

The fact that both in the letter and in the Elegy it is the evening meadow with which Rilke is concerned provides a key to the significance of the meadow in general: there is a sense of contentment and, above all, of calm repletion about these descriptions; the meadows have been exposed all day to the summer, and now they are, so to speak, full of it — they have absorbed it and now, enriched, are resting in the cool of the evening. The meadow, in other words, seems to be a symbol of that receptivity that Rilke described with the epithet 'offen'. Thus the fifth of the second group of the *Sonette an Orpheus*, the 'anemone Sonnet',[5] describes the flower-covered meadow's summer day from 'der Anemone / Wiesenmorgen' through to 'der Ruhewink des Untergangs', and concludes with the question:

> Aber *wann*, in welchem aller Leben,
> sind wir endlich offen und Empfänger?

The same idea of 'openness', in this case in the form of a totally passive, almost unwilling, exposure, is associated with the meadow in 'Die Liebende', from which a line has already been quoted:

> Was bin ich unter diese
> Unendlichkeit gelegt,
> duftend wie eine Wiese,
> hin und her bewegt, . . .   (SW, I, 622)

Finally, the adjective 'empfänglich', which Rilke applies to the meadow in the poem 'Neigung: wahrhaftes Wort!' of 1922, provides the clearest evidence of the associations of openness and receptivity that this landscape feature held for him:

> wo sich ein Hügel langsam, mit sanften Geländen
> zu der empfänglichen Wiese neigt . . .   (SW, II, 139f.)

The meadow's 'openness' in this rather specific sense is paralleled by the literal openness of all the plain landscapes: all of them provide a symbol of 'das Offene', that ideal unindividuated realm, Man's ignorance of which is lamented in the Eighth Elegy:

Dieses heißt Schicksal: gegenüber sein
und nichts als das und immer gegenüber.   (SW, I, 715)

On the open plain there was no question of being 'gegenüber', and this must have been an important factor in the development of Rilke as an 'Anhänger der Ebene'. The plain itself is nonetheless a comparatively rare feature in his writings, and only during the Russia and Worpswede years can it in any way be said to dominate his landscape vision. In fact the plain was probably too overwhelmingly open to be of much use to Rilke after he had moved beyond the quasi-pantheism of his youth; it, the whole, dominated too much the parts in which he now became interested. What really interested him during the greater part of his life was not so much the plain itself as the plain-like aspects, the elements of openness, that he found in other landscapes. Thus in Paris he loved above all the wide, open boulevards and the great skies – the feature that he found lacking in the constrictive environment of Rome (B Lou, 155; 12 May 1904) – at Toledo he enthused about the 'offene Menge der Landschaft', and even in the mountains of the Valais it was the openness of the landscape that attracted him to Muzot. The delicate balance between constriction and openness that in later years replaced Rilke's delight in the empty vistas of Russia and Worpswede is illustrated well in his reaction to the landscape of the Baselland in 1920 (see p. 57 above): when he arrived here it was the openness that first attracted him, it was, he said, 'das erste Mal in der Schweiz, daß ich wieder ein rechtes Gefühl der Weite aufbringe' (B Nölke, 44; 6 March 1920); soon, however, he found that this landscape was *too* open, the plain element too strong, and the individual parts became lost 'im zu Weiten, Offenen' (B Nölke, 48; 20 April 1920). At Schloß Berg, on the other hand, the situation was much more favourable: here order and openness fused happily in the way the park ran on into the adjoining meadows:

der Park vor den stillen Fenstern geht in die Wiesen über, die leicht nach dem Irchel ansteigen und dieser, ein bewaldeter nachgiebiger Hügel, schließt den Ausblick ohne ihn irgendwie zu beengen.   (B Nölke, 70; 21 November 1920)

In descriptions such as this one sees what has become of the plain in the later Rilke. The open realm has developed away from the total swamping of individuality of the early years to a constellated universe of 'Bezug', of perfectly balanced relationship, and the great overpowering expanse of the plain recedes accordingly. But the meadow, the plain's slightly 'tamed', gentle variant, remains as much as ever one of Rilke's favourite landscape features, a symbol of 'openness' in all its senses.

Forest

The forest, like the heath, is decidedly ambiguous in its relationship with Man: on the one hand it offers a protective, friendly refuge from the unnatural turmoil of the

76

city, yet on the other hand, it represents an ominous and confusing wilderness.

The friendly Eichendorffian forest is, like the friendly heath, predominantly a feature of Rilke's early poems, where it occurs in such uninspired lines as:

> auf goldnen Sonnenflügeln sachte
> umschwebt mich grüner Waldestrost.   (SW, I, 79)

The Romantic vocabulary appears again in the lines:

> Der hohe Wald war mir ein Hort,
> ein guter Freund, vielleicht mein bester   (SW, III, 429)

and in 1894 Rilke wrote a cycle of four poems under the title 'Waldesrauschen' (SW, III, 424ff.), in which the mysterious and enchanting voice of the forest is again evoked in a decidedly derivative idiom.

The hostile forest is less frequent in the early work, but at times it does emerge as an ominous undertone from the idyllic superficial impression, as in the following poem of 1898, where both sides of the Romantic forest are present in the form of the ambivalent enchantress whose bewitchment and capture of the poet could be an act of bountifulness as much as of evil — Rilke manages very well here to leave the ending totally ambiguous as a fitting climax to the wanderer's (literal) growing bewilderment:

> Du wacher Wald, inmitten wehen Wintern
> hast du ein Frühlingsfühlen dir erkühnt,
> und leise lässest du dein Silber sintern,
> damit ich seh, wie deine Sehnsucht grünt.
>
> Und wie mich weiter deine Wege führen,
> erkenn ich kein Wohin und kein Woher
> und weiß: vor deinen Tiefen waren Türen —
> und sind nicht mehr.   (SW, I, 153)

Perhaps the best known of the predominantly hostile forest images in Rilke is the strange internal landscape of the Third Elegy:

> . . . seines Inneren Wildnis,
> diesen Urwald in ihm . . .   (SW, I, 695)

This use of the image is not entirely new in Rilke — it has a prototype and a kind of female counterpart in the Worpswede essay on Heinrich Vogeler:

Ist nicht jedes Mädchens Einsamkeit ein solcher verworrener Wald, ein Wald aus tausend Dingen, Träumen und Heimlichkeiten, in den der Mann als der Fremde kommt . . .?   (SW, V, 132)

In both of these metaphorical forests both the friendly and the hostile elements are present, with the latter almost totally dominating in the later work.

Tree

In contrast to the forest the tree is a frequent and deeply significant image in Rilke's work. It is always the isolated tree standing on its own with which he is concerned (the Rilkean forest is never looked on as a collection of Rilkean trees, and its significance bears little relation to that of the individual tree), and thus the type of the tree for Rilke is the 'Baum an dem Abhang' of the First Elegy. The importance of the tree derives from the broad variety of the ideas it evokes, and in later years these fused for Rilke to such an extent that the tree became a kind of universal symbol of life itself; hence the meaningfulness for even the despairing questioner of the First Elegy of the simple 'Baum an dem Abhang', a meaningfulness that is not investigated at this point and can only be deduced from the cumulative effect of the trees that have gone before in Rilke's life and work. In the Fourth Elegy, the opening lines go further, actually equating, in the words 'Bäume Lebens', trees and life itself. Other instances of the tree in the later works — such as the Tenth Elegy's 'Tränenbäume' (a counterpart to the 'Jubel-Baum' of a 1914 poem (SW, II, 84)) or the first lines of the *Sonette an Orpheus:*

> Da stieg ein Baum. O reine Übersteigung!
> O Orpheus singt! O hoher Baum im Ohr!

— all suggest deeper meanings beyond their cryptic brief appearances. That the Sonnets in particular, the most affirmative of Rilke's German cycles, should open with such an ecstatic mention of the tree is an indication of the deep and positive meaning that this symbol had acquired for him over the years.

Of the tree's multiple associations three in particular stand out. These are the ideas of perfection and self-sufficiency, of organic maturation, and of integration with the environment; this is the order in which they become prominent in Rilke's work, and at the end all three have accumulated to produce the recurrent life-symbol of the later poems.

For Rilke the tree had much in common with the fountain (another highly evocative symbol)[6] and it is in the first of the tree's associations — that of perfection and self-sufficiency — that the two are most closely linked. Like the fountain the tree stands alone, yet with its own centre of gravity, just as the 'Kunst-Ding' (SW, V, 158) does:

> Arbre, toujours au milieu
> de tout ce qui l'entoure —   (SW, II, 658)

This is the idea evoked in one of the first references to the tree, a poem of 1903 in the *Buch von der Armut und vom Tode*, in which Rilke laments the plight of the city children and their need for a little corner of countryside in which to live:

> Sie brauchen ja nur eine kleine Stelle,
> auf der sie alles haben wie ein Baum.   (SW, I, 362)

78

Here the tree's self-sufficiency is very much in the forefront; the idea of perfection develops out of this, reaching a climax in the reference to Orpheus's perfect song at the beginning of the Sonnets. It had already been implicit in an even earlier mention of the tree, in the poem 'Verkündigung' of 1899, where the Angel is overcome with confusion at Mary's calm and self-sufficient perfection, and repeats, as a refrain throughout the poem: 'du aber bist der Baum' (SW, I, 409f.).

The idea of the isolated and self-sufficient tree was one that continued to attract Rilke in the Muzot years — the 'gestalteten Bäume' of the Seventh Elegy are an instance of this (SW, I, 710), as are the 'einzelne erwachsene Pappeln', the 'Rufzeichen des Raums' that he could see from his room in the Château[7] —, but this image probably originates, if anywhere, in Worpswede, where Rilke first learnt to appreciate the things that stood out sharp and solitary above the horizon (see above, p. 21). It is natural that the tree should take on this, its first significance, largely during the years when Rilke was concerned with the world of isolated 'Dinge', and it is natural too that the second significance, that of organic maturation, comes to the fore during the post-Paris period — the years when Rilke himself was waiting for the 'fruition' that finally came in Switzerland.[8] Here too, however, there is a comparatively early first reference, which reveals how Rilke felt from the beginning the potentialities of the tree symbol:

Künstler sein heißt: nicht rechnen und zählen; reifen wie der Baum, der seine Säfte nicht drängt und getrost in den Stürmen des Frühlings steht ohne die Angst, daß dahinter kein Sommer kommen könnte. Er kommt doch. Aber er kommt nur zu den Geduldigen, die da sind, als ob die Ewigkeit vor ihnen läge, so sorglos still und weit. Ich lerne es täglich, lerne es unter Schmerzen denen ich dankbar bin: *Geduld* ist alles!   (B, 51; 23 April 1903 to Franz Xaver Kappus)

The idea of slow maturation was one that Rilke developed in *Malte Laurids Brigge* (SW, VI, 724f.) and one with which he consoled himself during the long and barren years of the War. Being drafted to the Kriegsarchiv in Vienna came as a rude shock to him; it was too much like the Militärschule of his childhood, and he wrote in a letter of 15 April 1917 to Anton Kippenberg that he felt like a tree that had been turned upside down, with its crown buried in the earth, adding: 'Wozu immer noch hinzu zu wissen ist, daß diese Krone gerade im Augenblick damals des Vergrabenwerdens voll neuer Säfte stand, zu Blühen und Tragen bereit wie nicht seit lange' (B, 528f.) In the Elegies the idea of absorption, maturation and fruition took on a new form as the doctrine of 'Verwandlung', but the old image of the tree was not forgotten, and it was brought back into prominence in Rilke's mind when he came across Valéry's poem 'Palme' (Valéry, pp. 153ff.). The theme of this work and its use of the tree image is very much akin to the ideas Rilke had expressed some twenty years before in the letter quoted above, as the following lines, with their similar emphasis on patience, show:

> Patience, patience,
> Patience dans l'azur!
> Chaque atome de silence
> Est la chance d'un fruit mûr!

Other lines expressed perfectly those very ideas with which Rilke had sought to console himself during the sterile decade before the Elegies:

> Ces jours qui te semblent vides
> Et perdus pour l'univers
> Ont des racines avides
> Qui travaillent les déserts.

Valéry's palm represented too all the ideas of perfection and self-sufficiency that Rilke saw in the tree, for, as another line put it, 'Sa figure est accomplie'; and in its balancing between heaven and earth it even approached the precious moment that Rilke had found expressed in the image of the top of the fountain jet (See below, pp. 106f.):

> Admire comme elle ...
> Départage sans mystère
> L'attirance de la terre
> Et le poids du firmament!

Influenced presumably by this poem, Rilke wrote of himself in February 1923:

Moi, je suis lent intérieurement, j'ai cette lenteur intrinsèque de l'arbre qui compose sa croissance et sa floraison, oui, j'ai un peu de son admirable patience (il m'a fallu m'y éduquer depuis que j'avais compris la secrète lenteur qui prépare, qui distille toute oeuvre d'art).   (B, 813; 3 February 1923 to 'une amie')

A few days later he wrote of his reading and translations of Valéry in terms that leave no doubt about the affinity that he felt for the French poet's work — and in particular for 'Palme':

Ich habe *herrliche* Paul-Valéry Gedichte übertragen, Gipfel der Herrlichkeit, und nie noch, auch in meinen besten Übersetzungen, ist mir solche Annäherung gegeben gewesen. Das macht natürlich sehr glücklich, und die malaises des Körpers und ihr Zwiespalt sind von solchen Siegen dann im reinsten Bogen überbrückt. Hören Sie selbst diese Strophe aus dem Gedicht 'Palme', wo der künstlerischen Geduld, dem Reifenlassen der Früchte in scheinbar anstehender unleistender Zeit, das Wort geredet ist ... [then follows Rilke's translation of the 'Patience, patience ...' stanza] (B, 816; 7 February 1923 to Dory Von der Mühll).

The tree as a symbol of integration with the environment is found, at its simplest and most obvious level, in the opening line of the Fourth Elegy: 'O Bäume Lebens, o wann winterlich? ' The tree, as this question suggests, is normally at one with the seasons. Like the migratory birds of the next lines it is 'verständigt', fully in step with the progress of the year, and reacting accordingly when spring and autumn arrive. A more subtle form of integration appears in the image of the wavy edge of the tree's leaves, which are like 'eines Windes Lächeln', and the image of 'unsres Saums / Wellen-Gefühle' appears also in a poem of 1924 in which yet another aspect of the tree is taken as a symbol of integration. This time it is the leafless autumn tree with which Rilke is concerned:

> Oh hoher Baum des Schauns, der sich entlaubt:
> nun heißts gewachsen sein dem Übermaße
> von Himmel, das durch seine Äste bricht.
> Erfüllt von Sommer, schien er tief und dicht,
> uns beinah denkend, ein vertrautes Haupt.
> Nun wird sein ganzes Innere zur Straße
> des Himmels. Und der Himmel kennt uns nicht.   (SW, II, 180)

The bare tree, with the gaps between its twigs and branches now visible, has let in the sky around and beyond it; as Stahl says: 'Der kahle Baum, durch den das Licht hindurchkann und der die Sicht nicht mehr versperrt, ist Rilke wie eine Öffnung, wie eine Straße und ein Weg ins Ganze' (p. 85). Finally in this connection the tree with its array of branches is, as Stahl also points out later, a symbol of that peculiarly Rilkean form of integration – 'Verteiltsein'.[9]

These three associations – perfect self-sufficiency, patient organic maturation, and integration with the environment – make of the tree one of the most positive landscape images in Rilke's work. It is of even more manifold significance than the in many respects similar image of the fountain, and its human associations make it one of the most sympathetic of the 'natural' landscape features. Although it is entirely a creation of Nature, its *human* significances are so strong as to move it towards the ideal landscape that the Man-made fountain occupies in its turn by virtue of its *natural* appearance and associations – the tree and the fountain are Nature's and Man's joint contributions to the harmonious environment that Rilke sought as 'home'.

Island

One of Rilke's earliest treatments of the island theme occurs in a poem of the *Leben und Lieder* collection of 1894. The poem is one of a group written in the autumn of 1893 entitled 'Sehnsuchtsgedanken', and, in a style and idiom openly derivative of Goethe's 'Mignon', it tells of a fairy-tale paradise of childhood dreams to which the poet longs to escape; the second stanza is typical of the poem as a whole:

> Kannst du mir sagen, wo das Eiland liegt,
> an dessen Küsten sich gefügig schmiegt
> mit feuchten Armen die kristallne See?
> Kannst du es nicht? – wo dann nach allem Weh
> sich um die Stirn ein kühler Lorbeer flicht
> kannst du es nicht?   (SW, III, 78)

The ideas here are entirely conventional, the paradisiacal island merely a further figment of the adolescent poet's *Sehnsucht*, and this more or less arbitrary use of the island image is soon superseded by something more integral.

The significance that islands have in the work of the mature Rilke is the traditional one of the idea of isolation, a significance that Blume, in his article 'Die Insel als Symbol in der deutschen Literatur' (p. 240), has traced in several major authors, and one that, as he points out, is already contained in the etymology of the two words: 'Hält man sich . . . die Ableitung des Wortes "Isoliertheit" von Insula, Insel, vor Augen, dann muß man sich allerdings fragen, ob nicht das Bild der Insel eine besonders nahe Beziehung zum Thema der Einsamkeit hat'. For Rilke this isolation is at first seen as something negative, as the curse of individuation:

. . . die Kunst hat . . . bewiesen, daß wir jeder auf einer anderen Insel leben; nur sind die Inseln nicht weit genug um einsam und unbekümmert zu bleiben. Einer kann den Anderen stören oder schrecken oder mit Speeren verfolgen — nur helfen kann keiner keinem.   (SW, V, 415)

But in these lines of 1898 there is already a hint of the more peculiarly Rilkean evaluation of isolation that in later poems tends to set him apart from the conventions of the island image as it had become established in the nine-teenth and twentieth centuries — indeed, the later Rilke could be said to be to be re-establishing what Blume sees as the significance of the island in pre-Romantic poetry: isolation as a manly virtue rather than a curse ('Insel', pp. 245f.). The Rilkean slant appears in the words 'nur sind die Inseln nicht weit genug um einsam und unbekümmert zu bleiben' — the lack of union is regretted, but another ideal is envisaged that would be equally preferable to the existing confusion, and that is a state in which isolation would be so complete that the islands could be 'einsam' and 'unbekümmert'.

This movement from seeing isolation as a curse to coming to terms with it and even affirming it follows the pattern portrayed in the *Duineser Elegien*, where the conventionally negative — death, sorrow, unrequited love, transience — comes to be acclaimed as positive; it is the Rilkean pattern of 'Umschlag', and it provides a basic theme in such poems as 'Die Blinde' of the *Buch der Bilder* (SW, I, 465ff.). In this work of 1900 the blind girl says of herself:

Ich bin eine Insel und allein.
Ich bin reich. —

She describes how her sudden enforced isolation had brought her great suffering, until slowly she had learnt to accept it and discover her neglected inner self:

Dann wuchs der Weg zu den Augen zu.
Ich weiß ihn nicht mehr.
Jetzt geht alles in mir umher,

82

sicher und sorglos; wie Genesende
gehn die Gefühle, genießend das Gehn,
durch meines Lebens dunkles Haus.

In the trilogy 'Die Insel. Nordsee' (SW, I, 538ff.) the movement to acceptance of
isolation is equally apparent. The first two poems describe successive layers of
loneliness — isolated individuals in isolated farms on an isolated island —, but it
is a negative loneliness: these people are confused, sad and oppressed by the might
of the outside world. In the third section, however, the island is compared to a star
— not to one of the constellated stars of the later Rilke, but a totally isolated one
that defiantly and heroically asserts its loneliness, a star that

> ... unerhellt und überhört,
> allein
>
> damit dies alles doch ein Ende nehme
> dunkel auf einer selbsterfundnen Bahn
> versucht zu gehen, blindlings, nicht im Plan
> der Wandelsterne, Sonnen und Systeme.

Now the island is seen in a new light, the 'Umschlag' has taken place — at least in
the poet's mind — and all that the island stands for is affirmed, albeit rather grimly
and desperately. As Fletcher and Schiffer say in their analysis of these poems'
symbols:

The attitude toward [man's isolation] in the first two sections of 'Die Insel'
shows the fear of life that is to be found in the early Rilke; the recognition and
acceptance of this inevitable isolation points forward to the concept of life as a
task to be mastered. The determination to set out 'damit dies alles doch ein
Ende nehme,' is, of course, still far removed from the unqualified affirmation of
human existence expressed in the 'Hiersein ist herrlich' of the Seventh Elegy. But
this willingness to face consciously the nature of human existence with its
limitations and uncertainties represents a determined step out of insular
existence. (p. 287)

(This last phrase is misleading: the star's determination represents a step out of
'insular existence' only to the extent that this existence is equated with the unhappy
state of affairs portrayed in the first two of these poems; there is a total
affirmation of 'insular existence' when this latter is recognised for its positive
aspects.)

The clearest instance of the island's isolation being seen as something
positive occurs in the *Rodin* monograph, where Rilke attempts to describe the
perfect self-sufficient loneliness of the 'Kunst-Ding'. In the first part of the
monograph, written in 1902, he uses the image of the walled city, but the
language is closely reminiscent of that of 'Die Blinde' and 'Die Insel. Nordsee':

Das plastische Ding gleicht jenen Städten der alten Zeit, die ganz in ihren Mauern lebten: die Bewohner hielten deshalb nicht ihren Atem an, und die Gebärden ihres Lebens brachen nicht ab. Aber nichts drang über die Grenzen des Kreises, der sie umgab, nichts war jenseits davon, nichts zeigte aus den Toren hinaus und keine Erwartung war offen nach außen. Wie groß auch die Bewegung eines Bildwerkes sein mag, sie muß, und sei es aus unendlichen Weiten, sei es aus der Tiefe des Himmels, sie muß zu ihm zurückkehren, der große Kreis muß sich schließen, der Kreis der Einsamkeit, in der ein Kunst-Ding seine Tage verbringt. (SW, V, 158)

In view of this passage it follows naturally that in the second part of this monograph, written at the height of Rilke's preoccupation with 'Dinge' in 1907, the island image is quite unequivocally used: 'Erst dann war ein Ding da, erst dann war es Insel, überall abgelöst von dem Kontinent des Ungewissen' (SW, V, 217). Here the island symbol reaches the acme of its perfection, and it is at this point that, to all intents and purposes, it disappears from Rilke's work; Rilke's fascination with the idea of perfect isolation becomes replaced around 1910 by a concern with 'Bezug', with the balance of perfectly isolated elements in an integrated whole. One might surmise that the archipelago would be the natural next stage in the development of his island imagery, paralleling the place of the constellation in the star imagery, but the landscapes of Rilke's poetry tend to be those of his personal experience, and so the island, which in its ideal form had been equated in 'Die Insel' with an isolated star, gives way in the later work to the image of the constellated star.

b) WATER

River

The river image is found predominantly in the early Rilke, where big, powerful rivers are taken as symbols of an ideal, onward-going, integrated force. In a letter of 8 August 1903 to Lou Andreas-Salomé he writes:

. . . ich teile mich immer wieder und fließe auseinander, – und möchte doch so gerne in *einem* Bette gehen und groß werden. Denn, nicht wahr . . ., es soll so sein; wir wollen wie ein Strom sein und nicht in Kanäle treten und Wasser zu den Weiden führen? Nicht wahr, wir sollen uns zusammenhalten und rauschen? Vielleicht dürfen wir, wenn wir sehr alt werden, einmal, ganz zum Schluß, nachgeben, uns ausbreiten und in *einem* Delta münden . . .   (B, 62)

Earlier in the same letter Rilke had described Rodin as a mighty headlong river rushing through the world (B, 60). In the poetry of this early period the river is often an expression of the pantheist life-force, akin in this respect to the all-linking wind:

Das Leben ist groß,
wilder, wie Ströme, die schäumen,

84

wilder, wie Sturm in den Bäumen.   (SW, I, 141)

The parallel is not exact, however, for the wind and the storm are essentially external elements rarely explicitly equated with life itself, and never with an individual human life. This latter is almost invariably the case with the river image, as in the *Buch der Bilder* poem 'Fortschritt', which describes enthusiastically a sudden surge in the poet's sense of integration with the world about him, and begins with the lines:

Und wieder rauscht mein tiefes Leben lauter,
als ob es jetzt in breitern Ufern ginge.   (SW, I, 402)

Much of the sense of these early examples of the river image is contained in the imagery of the Sixth Elegy, the 'hero' Elegy — an erratic among the later works in this respect. Throughout this Elegy the hero's life is described in terms appropriate to a rushing torrent, and seven lines from the end the image becomes explicit in the description of the heroes' mothers as 'Ursprung reißender Ströme' (SW, I, 707).

An occasional corollary of Rilke's river imagery is its sexual connotations: the river is invariably seen as male, whilst the riverbed is female. This idea too is present in the Sixth Elegy, where the mothers are described as 'Schluchten' (ibid.), and it is even clearer in the Third Elegy, with its description of the 'Fluß-Gott des Bluts', and 'das trockene Flußbett / einstiger Mütter' (SW, I, 693ff.). This aspect of the image gives rise, in the poem 'Hetären-Gräber' of the *Neue Gedichte*, to one of Rilke's most individual and most lengthy exploitations of the river and its associations. The poem describes the graves of the hetaerae that Rilke had seen in Rome, and in the last two stanzas a river image is introduced that is very similar to that used in the Sixth Elegy:

Flußbetten waren sie,
darüber hin in kurzen schnellen Wellen
(die weiter wollten zu dem nächsten Leben)
die Leiber vieler Jünglinge sich stürzten
und in denen der Männer Ströme rauschten.
Und manchesmal brachen Knaben aus den Bergen
der Kindheit, kamen zagen Falles nieder
und spielten mit den Dingen auf dem Grunde,
bis das Gefälle ihr Gefühl ergriff:

Dann füllten sie mit flachem klaren Wasser
die ganze Breite dieses breiten Weges
und trieben Wirbel an den tiefen Stellen;
und spiegelten zum ersten Mal die Ufer
und ferne Vogelrufe —, während hoch
die Sternennächte eines süßen Landes
in Himmel wuchsen, die sich nirgends schlossen.   (SW, I, 541f.)

85

This image of the quasi-sexual relationship between river and riverbed is Rilke's only really original addition to this common symbol of the progress of human life. One thing that his consistent use of the river image does show is the close relationship between the ideas associated with the hero in his later work and his concern in earlier years with the unindividuated *élan vital.*

Pond

This rather unusual motif occurs in a number of Rilke's poems, particularly in the early and middle periods of his life. It was a symbol of considerable importance for him, and one whose significance remained consistent throughout his life. The key to the meaning of the 'Teich' lies in the frequency with which the word 'offen' is associated with it:[10] at its simplest level the image is that of an eye, as in one of the early poems with its line: 'die Teiche,offen, liegend ohne Schlaf' (SW, I, 167), or, more explicitly, in the poem 'Sturm' of the *Buch der Bilder*, where the poet says: 'meine Augen sind offen wie Teiche' (SW, I, 404); the same idea is present in 'Orpheus. Eurydike. Hermes', with its reference to 'jener große graue blinde Teich' (SW, I, 542).

The specifically Rilkean aspect of this metaphor lies in the way it is used to express a particular form of seeing, and, indeed, not only of 'seeing' in the simple normal visual sense: the pond is for Rilke an image of passive receptivity, of abandonment to the impressions of the outside world – in short, it is, as its commonest epithet suggests, an image of 'Offenheit', of openness in that subjective sense that Bollnow (p. 166) characterizes as 'das Geöffnet-sein für die auf den Menschen eindringenden Stimmen'. The never-closing pond is thus a close relative of the anemone that provides the subject of the fifth of the second group of the *Sonette an Orpheus*, the little flower that Rilke had seen in a garden in Rome, and that he described in a letter of June 1914:

... sie war tagsüber so weit aufgegangen, daß sie sich zur Nacht nicht mehr schließen konnte. Es war furchtbar, sie zu sehen in der dunkeln Wiese, weit offen, immer noch aufnehmend in den wie rasend aufgerissenen Kelch, mit der vielzuvielen Nacht über sich, die nicht alle wurde. Und daneben alle die klugen Schwestern, jede zugegangen um ihr kleines Maß Überfluß.[11]

This is the situation of the poet as Rilke describes it in 'Wendung', where again the pond imagery is never far away:

> Aber wie oft, die vom Tag
> überladene Landschaft
> ruhete hin in sein stilles Gewahren, abends.
>
> Tiere traten getrost
> in den offenen Blick ...   (SW, II, 82)

An important point of distinction must, however, be made between the openness of the anemone or of the poet in 'Wendung', and that of the pond. In the passages just quoted, the accusatives ('in den . . . Kelch', 'in sein . . . Gewahren', 'in den . . . Blick') indicate the outside world's penetration into the depths of the receptive subject; in the pond imagery, on the other hand, Rilke is concerned with the reflections captured on the surface. Thus in 'Sturm' he describes the clouds rushing across the sky, and concludes:

> Überdunkelt und überschienen
> lieg ich flach unter ihnen,
> wie Ebenen liegen;
> meine Augen sind offen wie Teiche,
> und in ihnen flüchtet das gleiche
> Fliegen.   (SW, I, 404)

Here the dative ('in ihnen') indicates a distinctly different movement from that of absorbing the environment. The pond's surface reflections thus represent a kind of receptivity that in later years Rilke was to find too superficial, lacking in 'Verinnerlichung', in that love that 'Wendung' extols. One poem, however, does endue the pond with this profounder nature, and that is 'Waldteich, weicher, in sich eingekehrter', a poem that was written at the same time – indeed, in part on the same day – as 'Wendung', and one that in its later stanzas expresses precisely the same themes as 'Wendung'. This poem is one of the last of Rilke's references to the pond, but it is at the same time the only poem in which the pond is the initial subject; the description stems from a real experience, as Rilke disclosed shortly after:

Vor ein paar Tagen schrieb ich ein Gedicht . . . [das] von dem gewissen kleinen Waldteich im linken Strandwald seinen Ausgang nahm; plötzlich wurde mir dieses Stück Heiligendamm ganz überaus fühlbar. [12]

This pond Rilke saw as a haven of peace and restrained introversion; its distinctive feature in the context of the development of his imagery is the accusative following the word 'spiegeln' – the reflections are now absorbed, and no longer left to play on the surface:

> Waldteich, weicher, in sich eingekehrter –,
> draußen ringt das ganze Meer und braust,
> aufgeregte Fernen drücken Schwerter
> jedem Sturmstoß in die Faust –,
> während du aus dunkler unversehrter
> Tiefe Spiele der Libellen schaust.
>
> Was dort jenseits eingebeugter Bäume
> Überstürzung ist und Drang und Schwung,
> spielgelt sich in deine Innenräume
> als verhaltene Verdüsterung . . .   (SW, II, 79ff.)

The simple substitution of an accusative for a dative adapts the pond to an ideal
of Rilke's newly-developing mature vision of the world, and the poem, after
discussing and regretting his violation of the Non-Self by a too superficial
'Erringen', concludes with lines that again evoke the pond's absorption of the
world outside:

> Oh, ich habe zu der Welt kein Wesen,
> wenn sich nicht da draußen die Erscheinung,
> wie in leichter vorgefaßter Meinung,
> weither heiter in mich freut.

Occasionally the pond takes on a totally different significance, when Rilke
considers the surface of the water as a symbol of suspension above an abyss. This
idea appears in 'Orpheus. Eurydike. Hermes':

> Brücken über Leeres
> und jener große graue blinde Teich,
> der über seinem fernen Grunde hing
> wie Regenhimmel über einer Landschaft.   (SW, I, 542)

This image of precarious suspension (akin to that which Blume suggests Rilke saw
in the 'floating' city of Venice, (see above, pp. 33f.) does not, of course, rule out the
symbol of openness — they stem from different aspects of the pond's appearance
— here, indeed, the word 'blind' indicates that these more usual associations are
also present. Both suspension and openness are even more clearly present in a poem
of 1900, addressed to Paula Becker-Modersohn, in which Rilke describes his
affection for the way of life of the Worpswede artists. In fact, five lines of this
early work capture perfectly the whole significance of the pond for Rilke: here he
uses the image to express the heightening transformation of reality achieved by the
artist's receptive openness, and at the same time he brings in the theme of life above
the abyss — life always potentially threatened with collapse, but still firm under the
weight of the outside world; the collapse was to come in *Malte*, where the outside
world was no longer so congenial:

> Einfaches Sein, den Himmeln hingegeben,
> wie Teiche, welche immer offen sind,
> schöner erzählend, was die Lüfte leben,
> und über allem Abgrund, ewig eben,
> die Tage tragend und den Abendwind.   (SW, III, 706)

Sea

The underlying significance in Rilke's references to the sea is that of a unity to
which one abandons oneself; as one would expect of a landscape feature with these
associations, it is commonest in the early works. Some of the first references to the sea
appear in poems written in 1895, where the poet's relation to the sea has

connotations of a sexual nature — the sea is explicitly equated with a woman:

> ... nur für dich, du See, empfinde
> ich so, wie für ein schönes Weib.   (SW, III, 429)

Contemporaneous with these lines is a poem entitled 'Bad', which Rilke published in the cycle *Strandgut*; here the abandonment to the sea is literal — the bather allows himself to be carried out by the waves:

> Ins Meer! Die Welle naht, die scheue,
> und zieht mich leise vom Gerüst,
> und küßt mich zart, so wie die neue
> Geliebte dich, die bange, küßt.
>
> Wie weich sie mich umfängt! Ich spüre
> den frischen Odem glückbewußt.
> Sie legt mir ihre Perlenschnüre
> mit Schmeicheln um die bleiche Brust.   (SW, III, 432)

Rilke's most vivid statements about the sea stem from the 1903 visit to Viareggio. Here too he enjoyed close physical contact with the elements, exercising and sunbathing on the beach, taking 'Luftbäder', and swimming and bathing in the sea. His feelings about the sea at this time are epitomized in a letter to Clara:

Wenn bange, unruhige und böse Gedanken kommen, so gehe ich ans Meer, und das Meer übertönt sie mit seinen großen, weiten Geräuschen, reinigt mich mit seinem Lärm und legt einen Rhythmus allem in mir auf, was verstört und verwirrt ist. (B92-04, 318; 27 March 1903)

The soothing, purifying effect of the sea is here exemplified in the rhythmic noise of its waves, but the nature of this effect is again one of abandonment, of subjugation, as witness the words 'übertönt', 'legt einen Rhythmus allem ... auf'; in short we have here an example of the underlying pattern of all the early Rilke landscapes — of the dominance of Non-Self over Self, of that form of integration, which he was later to reject, that involved a passive abandonment to the environment. The significance of the sea for the writers of the turn of the century has been described by Wolfdietrich Rasch in his 'Aspekte der deutschen Literatur um 1900'; many of the ideas that he discusses are evoked in Rilke's early encounters with the sea, and it is clear that the sea with its totally integrated subordinate parts, the waves, had for Rilke — as for many of his contemporaries — a meaning akin to that of the wind and the storm, other early images of totality and unity:

Der Aublick des Meeres scheint fast die Anschauung des nicht sinnlich wahrnehmbaren Gesamtlebens zu ersetzen. Denn das Meer hat eine unübersehbare, grenzenlos scheinende, ins Ungewisse sich verlierende Weite, eine ständige Bewegtheit und den jähen Wechsel von relativer Ruhe und Sturm. Es ist sowohl einladend und schön wie bedrohlich und vernichtend. Vor allem aber bildet das Verhältnis der Welle zum Meer in unvergleichlicher Genauigkeit das Verhältnis des Individuums zur Lebens-

ganzheit ab. Aus der gewissermaßen amorphen Masse des Wassers bilden
sich in jedem Augenblick neue Wellen, die aber sofort wieder sich auflösen, in das
Ganze zurücksinken. Dieses aber erzeugt sogleich wieder neue Wellen, wie der
schöpferische Urgrund neue individuelle, schnell vergängliche Gestalten
hervorbringt.[13]

Rilke's use of the sea image is limited in scope and frequency, and he does not
seem to have pondered for long on its symbolic potentialities – he was more
content to relax and to describe his relaxation–, but the occasional references in
these early years do reveal a distinctive and consistent pattern of associations.

    Although Rilke is mainly concerned with the surface of the sea – the only later
reference of note is a brief description of the colours of the sea around Capri
(SW, VI, 987f.) – there are in his work a few strange and unusual submarine
landscapes. He used the image of the underwater world in a number of letters in
his period of depression around the beginning of the war: in 1914 he wrote to Lou
of the 'Trübe und Dichte meiner Unterwasserwelt' (B, 458; 8 June); in 1915 he
wrote to the Fürstin of 'die Herzen alle die jetzt unter Wasser sind' (B Taxis, 396;
5 January), and the next summer he wrote to the same correspondent of the
Scirocco, 'der mit ungewöhnlichem Druck die ganze Landschaft tagelang, ja mehr
als eine Woche, niederhielt, so daß man wie auf dem Grunde eines lauen
stehenden Wassers lebte' (B Taxis, 486f.; 2 June 1915). In a poem of this period Rilke
goes well beyond these simple pictures of oppressive submergence to work out the
submarine imagery in considerable detail, describing a weird landscape almost
unique in his work:

> Fast wie am Jüngsten Tag die Toten sich reißen
> aus der Umarmung der Erde, und der erleichterte Ball
> hinter ihnen empor sich in die Himmel verliert – ;
> so fast stürzen sich jetzt diese, die leben, ins Erdreich,
> und die beladene sinkt, die Erde, zum Weltgrund
> in der Jahrtausende Tang, wo die Schicksale noch –
> stumme mit stumpfem Fischblick –
> kalte Begegnungen haben. Wo aus Röhren hervor,
> wie See-Anemonen,
> prachtvoll die Wunden erblühn, und dem furchtbaren Pulp
> selber die Strömung den Tast-Arm
> an das zu Fassende trägt. Da bildet
> aus dem gebeinernen Kalk sich die blasse Koralle
> starrlebendigen Grauns, die sich schweigend verzweigt.   (SW, II, 423)

Even here, though it is now modified into the idea of falling, there are still those
associations of abandonment that had accompanied the earlier mentions of the sea.
The imagery is not entirely new, for thirteen years before, in the *Stunden-Buch*,
Rilke had described another, similar underwater scene; here too the ideas evoked
are of falling into the depths of an alien, frightening and oppressive world:

90

Ungläubig sah er sich mit einem Mal
herabgelassen auf die fremde Stätte
und auf den grünen Meergrund seiner Qual.
Und war ein Fisch und wand sich schlank und schwamm
durch tiefes Wasser, still und silbergrau,
sah Quallen hangen am Korallenstamm
und sah die Haare einer Meerjungfrau,
durch die das Wasser rauschte wie ein Kamm.   (SW, I, 335)

These two submarine landscapes are unique erratics in Rilke's work, all the more remarkable for the lengthy interval that separates them, and there are no other instances of this world that, presumably, Rilke had no personal experience of. If anything, they are more closely linked with the motif of the pond than with that of the sea, for, although their references are undeniably marine, they present in literal terms a descent into that abyss above which, in certain poems, the pond's surface is precariously suspended; the sea's surface, on the other hand, seems never to have held quite this same significance for Rilke.

Watershed

Although this image appears only once in the poems[14] it does recur in the letters in which Rilke describes the turning point that he felt his life had reached after the completion of *Malte Laurids Brigge*. This was the point — described in the poem 'Wendung' (SW, II, 82ff.) — at which he began to despair at the active and wilful delineation of 'Dinge', now felt as an unwarranted violation of the Non-Self, and to propound instead a doctrine of love, of nurturing the captured world and allowing it to mature inside him:

Denn des Anschauns, siehe, ist eine Grenze.
Und die geschautere Welt
will in der Liebe gedeihn.

Werk des Gesichts ist getan,
tue nun Herz-Werk
an den Bildern in dir, jenen gefangenen; denn du
überwältigtest sie: aber nun kennst du sie nicht.   (SW, II, 83f.)

At first the 'watershed' was full of promise; Rilke did not know where the new direction of flow would take him, but something positive seemed to be happening. On 30 August 1910 he wrote to the Fürstin Marie of his recent stay in the Bohemian castle of Lautschin:

Lautschin war eine rechte Wasserscheide, nun fließt alles anders ab, ich weiß nicht wohin, ich seh nicht hinaus, es nimmt mich ganz in Anspruch, daß auf einmal Quellen da sind, die das neue Gefälle ausnutzen und sich weitertreiben. Das ist gar nicht von meiner Arbeit zu verstehen, die ruht, aber innen im Leben bewegt sich etwas, die Seele wird etwas lernen, sie fängt bei neuen Anfangsgründen an, und

91

das Beste dabei ist mir, sie so bescheiden zu sehen. Vielleicht lern ich nun ein wenig menschlich werden, meine Kunst kam bisher eigentlich nur um den Preis zustande, daß ich auf lauter Dingen bestand; das war ein Eigensinn und, ich fürchte, auch ein Hochmut, lieber Gott, und eine ungeheure Habgierigkeit muß es gewesen sein. (B, 269)

Six months later he was not quite so sure about the way things would turn out:

... Welt liegt da aufgehäuft zwischen damals und jetzt, ein Berg von Welt, und selbst wenn er, ärgsten Falls, unfruchtbar bleiben sollte, so ists eine Grenze, eine Wasserscheide, ich werde gar nicht anders können, als von da mit allen Antrieben nach der neuen Seite hin abfließen.   (B Taxis, 30f.; 27 February 1911)

Finally, at the end of 1911, Rilke wrote to Lou Andreas-Salomé (the recipient of most of his more self-pitying letters) in terms that reveal his growing awareness of that period of comparative creative sterility — in terms of production — that was to occupy the decade between *Malte Laurids Brigge* and the completion of the *Duineser Elegien.* Again he exploits the potentialities of the watershed image to express his situation:

Kannst Du's begreifen, daß ich hinter diesem Buch [scil.: *Malte*] recht wie ein Überlebender zurückgeblieben bin, im Innersten ratlos, unbeschäftigt, nicht mehr zu beschäftigen? Je weiter ich es zu Ende schrieb, desto stärker fühlte ich, daß es ein unbeschreiblicher Abschnitt sein würde, eine hohe Wasserscheide, wie ich mir immer sagte; aber nun erweist es sich, daß alles Gewässer nach der alten Seite abgeflossen ist und ich in eine Dürre hinuntergeh, die nicht anders wird.   (B, 300; 28 December 1911)

The insistence with which Rilke uses this image to express this important point in his life contrasts with the absence of the watershed in the poetry of this — or indeed any other — period. Possibly he found the image too trite — it is certainly a very straightforward and obvious one. More likely it was too abstract: nearly all the landscape features in Rilke's poetry represent something he has personally experienced, and even if he had ventured into the high mountains (for which there seems to be no evidence), a watershed is not a feature that one can experience as such. It is highly unlikely that Rilke ever actually saw water flowing off a mountain in different directions. The way the image is used in these latters points to its artificial nature, from which a certain inconsistency arises that would be unlikely had Rilke had a specific experience in mind: the poet, partially identified with the water, nonetheless sees himself *crossing* the watershed, thus confusing the single direction of the flow of his life with the two directions taken by the two different pieces of water that the mountains divide in reality.

Summary and Conclusions

Each of the images in this chapter has a peculiar significance appropriate to itself: the mountain is a symbol of ineffable and terrifying perfection, and in it one can see the type of the 'untamed' landscape; the plain, whilst still essentially 'untamed', is not seen so much in the light of this fact, but rather as a feature representing unity, and, in its variant the meadow, an ideal receptive openness and gentleness; the forest, like the plain's other variant the heath, is an ambiguous mixture of hostility and refuge; the tree — one of Rilke's most positive symbols — unites self-sufficiency, organic maturation, and integration with the surrounding world; the island provides an image of a distinctively positive type of isolation. Of the aquatic landscape features the river has associations of a masculine life force, with the river-bed providing an image of femininity; the pond symbolizes both receptive openness and a sense of suspension above the abyss; the sea represents an invitation to integration through self-abandon, whilst finally the watershed, in its attempt to represent a turning-point, shows what confusion can arise when a poet too loosely uses a landscape feature he has not himself experienced.

Beyond these peculiar individual meanings there are patterns and common associations that make these features significant as a group. Some images are, for instance, predominant at certain stages in Rilke's life: this is particularly true of the plain, the island, the sea, and the river, all of which are very largely features of Rilke's early years. This may be ascribed in part to the simple biographical fact that these were landscape features typical of the lowland countryside with which Rilke was most often in contact at this time; but nonetheless in their common associations of unindividuated unity, and, in the island, absolute individuation, they point very distinctly to the polar modes of being with which Rilke wrestled in the early stages of his life before finding a reconciliation of them in the later years. The various water images also seem to be further linked by certain associations of 'life': certainly this idea was evoked for Rilke by the water-filled monuments of ancient Rome,[15] and it is at least implicit in his use of the sea, whilst individual lives are suggested in his rivers, ponds, and watersheds.

The one theme that emerges as common to all these features is, however, the concern that was séen in Part One to underlie all Rilke's dealings with landscape: the relation of Self and Non-Self, of part and whole. This is the notion behind the idea of 'taming': the mountain represents the Non-Self that is totally beyond the Self's control, whilst the forest and the heath, in their hostile aspects, are similarly threatening and unaccommodating. In the river the Self is taken up by the unindividuated *élan vital*; in such features as the sea and the plain it is overwhelmed and fused with the Non-Self, whilst in the island the two are utterly separate. The tree and the pond also show the life of the Self in the context of its surroundings, and portray ways in which it may integrate with and embrace the Non-Self.

In Rilke's use of these natural landscape images a scale of preference may be detected that runs from such sympathetic and well liked features as the tree, the meadow, the valley and the pond, through the plain, the river, the sea and the island, to the more ambivalent heath and forest, arriving finally at the distinctly hostile mountain, whose exposed, monumental, utterly wild summit is felt to be least attractive. Among these essentially 'untamed' natural settings the most favoured are thus those that do not exhibit this characteristic too strongly — landscape features that, while still being predominantly part of Nature, present a certain accommodation to Man, whether it be in their usefulness, as in the meadow, or in their abundance of positive human significance, as in the tree and the pond, or both, as again is the case with the meadow. This scale of preference is a revealing mirror image of that discernible in Rilke's attitude to the features of the Man-made landscape that are now to be discussed.

NOTES TO CHAPTER 2

1. Beda Allemann, 'Rainer Maria Rilke', pp.24f. This interpretation seems much more satisfactory than Steiner's rather meandering and inconclusive comments on these lines (Steiner, p. 41).
2. SW, II, 95. See in this connection 'River', below. See also Steiner, pp. 64-66.
3. SW, II, 220. See also Albert-Lazard, pp. 50f.
4. See 'Das Bild der inneren Landschaft' in Bollnow, pp. 74ff.
5. SW, I, 753ff. See also 'Pond', below.
6. See Chapter 3, 'Fountain'.
7. B, 701; 26 November 1921 to Gertrud Ouckama Knoop.
8. This theme of organic maturation is the principal — indeed, almost the only — topic of Pierre Laurette's thesis Le thème de l'arbre chez Valéry et Rilke.
9. Stahl, p. 114. Rilke encountered an instance of the tree's integration both with the earth and with the air in Maurice de Guérin's Le Centaure, for in his translation of this work there occurs a passage describing trees as 'fest in der Erde und teilnehmend am Bewegten nur durch das Gezweig, das die Hauche der Luft in ihrer Macht haben und seufzen machen' (GW, VI, 60).
10. See for instance SW, I, 167; SW, I, 404; and SW, III, 706. Compare 'aufgetan' (SW, I, 456).
11. B, 465; 26 June 1914 to Lou Andreas-Salomé. See also SW, II, 19.
12. Letter of 24 June 1914 to Helene von Nostitz, published by Ernst Zinn in Dichtung und Volkstum (Euphorion), 40 (1939), 122f.; also as note to B Lou, 604f.
13. Rasch, p.25 . Rilke never formulated so explicit a vision of the sea as this, but he does approach it in 'Zur Melodie der Dinge' of 1898, where he talks of life as combining 'die große Melodie' and 'die einzelnen Stimmen', and says: 'man muß aus den rauschenden Tumulten des Meeres den Takt des Wogenschlages ausschälen . . .' (SW, V, 418). Reference has already been made to Valéry's preoccupation with the sea (p. 30 above), and here again there is a close contact between his vision and Rilke's. A more 'decadent', but basically similar attitude is portrayed at the turn of the century in Thomas Mann's Aschenbach as he sits meditating on the shore at Venice: 'Er liebte das Meer aus tiefen Gründen: aus dem Ruheverlangen des schwer arbeitenden Künstlers, der vor der anspruchsvollen Vielgestalt der Erscheinungen an der Brust des Einfachen, Ungeheueren sich zu bergen begehrt . . .' (Thomas Mann, Sämtliche Erzählungen, Frankfurt a.M., 1963, p. 378). Another point of similarity between Rilke's and Mann's early portrayals of Venice is mentioned in Chapter 1, note 29 above.
14. In the poem 'Der Reisende' (SW, II, 141).

15.   See Chapter 1, 'Rome'. A poem of October 1924 similarly describes the animation of
        the landscape around Muzot – which normally appears as a singularly dry setting – by
        the autumn rains:

> Wasser, die stürzen und eilende . . .
> heiter vereinte, heiter sich teilende
> Wasser . . . Landschaft voll Gang.
> Wasser zu Wassern sich drängende
> und die in Klängen hängende
> Stille am Wiesenhang.   (SW, II, 501)

3

MAN-MADE LANDSCAPE FEATURES

City

For Rilke two cities in particular stood out as representing the type of the modern metropolitan 'Großstadt', and these were Prague and, still more forcefully, Paris. There were other cities, such as Berlin, to which he reacted in a similar way, but these were brief and far less influential experiences. His reaction to other cities — and these are numerically in a large majority — was less extreme and more individual: these were places such as Moscow, Venice, Florence, Toledo, Geneva and Bruges. There were also places such as Rome and Munich, which were felt of more in their capacity as cities, and which occupied an uneasy position somewhere between 'Großstadt' and 'Kleinstadt'. Rilke's attitude to the city has been largely covered in the earlier sections dealing with these individual places — in particular in that dealing with Paris — and the following is accordingly intended as a drawing of conclusions from the material already presented in those sections.[1]

In his experience and depiction of urban landscapes Rilke displays his fundamental preference for that delicate mid-point where Man and Nature co-exist in harmony and mutual enhancement. This preference shows itself not only in his sympathy for the less oppressively urban cities, but also — and perhaps more clearly — in his dual attitude to Paris: his horrified and anguished rejection of its squalid and stale slums, its noise, and its overwhelming vastness, and on the other hand his delight in the liberating sweep of its open boulevards, its wide skies, and, above all, its parks. In its negative aspects the city represents the worst kind of 'taming'; Nature has here been 'humanized' so excessively that the environment created is in the end totally inhuman. In the early works Rilke reveals a straightforward Romantic displeasure at the unnaturalness of city life; both the Prague poems and the early Paris works and letters have this as one of their central themes:

> Ich liebe die leisen blassen
> Stunden über dem Land:
> Die Kinder in allen Gassen
> stehn vor den Häusern und fassen
> sich heimlich bei der Hand.

Sie müssen ein Rufen spüren,
das weit in den Wiesen beginnt;
sie wollen einander führen
fort von den schwarzen Türen,
die nicht ihre Heimat sind. (SW, III, 452)

This poem ('Abendkinder' of 1897), for all its juvenile sentimentality, introduces a
theme that runs through Rilke's vision of the city for the rest of his life and
culminates in the Tenth Elegy's picture of the vulgar, noisy, brash, and above all,
false 'Leidstadt'. All that the city, in its negative aspect, had come to mean for Rilke
is negated in the one word '*wirklich*', with which, in this Elegy, he describes the
land beyond the city boundary. The picture is not so far removed from that of
'Abendkinder': again the call is to the distant meadows, and again children are
inhabitants of the realm of authenticity:

gleich im Rücken der Planke, gleich dahinter, ists *wirklich.*
Kinder spielen, und Liebende halten einander, – abseits,
ernst, im ärmlichen Gras, und Hunde haben Natur.
Weiter noch zieht es den Jüngling; vielleicht, daß er eine junge
Klage liebt . . . . . Hinter ihr her kommt er in Wiesen. (SW, I, 722)

The theme of the city's inauthenticity occurs many times in the third section of
the *Stunden-Buch*, the *Buch von der Armut und vom Tode*, which, together with
Malte Laurids Brigge, represents Rilke's principal poetic statement on the horrors
of metropolitan life. The most direct presentation of the theme appears in the
lines:

Die großen Städte sind nicht wahr; sie täuschen
den Tag, die Nacht, die Tiere und das Kind;
ihr Schweigen lügt, sie lügen mit Geräuschen
und mit den Dingen, welche willig sind. (SW, I, 352)

Here there is already a hint, in the last line, of a second major theme in Rilke's
vision of the big city: the theme of fragmentation, for, as Damian says, the big
city 'bildet mit ihrer Verwirrung und Auflösung den Gegensatz zur Ganzheit und
Einheit der Landschaft'.[2] The things that are willing to accept falsity recall the
chaotic and broken world of *Malte Laurids Brigge*, where the whole is overwhelmed
by the parts' 'misbehaviour'. Another of these early Paris poems expresses the same
idea in the word 'aufgelöst' – in the cities harmony and balance are undone and
chaos is let loose:

Denn, Herr, die großen Städte sind
verlorene und aufgelöste . . . (SW, I, 345)

The anarchic fragmentation of city life is a major theme of *Malte Laurids Brigge*
and it arises again in the third part of the 'Spanische Trilogie', where Rilke

97

contrasts the countryside with the city not so much because of the former's greater 'authenticity', but because of its monumental harmony, symbolized in the unified and integrated figure of the shepherd, as opposed to the city's noisy confusion:

> Daß mir doch, wenn ich wieder der Städte Gedräng
> und verwickelten Lärmknäul und die
> Wirrsal des Fahrzeugs um mich habe, einzeln,
> daß mir doch über das dichte Getrieb
> Himmel erinnerte und der erdige Bergrand,
> den von drüben heimwärts die Herde betrat.
> Steinig sei mir zu Mut
> und das Tagwerk des Hirten scheine mir möglich,
> wie er einhergeht und bräunt und mit messendem Steinwurf
> seine Herde besäumt, wo sie sich ausfranst.   (SW, II, 45f.)

The faults of the city, then, in Rilke's eyes may be summarized as falsity and fragmentation. Each of these is a function of the other, and the two are united in the worst fact of all about the city — its total divorce from the integrated world of Nature (illustrated too in the sorry lack of real contact at the edge of town, discussed in the next section). Falsity and fragmentation are precisely those features of modern life that are lamented in the *Duineser Elegien*, where they are ascribed to the sin that Rilke calls, amongst other things, 'deuten' — that procrustean imposition of false identities, of divisions where none in reality exist, of 'zu stark unterscheiden'. The city can thus be seen as the supreme image in Rilke's work of the 'gedeutete Welt', in the form of a violently 'overtamed' landscape. This is a setting in which Man has violated and rejected Nature, replacing it with a false and fragmented monster in which he can never, in the Rilkean sense, be truly at home; an environment whose only redeeming features are those where Nature has been brought back into partnership with Man in its parks and open spaces.

Edge of Town

This landscape feature is noteworthy for the frequency with which it recurs in Rilke's poetry, especially, though by no means exclusively, during the early years. The edge of — presumably — Prague is a favourite setting in the juvenilia; thus one of Rilke's first poems, the heavily sentimental 'Der alte Invalid', which he wrote at an unknown date during his teens, reaches its trite climax

> hier, wo die letzten Häuser
> schon stehn am äußern Tor.   (SW, III, 12)

Another poem, entitled 'Abend', and published a year later in the *Larenopfer*, begins with the lines:

> Einsam hinterm letzten Haus
> geht die rote Sonne schlafen, (SW, I, 20)

whilst the whole of an 1897 poem — included in the 'Landschaft' section of *Mir zur Feier* — treats of this setting:

> Das ist dort, wo die letzten Hütten sind
> und hohe Häuser, die mit engen Brüsten
> sich drängen aus den grauen Baugerüsten
> und schauen wollen, wo das Feld beginnt.
>
> Dort bleibt der Frühling immer bang und blaß,
> der Sommer fiebert hinter diesen Planken;
> die Kirschenbäume und die Kinder kranken,
> und nur der Herbst hat dorten keinen Haß.
>
> Und seine Abende sind manchesmal
> windschwingenstill und schön in ihrem Schmelze:
> Die Schafe schimmern und der Hirt im Pelze
> lehnt sich lauschend an dem letzten Lampenpfahl. — (SW, III, 226)

The same setting occurs again on various occasions throughout Rilke's work, perhaps the best known being the edge of the 'Leidstadt' and its 'Jahrmarkt' in the Tenth Elegy:

> .... Oh aber gleich darüber hinaus,
> hinter der letzten Planke, ...
> gleich im Rücken der Planke, gleich dahinter, ists *wirklich.* (SW, I, 722)

At the simplest level Rilke's fascination with the edge of towns can be seen as an interest in the crucial point of contact between the over-humanized city and the 'untamed' world of nature. Almost invariably there is something squalid and depressed about this aspect of the setting; there is no happy marriage between town and country, only a despoliation of the latter by the former, and to this extent the image is another aspect of the negative side of Rilke's vision of the city. This is especially true of the Prague poems, as in the first two stanzas of 'Das ist dort . . .', and the same idea is still present in the Tenth Elegy, where the real wild landscape of the 'Klagen' is much further out beyond this initial little piece of semi-nature with its 'ärmlichen Gras' (ibid.), which, one may imagine, is still polluted by the vulgar din of the nearby fair.

At this level, then, the edge of town is a rather unhappy instance of the world of nuance: an example of Rilke's concern with the interstices of existence, of those phenomena neglected in a world where we all 'zu stark unterscheiden'; unhappy because here the nuance between 'town' and 'country' reveals itself as not really viable — there are bits of town and bits of country, but no real harmony between the two. Except, that is, for such rare moments as the autumn in the last stanza of 'Das ist dort . . .'; it alone knows no divisive enmity: '. . . nur der Herbst hat dorten keinen Haß'. One can only surmise that this 'link season', which is at the same time a 'decadent' season, was able, for the young Rilke, to embrace and express best the disparate aspects of this sickly link setting.

The insurmountable divisions of the edge of town landscape are emphasized by the recurrence both in 'Das ist dort, . . .' and in the Tenth Elegy of references to 'Planken'; the fence is a natural enough feature of the suburban landscape, and the repetition after an interval of two and a half decades is probably entirely unconscious, but it does still help to indicate how much the idea of division, of a border, was in Rilke's mind when he described these landscapes. What exactly the fence separates is not very clear in the early poem, but in the Elegy the 'letzte Planke' is the critical borderline between the vulgarly tame human world and the outside realms of Nature's deeper authenticity. There is thus here an image of the relationship between the human world and the world of Nature, between Man and environment – in short, of the relationship between Self and Non-Self, and this seems to be one of the underlying attractions of the whole of the edge of town setting for Rilke. This distinction between the 'tamed' and the 'untamed' worlds becomes somewhat clearer if one brings into consideration the first lines of 'Ausgesetzt auf den Bergen des Herzens':

> Ausgesetzt auf den Bergen des Herzens. Siehe, wie klein dort,
> siehe: die letzte Ortschaft der Worte, und höher,
> aber wie klein auch, noch ein letztes
> Gehöft von Gefühl.   (SW, II, 94)

In this, the most exposed and 'untamed' of Rilke's landscapes, the poet seeks to find his bearings by referring to the last outposts of the 'tamed' world, the world that Man has subjugated with his mind – 'die letzte Ortschaft der Worte' – and with his feelings – 'ein letztes / Gehöft von Gefühl'. The situation of these two outposts, both qualified by the word 'letzt', is a close parallel to the edge of town: in each case the image is that of a Man-made, built-up landscape beyond which the wild, exposed countryside begins. The exposed state of these frontier areas is brought out equally clearly in the following lines from the *Stunden-Buch*, where again the image is that of the edge of a human settlement:

> In diesem Dorfe steht das letzte Haus
> so einsam wie das letzte Haus der Welt.   (SW, I, 323)

In a poem of the *Buch der Bilder* Rilke uses this same image of the last house, but this time he has attained a state of elated integration, and the world beyond the 'fence' has become sympathetic to the point of confusion:

> Dort draußen ist, was ich hier drinnen lebe,
> und hier und dort ist alles grenzenlos . . .
> der erste Stern ist wie das letzte Haus.   (SW, I, 458)

The significance of the last house and the edge of town is illustrated most clearly of all in the first poem of the *Buch der Bilder*, 'Eingang':

> Wer du auch seist: am Abend tritt hinaus
> aus deiner Stube, drin du alles weißt;
> als letztes vor der Ferne liegt dein Haus:
> wer du auch seist.
> Mit deinen Augen, welche müde kaum
> von der verbrauchten Schwelle sich befrein,
> hebst du ganz langsam einen schwarzen Baum
> und stellst ihn vor den Himmel: schlank, allein.
> Und hast die Welt gemacht. Und sie ist groß
> und wie ein Wort, das noch im Schweigen reift.
> Und wie dein Wille ihren Sinn begreift,
> lassen sie deine Augen zärtlich los . . .   (SW, I, 371)

Here the whole process of perception, conception and the 'taming' of the Non-Self is portrayed in terms of the 'last house' image. The image is universalized — every being, every Self, borders on a Non-Self. Rilke admonishes us to extend the boundaries of this Self, to leave the confines of the familiar room and cross the threshold — the word is used again, also with the word 'verbrauchen', in the Ninth Elegy, testifying once more to the importance in Rilke's work of this border between the 'tamed' and the 'untamed' worlds:

> Schwelle: was ists für zwei
> Liebende, daß sie die eigne ältere Schwelle der Tür
> ein wenig verbrauchen, . . .
> leicht.   (SW, 1, 718)

In 'Eingang' the Self extends itself beyond this threshold and 'tames' something from outside, from Nature — a tree, by isolating it, and by extension the whole world is captured as if by a word, by naming, by being given a human significance and becoming a concept. (It was this rather facile 'annexation' that Rilke later rejected as a loveless violation of the Non-Self in the poem 'Wendung' of 1914, and in the criticism of 'deuten' in the Elegies.)

The edge of town image rarely occurs in a single situation where its significance is very clear, but taking the various instances together, and particularly in the context of Rilke's work as a whole, one may fairly conclude that it represents more than a simple 'in between' situation. The city, as the ultimate 'tamed' landscape, has a relationship to the surrounding countryside that mirrors closely that between Man and his environment, between Self and Non-Self. The edge of town is the place where this relationship takes place, and in it Rilke portrayed on several occasions a setting that symbolized — possibly without his being fully aware of it — one of the major preoccupations of his work.

101

Tower

The associations of this motif for Rilke are fairly straightforward. The tower, as Bollnow says, represents in Rilke's works 'das Feste, das Ragende, das Gewaltige, zugleich aber auch in eine alte Vergangenheit Zurückreichende' (p. 76). Probably the most notable of Rilke's tower descriptions is 'Der Turm', inspired by the Tour St-Nicolas at Veurne during his visit to Flanders in 1906; here the impression is certainly one of 'das Ragende', but the impression of height is, initially at least, combined with one of claustrophobia – the poem begins with the word 'Erd-Inneres' – as the poet climbs up the terrifying abyss of the dark stairwell (SW, I, 532f.). In the poems of the War years the tower tends to take on significance as a phallic symbol, as in the second of the 'Gedichte für Lulu Albert-Lazard' of 1914, where sexual imagery is fused with that of poetic creation around the central image of the tower (SW, II, 218), and as in the fourth of the 'Sieben Gedichte' (SW, II, 436f.) written a year later. The quite minor role played in most of Rilke's work by the tower would seem to be belied by the ecstatic references made in the Elegies – the objects of the Elegies are largely ones that have, over the years, gathered considerable and rich associations for the poet –, but presumably the immediate everyday evocations of the word 'Turm' are taken by Rilke to be sufficient in themselves to provide an image of the magnificence of Man's aspirations and achievements, and to carry such lines as

> Aber ein Turm war groß, nicht wahr? O Engel, er war es, –
> groß, auch noch neben dir?   (SW, I, 712)

in the Seventh Elegy, and

> Sind wir vielleicht *hier*, um zu sagen: Haus,
> Brücke, Brunnen, Tor, Krug, Obstbaum, Fenster, –
> höchstens: Säule, Turm . . . .   (SW, I, 718)

in the Ninth. Associations of the pillar at Karnak and of the cathedrals of northern France certainly also play their part in contributing to the significance of these references to the tower in the Elegies.

Cathedral

The cathedral in Rilke's work plays a role similar to that of the tower, and, quite naturally, the two are at times inseparable. Both exemplify human achievement in their vertical vastness, but the cathedral, more than the more frequent tower, represents the heightened world of the aesthetically transformed object, as in the Seventh Elegy:

> . . . das strebende Stemmen,
> grau aus vergehender Stadt oder aus fremder, des Doms.   (SW, I, 712)

102

In its skyward aspirations in both the concrete and the spiritual sense the cathedral is literally and metaphorically raised above the surrounding town; imbued with immense human significance like the objects described in the Hulewicz-Brief, 'in die Hoffnung und Nachdenklichkeit unserer Vorväter eingegangen war',[3] it stands out as a permanent monument to humanity amidst the transitory — and thus alien — huddle of the city's houses.

The setting here is almost certainly that of Chartres, especially as this town is mentioned by name a few lines later. Chartres, more than any other, was *the* cathedral for Rilke, and although he did sometimes mention others, the impression made on him there remained uppermost in his mind throughout his life — as this reference in the Seventh Elegy testifies. A more immediate and much lengthier result of his excursion to Chartres was a series of poems written in the summer of 1906, and included in the *Neue Gedichte*: 'L'Ange du Méridien, Chartres', 'Die Kathedrale', 'Das Portal', 'Die Fensterrose', 'Das Kapitäl', and 'Gott im Mittelalter' (SW, I, 497ff.). In these poems the cathedral is seen as the mighty product of all that is deep and fervent in Man — an idea that develops naturally from the *Stunden-Buch* image of God as the product of the monks' infinite labour:

> Wir bauen an dir mit zitternden Händen
> und wir türmen Atom auf Atom.
> Aber wer kann dich vollenden,
> du Dom.   (SW, I, 261)

At Chartres the cathedral has been more than completed; it has outgrown its human creators, and in superior isolation rears above the everyday world:

> in jenen kleinen Städten kannst du sehn,
> wie sehr entwachsen ihrem Umgangskreis
> die Kathedralen waren. Ihr Erstehn
> ging über alles fort, . . .   (SW, I, 498)

In these lines from 'Die Kathedrale' the meaning of the cathedral for Rilke is summed up in the dual meaning of 'entwachsen', a pun that has its English equivalent in the phrase 'grown out of': the cathedral is both a product of its environment, of the richest human feelings of the city that it dominates, but also it has, by taking on such significance, outgrown the town that produced it. The cathedral thus stands alone like some gigantic 'Kunstding', a testimony, more magnificent than the tower, to the aspirations and achievements of the human spirit, and thus worthy to be shown with pride to the 'Angel' of the Elegies.

Fountain
    Of the man-made landscape features in Rilke's life and work the fountain was

103

probably the most meaningful, and the one that most consistently delighted and intrigued him. It occurs at all stages of his life, at first as a rather trite focus of Romantic *Stimmung* –

> Fern hör ich die Fontäne lallen
> ein Märchen, das ich längst vergaß, –   (SW, I, 81)

– but soon developing into a symbol evocative of more peculiarly Rilkean ideas summed up in the French poem 'La Fontaine' of February 1924:

> Je ne veux qu'une seule leçon, c'est la tienne,
> fontaine, qui en toi-même retombes, –
> celle des eaux risquées auxquelles incombe
> ce céleste retour vers la vie terrienne.
>
> Autant que ton multiple murmure
> rien ne saurait me servir d'exemple;
> toi, ô colonne légère du temple
> qui se détruit par sa propre nature.
>
> Dans ta chute, combien se module
> chaque jet d'eau qui termine sa danse.
> Que je me sens l'élève, l'émule
> de ton innombrable nuance!
>
> Mais ce qui plus que ton chant vers toi me décide
> c'est cet instant d'un silence en délire
> lorsqu'à la nuit, à travers ton élan liquide
> passe ton propre retour qu'un souffle retire.   (SW, II, 530)

It is uncommon for Rilke to state explicitly in his poetry that a particular object is meaningful for him; the importance for him of the fountain is emphasized all the more by the fact that he does precisely this at the beginning of 'La Fontaine'. Nor is this an isolated instance: some twenty-three years earlier he had begun the poem 'Von den Fontänen' with the line: 'Auf einmal weiß ich viel von den Fontänen' (SW, I, 456), whilst a fragmentary Elegy of 1912 contains the lines:

> . . . wem Aufstieg und Rückfall
> alter Fontäne nicht mehr . . .
> . . . die Seele erschreckt und verwandelt, der gehe
> . . . hinaus und tue sein Tagwerk; wo anders
> lauert das Große auf ihn und wird ihn wo anders
> anfalln, daß er sich wehrt.   (SW, II, 386)

Such direct pronouncements are reminiscent of the first line of the Sixth Elegy – 'Feigenbaum seit wie lange schon ists mir bedeutend' –, and even here thoughts of the fountain are not far away, for four lines later come the words:

> Wie der Fontäne Rohr treibt dein gebognes Gezweig
> abwärts den Saft und hinan . . .   (SW, I, 706)

At the centre of Rilke's fascination with the fountain lies the fact that the jet of water that rises and falls and rises again was a perfect embodiment of the idea of unbroken self-sufficient circularity, of that perfection of being attained by the 'angels' of the Elegies. The whole of the forty-one-line-long poem 'Von den Fontänen' is concerned with the manifold instances of rising and falling that are conjured up in the movement of the fountain, whilst the well-known 'Römische Fontäne' describes the fall of the water against the rising stem and basins of the old Roman fountain (SW, I, 529). The rising and falling movement that runs through all the Elegies is also condensed into the image of the fountain in the Seventh, where the delightful and subtle interplay of the two inseparable movements is expressed with a remarkable combination of complexity and succinctness, expressing the deep significance behind the fountain's outward simplicity:

> ... Fontäne,
> die zu dem drängendem Strahl schon das Fallen zuvornimmt
> im versprechlichen Spiel ...   (SW, I, 709)

In later years the emphasis on the fountain's self-sufficiency grows stronger; this is the idea expressed in the second line of 'La Fontaine' — 'qui en toi-même retombes' — and in a letter of 1919 Rilke even goes so far as to equate the fountain with the 'Kunst-Ding' in this respect:

Das Kunst-Ding kann nichts ändern und nichts verbessern; sowie es einmal da ist, steht es den Menschen nicht anders als die Natur gegenüber, in sich erfüllt, mit sich beschäftigt (wie eine Fontäne), also, wenn man es so nennen will: teilnahmslos. (B, 585; 2 August 1919 to Lisa Heise)

In Rilke's life one fountain in particular stood out as making a particularly deep impression on him, and that was the fountain in the garden of Schloß Berg am Irchel, where he stayed during late 1920 and early 1921. He could see and hear this fountain from his room, and he often mentioned it in his letters of the time. Here too he was struck by the self-sufficient, indeed, self-enriching, nature of this circle of moving water:

c'était elle qui vivait de sa vie impalpable, se jetant dans l'espace et retombant dans son propre sein —, enrichie de quoi? : d'elle-même. Oh qu'elle était légère, non, il n'y a pas une parole d'ici qui saurait exprimer son existence, éphémère tant qu'éternelle.   (B Merline, 98; 26 November 1920)

This fountain was the focal point of the whole garden — 'Le rôle principale incombe à la fontaine', he had written to the same correspondent a week earlier (p. 94; 18 November) — and its noise too became important for him: 'Und die, mit ihrem immerfort abgewandelten Niederfall ist nun wirklich das Maß der Geräusche, selten reicht etwas über ihr Rauschen hinaus!'[4] Like the sea at

Viareggio the splash of the fountain imposed a soothing background on Rilke's stay at Berg, but much more than the sea ever did it provided him with an exemplary image of the ideal he was seeking to attain in himself, and he talked of it accordingly as:

cette fontaine qui tout ce temps, même aux jours tant angoissés me répétait: reste, reste –, je suis là, je te donne l'exemple du mouvement que tu dois accomplir en toi-même.[5]

Undoubtedly the fountain at Berg was in Rilke's mind when he wrote 'La Fontaine', and this, his last major pronouncement on this theme, represents the climax of his lifelong fascination with fountains. Here, as at Berg, he is interested not only in the sight, but also in the sound of the fountain, its 'multiple murmure', which more than anything else is an example for him. It is an example, as in the earlier poems, of circular and self-sufficient movement, but it is much more than this, for in this late poem ideas more peculiar to Rilke's final period are also evoked in this fountain. In its synthesis of rise and fall the fountain had presented an image of the totality of life, and now this totality appears again in its 'innombrable nuance': Rilke now sees in the fountain a picture of the unindividuated realm of nuance where the human mistake of 'Deutung', of 'zu stark unterscheiden' (SW, I, 688), is made good. The crude divisions we make with our names and our concepts are healed, the apparent gaps reveal themselves as a deeper, more genuine continuum – the fountain's world of nuance is 'innombrable', in other words beyond division by number, or to use one of the most positive words in the late Rilke's vocabulary, 'überzählig' (SW, I, 720). The fountain is evidence of the ultimate unity of all that is apparently disparate, of rising and falling, of creation and destruction, of 'Verwandlung' and form. In the lines:

celle des eaux risquées auxquelles incombe
ce céleste retour vers la vie terrienne

the fountain also comes to express that enrichment through exposure, the joyful fulfilment of returning from 'Geworfensein' that Rilke, in one of his last poems, described as 'Heimgewicht':

Ach der geworfene,   ach der gewagte Ball,
füllt er die Hände nicht   anders mit Wiederkehr:
rein um sein Heimgewicht   ist er mehr.   (SW, II, 319)

The ball that was thrown, and, for a brief moment, stood still between rise and fall, fascinated Rilke.[6] It too, at this critical point, symbolized perfect balance and self-sufficiency, and 'La Fontaine' concludes with a similar image of this infinitesimal but immensely significant stage in the water's trajectory. Here at the top of the fountain all the tensions and balances, the syntheses and harmonies of this rich

image are perfectly combined, and as its literal climax provide a fitting
conclusion to Rilke's poem:

> Mais ce qui plus que ton chant vers toi me décide
> c'est cet instant d'un silence en délire
> lorsqu'à la nuit, à travers ton élan liquide
> passe ton propre retour qu'un souffle retire.

Summary and Conclusions

The five features discussed in this chapter represent the most unambiguously
Man-made elements in Rilke's landscape imagery. Although buildings are, on the
whole, less prominent in his work than the more natural landscape features, or
those formed by Man and Nature in concert, these five are quite important, and, in
both their similarities and dissimilarities, revealing.

Their common element is, of course, their artificiality — the fact that, as products
of Man's spirit and hands, they are largely beyond the control of Nature. What
distinguishes them, however, is the marked variation in Rilke's preferences for them:
the city is without doubt one of the most negative motifs in Rilke's work, and the
edge of town is only slightly less disliked. The tower, the cathedral, and, above all,
the fountain are, on the other hand, affirmed as creations of the highest order.
Outwardly the difference between these two groups lies in the size and degree of
artificiality: the city and the edge of town reveal an oppressive and heavy-handed
assertion of Man over Nature that results only in a degradation of both. In the other
three features there is a much greater cooperation between Man and Nature — indeed,
in all of them Rilke found close correlations with Nature's own creations: the
fountain, he felt, was like a Man-made tree, and he talked of 'den Fontänen, / den
unbegreiflichen Bäumen aus Glas' (SW, I, 456), or compared the rise and fall of the
water to that of the fig-tree's sap (SW, I, 706); the stairwell of the tower at Veurne
reminded him of the steep bed of underground streams (SW, I, 532); the
cathedrals in Paris were 'ein Stück Natur in dieser Stadt',[7] and he quoted
approvingly a comment by Rodin about the cathedral tower at Bruges: 'ça monte,
monte, monte et puis ca commence à fleurir tout en haut —, comme les rochers qui
fleurissent aussi tout en haut'.[8] These features, in addition to their peculiar
individual symbolic associations — which in themselves are almost invariably
positive — are thus seen as monuments to Man's working freely in harmony with
Nature, to his adaptation of her patterns and designs to relatively non-functional
expressions of his spirit's deepest aspirations, and they are neither eyesores nor
despoliations of the landscapes in which they stand.

The city has for Rilke much in common with the mountain, but there is also
much that makes them polar opposites. Both represent extremes and both are
terrifyingly hostile to the poet; but whereas the mountain's threat lies in its total

a-humanity, the city's horrors derive from its all too human nature: it is, in other words, a horribly 'overtamed' landscape feature that, like the 'untamed' mountain, demands to be brought nearer to the mid-point where Man and Nature meet. This is the point where Man's fountain and Nature's tree coexist by virtue of their metaphorical similarities. The metaphorical nature of this sympathy is, however, surpassed for Rilke by the literal cooperation of Man and Nature in the landscape features of the following chapter, where his most positive landscape symbols are discussed.

NOTES TO CHAPTER 3

1.   See also Blume, 'Stadt'. Blume, however, seems to be misled by Rilke's emphatic rejection of the 'Großstadt': the horrors of Paris may have led to expressions of longing for the countryside, but, as his letters show, Rilke was almost equally averse to the other extreme of the wild, totally untamed wilderness.
2.   Damian, p. 163. 'Landschaft' here has, of course, the restricted sense of 'country-side'.
3.   B, 899; 13 November 1925 to Witold Hulewicz.
4.   B, 639; 25 November 1920 to Gräfin M.
5.   Compare the following lines from Valéry's 'Palme', which Rilke was shortly to read and translate:

> – Calme, calme, reste calme!
> Connais le poids d'une palme
> Portant sa profusion!   (Valéry, p. 154)

6.   See 'Der Ball'; SW, I, 639f.
7.   B, 92-04, 270; 26 September 1902 to Clara.
8.   B, 04-07, 166; 20 July 1906 to Clara.

4

GENTLY 'TAMED' LANDSCAPE FEATURES

Park

The word 'Park' in Rilke refers almost always to the large rural parks of the type surrounding country mansions and castles; only in the earliest years did he write poems about city parks.[1] The park is a frequent feature in his work, and his letters too contain many descriptions of parks — he stayed at country houses many times during his life (mainly as a result of having a large number of aristocratic patrons), and invariably acquainted himself enthusiastically with the parks in which they were set. Parks never failed to find a positive response in Rilke, and of the many descriptions that he wrote, the following from a letter of 1923 is, in this respect, no exception; in it he reveals much of what it was that attracted him in the park landscape, and the passage, which is notable for the careful detail with which he portrays even a setting he has not seen, is worth quoting at some length:

Ihr Bericht über Weltrus (das ich — dem Namen nach — seit Kindheit kenne) hat mich außerordentlich interessiert; dieser Park voll baulicher Überraschungen, wie man sie im ausgehenden achtzehnten Jahrhundert so sehr liebte, als gälte es, eine solche, an einen Wohngedanken repräsentativ angeschlossene Umgebung, nicht nur zum zentralen Schloß hin gebunden zu halten, sondern auch wieder diese zu steife und stramme Bindung zu lockern, durch das Nebenspiel kleiner Architekturen, die sich ihrerseits auch wieder wichtig nehmen und, jede einzelne, stark genug sind, ein paar Bosketts zu beschäftigen und ein paar Wege zu sich zu verführen. Diese Solo-Stimmen im Großen und Ganzen der orchestralen Disposition können von unbeschreiblicher Bezauberung sein, manchmal sind sie wie ein Solo der Stille, wenn man den übrigen Park in seiner vielfältigen Musik plötzlich aus dem Gefühl verliert, um auf das Abseitssein einer solchen Mühle, eines solchen Tempelchens oder einfach einer 'chaumière de plaisir' einzugehen. — Wieviel wunderbare Übersetzungen seiner Erfahrung und Selbstkenntnis hat sich doch der menschliche Geist geschaffen —, wie diskret und geständig zugleich übertrug er sich in das Wesen einer solchen Anlage, spannte und rühmte sich in ihr auf seine Art, wie die Welt sich im Sternen-Himmel spannt und rühmt. . . . [Rilke then describes a 'chambre de verdure' — 'ein kleiner hochgewachsener Saal aus sorgfältig verbundenen, einst beschnitten gewesenen Taxus-Bäumen' — in another park and continues:] was aber noch ohne weiteres fühlbar bleibt, ist die wunderbare Berechtigung dieses dunkeln Intérieurs in seiner Funktion, einen

Übergang darzustellen, zwischen der ganz in Buchs gerahmten Ordnung des Schloßgartens und, draußen, der ausgedehnten, von zerstreutem Baumbestand überwachten Wiese, die ihre Schloßzugehörigkeit dann erst am Ausgang durch zwei Pappeln zu erkennen gibt. Auch da gibt es dann übrigens, rechts und links von dem Taxus-Zimmer, oder besser überhalb und unterhalb seiner (da sich die ganze Anlage in Terrassen abspielt) zwei bauliche Dépandancen: die 'Ruine' und die 'Volière', beide heute verfallen –, und die Wiese drüber hinaus heißt und hieß, als ob diese Ländlichkeit denn auch durch einen Namen bestätigt sein sollte (kein Mensch weiß wieso): 'Das Josephle'. Draußen im 'Josephle', ein paar hundert Schritte vom Schloß, aber jenseits jener Chambre de Verdure, in der man offenbar vergaß, was man hinter sich ließ, wurde in früheren Zeiten der Tee oder sogar eine Art Picknick eingenommen, um dieser proponierten Landschaftlichkeit in jeder Weise recht zu geben. Man sah hin, unwillkürlich, mit dem Wunsch, unter den alten Bäumen lichte Kleider zu sehen, die Frauen und Mädchen von einst –, ebenso vergangen nun (würde ein melancholischer Dichter aus ihren Tagen versichern) wie das zitternde Spiel der Laubschatten auf ihren Sommerkleidern . . . Nein, *nicht* ebenso vergangen vielleicht, denn: was wissen wir . . .   (B Sizzo, 51ff.; 16 December 1923)

The predominant concerns of the two parts of this passage are the balance of the park's layout, and the balance between Man and Nature that the park represents: the overall sense of harmony that the park evokes is thus presented in its constituent parts. In the first sentence Rilke describes the role of the castle: it is, quite simply, that of centre of gravity – it is the one object to which, ultimately, everything else is related. But the relationship is nevertheless a balanced one: the castle is not allowed to dominate, for it is surrounded by smaller centres of gravity,

die sich ihrerseits auch wieder wichtig nehmen und, jede einzelne, stark genug sind, ein paar Bosketts zu beschäftigen und ein paar Wege zu sich zu verführen.

The castle is, in the words of a letter Rilke had written earlier to the same correspondent, one of those that are '*für die Gärten* gemacht', unlike the strictly dominating castles of the French parks where the priority is reversed (B, 784; 12 April 1922). In the second sentence Rilke sums up this harmony and balance in the musical analogy – an image that is often at least implicit in his descriptions of parks, as in this passage of 1902: 'Und plötzlich heben, wie die Strophen eines Gedichts, Parkwege an, rhythmisch angelegt und mit einer gewissen graziösen Müßigkeit Halbkreise beschreibend zu dem nächsten Platze hin, statt gerade auf ihn zuzugehen' (SW, V, 86). More explicitly, in a letter to Clara of 1 June 1906 Rilke described the park at Chantilly as a 'Menuett des Raumes' (B04-07, 149f.) Like a piece of music, the park is a free creation of the human spirit, Rilke concludes in the third sentence, and even here there is a delicate balance, for Man's self-expression in the park he creates is 'diskret und geständig zugleich'. The last phrase of this sentence is especially noteworthy, for here Rilke brings in the image of the constellation: in the park the human spirit 'spannte und rühmte sich . . . auf seine Art, wie die Welt sich im Sternen-Himmel spannt und rühmt'. In

110

the park Man achieves a state of 'Bezug', of ideal constellated balance, and it is precisely this relationship that Rilke has portrayed in the two preceding sentences: the various elements of the park are independent and yet at the same time integrated into a pattern as 'Solo-Stimmen im Großen und Ganzen der orchestralen Disposition'. Here whole and part mutually enhance one another in what is in effect a vast work of art in which Man can walk about, enjoying the meaningful proportions that perfectly express his own spirit.

The park is not, however, by any means a creation of Man alone, and in the second part of this passage Rilke turns to the element of Nature in this landscape. Here too there is balance in the form of the gentle gradation represented by the all-important 'Übergang' between the slightly over-tamed 'Schloßgarten' and the much more casual meadow beyond. The meadow has been given a name, but this ascription of human significance is no heavy-handed violation of the 'deuten' type; this is an act of 'sagen' by which the very wildness – 'Ländlichkeit' – of this meadow has been, if anything, confirmed and intensified – 'bestätigt'. Here, more than anywhere, the balance between Man and Nature is most apparent, and Rilke sums it all up in the words 'dieser proponierten Landschaftlichkeit' – a phrase that could well apply to all the parks of his life and work in its expression of the coexistence of human order and natural wilderness. This aspect of the park is one that Rilke had mentioned in the Rodin monograph:

In den Häusern des achtzehnten Jahrhunderts und seinen gesetzvollen Parken sah er wehmütig das letzte Gesicht der Innenwelt einer Zeit. Und geduldig erkannte er in diesem Gesicht die Züge jenes Zusammenhangs mit der Natur, der seither verloren gegangen ist. (SW, V, 242)

The nostalgic sense of transience described in these lines is one that Rilke turns to in the last sentence of the letter above, and this again is a recurrent feature in his description of parks – it provides, for instance, the dominant theme in the cycle 'Die Parke' in the Neue Gedichte, which is one of Rilke's most lengthy exploitations of a single landscape feature and evidence enough in itself of his deep interest in the park.[2] There is about nearly all the parks in Rilke's work a heavy mood of mystery at the passing and yet at the same time distinctly felt presence of an age of genteel glory,[3] a mystery expressed not only by the rhetorical question of the last sentence in the letter above, but also, typically, by the dots with which the last two sentences end – or rather, do not end. More than anything this atmosphere seems to depend on the big old trees that occur in all of Rilke's parks, for, in addition to the significance that the tree has anyway for Rilke, these are the magnificent features that remain long after the people have gone, thus emphasizing all the more the evanescence of human life, whilst at the same time capturing and preserving the meaningfulness with which these long-dead people have imbued them in the manner of the 'uns mitwissenden Dinge' of the Hulewicz-Brief (B, 899; 13 November 1925). The juxtaposition of permanence

111

and transience is in fact literal here: 'unter den alten Bäumen lichte Kleider
... die Frauen und Mädchen von einst', and past and present, fantasy and fact,
become confused in the symbolic 'zitternde Spiel der Laubschatten'. For all its
permanence, the tree still, in its recurring annual cycle, is an embodiment of
transience, against which it gloriously reasserts its living self each spring, and thus
in a way it symbolises the whole park, where past and present, the passage of time
and stately timelessness coexist. This is the image that seems to underlie the first
stanza of 'Die Parke':

> Unaufhaltsam heben sich die Parke
> aus dem sanft zerfallenden Vergehn;
> überhäuft mit Himmeln, überstarke
> Überlieferte, die überstehn ... (SW, I, 603)

The park's old trees were a feature that attracted Rilke from the beginning; thus
in a letter of 25 June 1902 he wrote from Schloß Haseldorf in Holstein: 'Der große
Park um das Schloß ist nicht zu gepflegt und wirkt vor allem durch seine
Riesenbäume' (B, 36; to Otto Modersohn). But it was probably in the park at
Borgeby-Gård that Rilke was most impressed by the trees; in 1904 he described
this southern Swedish landscape to Clara in a letter in which he constantly returns
to mention them:

Das Land ganz eben — Felder, einzelne Höfe. Sehr große Kühe weiden auf
schönen Wiesen. Endlich kommen große, sehr große Bäume, — Wirtschaftsgebäude,
eines mit einem Storchnest! ... Ein großer Wirtschaftshof, eine Biegung des
Weges aus großen Bäumen: wir fahren in das Einfahrtstor des mittleren Turmes ...
— fahren auf der anderen Seite wieder heraus, an einer Allee aus Riesenkastanien-
bäumen vorbei, sehen links den Park mit Wiesen, die dunkel und frisch von Regen
sind, mit schönen langlangen, gepflegten Wegen und Bäumen — Bäumen.   (B, 82;
26 June 1904)

A postscript to the same letter, written the next day, again mentions the big trees:
'Gestern nach Tisch war ich allein im Park, der groß, wie ein Gebäude aus
Kastanien und Linden, in der Ebene liegt' (B, 86). This may well have been the
experience that led to the first lines of 'Abend in Skåne':

> Der Park ist hoch. Und wie aus einem Haus
> tret ich aus seiner Dämmerung heraus
> in Ebene und Abend.   (SW, I, 404)

Borgeby-Gård became for Rilke the type of the semi-wild park, a place heavy with
an atmosphere of brooding Nordic mystery, which he evoked in the Scandinavian
reminiscences of *Malte Laurids Brigge*, and in such poems as 'In einem fremden
Park. Borgeby-Gård' (SW, I, 517) — where every stanza takes the form of a question
as to the nature of this setting's intangible past-laden mystery —, and possibly also
the more ominous 'Vor dem Sommerregen' (SW, I, 520).

The parks of the 'Die Parke' cycle are of a slightly different kind: with their terraces and fountains, their basins, ponds and steps, they are more 'tamed' than Borgeby-Gård was, and are probably the result of experiences Rilke had in France. He expresses their arrogant grandeur in the words 'huldvoll, prunkend, purpurn und pompös', with which the first poem ends (SW, I, 603), but as the fourth poem emphasizes, these are still landscapes in whose creation Nature has – albeit not without a certain vanity – complied with the ordering hand of Man:

> Und Natur, erlaucht und als verletze
> sie nur unentschloßnes Ungefähr,
> nahm von diesen Königen Gesetze,
> selber selig, um den Tapis-vert
>
> ihrer Bäume Traum und Übertreibung
> aufzutürmen aus gebauschtem Grün
> und die Abende nach der Beschreibung
> von Verliebten in die Avenün
>
> einzumalen mit dem weichen Pinsel ...   (SW, I, 605)

In later years Rilke found at Berg am Irchel a park that represented a mid-point between the slightly wild landscape of Borgeby-Gård and the more tamed one of 'Die Parke'. The park at Berg, in spite of being fairly small, had, to a certain extent, reverted to Nature, so that from his window Rilke could see 'einen etwas vernachlässigten Park',[4] 'ein verlassener Park, der gegen die stille Landschaft zu offen steht'.[5] If at Borgeby-Gård Rilke had been impressed by the trees, here at Berg it was this openness of the edge of the park that he most frequently mentioned:

der Park vor den stillen Fenstern geht in die Wiesen über, die leicht nach dem Irchel ansteigen und dieser, ein bewaldeter nachgiebiger Hügel, schließt den Ausblick ohne ihn irgendwie zu beengen.[6]

Here not only was there an ideal non-constricting framework, together with an image of 'openness', but also a perfect interfusion of the 'tamed' and the natural landscapes, both represented here in their most reconcilable, sympathetic forms. The park at Berg was thus perfectly integrated into the landscape – complete in itself yet 'open'; a similar ideal situation had been the subject of the sixth of 'Die Parke', where Rilke described how the paths led the eye onwards and outwards across the park:

> bis zu den weiten Teichen,
> wo sie (wie einem Gleichen)
> der reiche Park verschenkt
>
> an den reichen Raum ...[7]

The park, then, represents for Rilke one of the most ideal of landscapes. In it he saw a harmonious balance in both the temporal and the spatial spheres, and a perfect accord between Man and Nature. In the park he saw achieved what he himself set out to do –a work of art in which transience was transmuted into permanence, in which neither the whole nor the part existed at the other's expense, but rather set off one another in a relationship of mutual enhancement, just as the park itself was distinct from and yet integrated into the surrounding countryside. Above all he found here a setting in which one could be perfectly at home, for in this 'proponierte Landschaftlichkeit' the human spirit had achieved a self-expression with which Nature was in full accord.

Garden

The garden is, of course, in many respects similar to the park, and the two are not always clearly distinguishable; Rilke's attitude to the garden reflects this affinity in being fundamentally similar to his attitude to the park. Thus his garden descriptions often tend to use the same imagery as his descriptions of parks, as in the musical analogy he brought into a reference to the garden at Soglio: 'der melodische Garten, in dem man die Notenzeilen noch erkennt unter der verwilderten Musik seiner Blumen';[8] or in his description of a garden on the Giudecca at Venice, where he talked of the openness of this tamed landscape, which only a strip of grass separated from the sea:

nichts ist ergreifender, als dieser Streifen Zwischen-Welt, als sollte man sich in ihm der Vielfältigkeit entwöhnen und auf ein Ewiges vorbereiten, das einfach ist. (B, 622; 26 June 1920, postscript to 25 June to Gräfin M.)

Like the park, the garden is a 'tamed' landscape, a fact that emerges clearly from the following passage from the story 'Der Totengräber', written around 1901, where there is already a hint of that ideal relationship between the 'tamed' and 'untamed' landscape that Rilke later saw in the way his parks fitted into the surrounding countryside:

Er hat das Gefühl: so lang er Herr ist hier, in diesen vier Hecken, so lang er hier ordnen kann und bauen, und wenigstens außen, wenigstens durch Blumen und Beete, diesem wahnwitzigen Zufall einen Sinn geben und ihn mit dem Land ringsherum versöhnen und in Einklang bringen kann, so lange hat der andere nicht recht . . . (SW, IV, 702)

The same idea was still with Rilke in 1920, though by now he was formulating it in the language of his later years:

Was mir hier sehr fehlt ist der Garten . . . die Häuser des Gutes liegen in der unabgegrenzt offenen Landschaft . . . Da verliert sich denn manches im zu Weiten, Offenen, was man gerne an geordneten Wegen beisammen sähe. (B Nölke, 48; 20 April 1920)

Steiner, in his commentary on the Third Elegy, mentions this 'tamed' aspect of the garden as being one of its essential features, and one that lies at the root of its significance in Rilke; Steiner sees the garden as a place of 'Bezug', or, as he puts it in the words of the Fourth Elegy, of 'Maß des Abstands':

in diesem (Urwald) wächst alles wahllos, unkultiviert, stürzt durcheinander, und jedes lebt auf Kosten des andern; im Garten dagegen ist Ordnung, jedem sein Platz angewiesen, und keines zerstört durch seine Existenz die des andern. Im Garten ist das tierhafte Leben der Urlandschaft gebändigt und das Maß des Abstands gewonnen. (p. 71)

Hence the entreaty to the girl at the end of this Third Elegy:

> führ ihn
> nah an den Garten heran . . .

She is to bring the youth into contact with a more serene and balanced realm, away from the violent chaos of 'seines Inneren Wildnis'; the garden image here is evidence of the consistency with which the meaning of this Elegy is carried on its landscape symbols. Exceptionally the garden in Rilke is 'overtamed', 'gedeutet': an instance of this occurs in the Fourth Elegy, with its reference to 'Der bekannte Garten' (SW, I, 697). Steiner describes this as

die Vorstellung des spießbürgerlichen Gärtchens . . . in dem alles in Kleinheit und Enge vorausberechnet und herausgeputzt ist, nichts frei sich entfalten und entwickeln kann oder sonst wieder auf das stereotype Maß zurückgeschnitten wird.[9]

Although the park and the garden are fundamentally alike in the meaning they have for Rilke, there is frequently a noticeable difference in the manner in which he uses them. This lies in the fact that the park is almost invariably presented literally, whereas the garden is often used metaphorically — possibly because it is a commoner conventional symbol than the park; the garden is also more distinctly 'tamed', more 'humanized', than the park, and thus lends itself more readily to the human associations that it expresses in much of Rilke's imagery. In Rilke's early work especially the garden is a common metaphor for a person: a poem of November 1897 begins with the line: 'Ich bin ein Garten, und der Frühling schneit' (SW, III, 582), whilst another, written some six weeks later, begins: 'Ich will ein Garten sein . . .' (SW, I, 147). Similarly a poem of March 1898 starts:

> Ihr Mädchen seid wie die Gärten
> am Abend im April . . .   (SW, III, 602)

A later poem, of 1914, describes how lovers intensely feel and then *become* the garden about them (SW, II, 222), and a letter of 29 December 1921 talks of Woman as the 'Garten der Liebe', continuing:

die Frauen . . . *sind* dieser Garten und dieses Gartens Himmel und Wind und Windstille dazu, können sich nicht rühren, als *in* sich, können nur Dasein und Jahreszeiten hinnehmen im Rhythmus von Erwartung, Erfüllung und Abschied. (B, 722; to Ilse Blumenthal-Weiß)

Common to all these instances of the garden image is the idea of integration: the garden, as a mid-point between Man and Nature, is aptly used here to symbolize a state of harmony with Nature, either by the poet's 'Ich', as in the first stanza of this 1897 poem:

> Ich bin so jung. Ich möchte jedem Klange,
> der mir vorüberrauscht, mich schauernd schenken,
> und willig in des Windes liebem Zwange,
> wie Windendes über dem Gartengange,
> will meine Sehnsucht ihre Ranken schwenken . . .   (SW, I, 147)

or by those more integrated beings of Rilke's world, lovers and women, as in the other quotations above. The connection between love and gardens was one that Rilke encountered in *Die Liebe der Magdalena*, as the following passage from his translation shows:

die Liebe, die gerade anfängt . . . ganz besonders liebt die Gärten, die Blumen, die gepflegten und gefälligen Ländereien, die, wenn ich mich so ausdrücken darf, durch ihr lachendes Gesicht an ihrer Freude mitwirken.   (GW, VI, 96)

This use of the garden image as a symbol of integration reaches its climax in the seventeenth of the second group of the *Sonette an Orpheus*, for here, in the 'immer selig bewässerten Gärten', Rilke presents a picture of that ideal realm that the angels inhabit — a place where there are 'Bäume, von Engeln beflogen'. Here, for once, the perfection symbolized by the garden reaches a superhuman intensity. Conversely, in 'Das Lied des Zwerges', absence of integration is symbolized by the absence of a garden — referring to his misshapen body the dwarf says:

> Meine Seele . . .
> . . . hat keinen Garten, sie hat kein Bett . . .   (SW, I, 454)

Finally, there is, in a letter of May 1922, an instance of a metaphorical use of the verb 'gärtnern', where Rilke takes up again the youthful image of himself as a garden. He describes his comparative lack of success in cultivating the garden at Muzot — due mainly to impatience and lack of 'Können' on his part — but then, referring to the production of the Elegies and Sonnets, he continues:

Mein inneres Gärtnern war herrlich diesen Winter. Das plötzlich wieder heile Bewußtsein meiner tief bestellten Erde ergab mir eine große Jahreszeit des Geistes und eine lange nicht mehr gekannte Stärke des Herzstrahles.[10]

Orchard

With one noteworthy exception this is distinctly a feature of the later Rilke's
work. Together with the vineyard it tends to replace the earlier park and garden
imagery during the Valais years. The exception is the 1907 poem 'Der Apfel-
garten, Borgeby-Gård':

> Komm gleich nach dem Sonnenuntergange,
> sieh das Abendgrün des Rasengrunds;
> ist es nicht, als hätten wir es lange
> angesammelt und erspart in uns,
>
> um es jetzt aus Fühlen und Erinnern,
> neuer Hoffnung, halbvergeßnem Freun,
> noch vermischt mit Dunkel aus dem Innern,
> in Gedanken vor uns hinzustreun
>
> unter Bäume wie von Dürer, die
> das Gewicht von hundert Arbeitstagen
> in den überfüllten Früchten tragen,
> dienend, voll Geduld, versuchend, wie
>
> das, was alle Maße übersteigt,
> noch zu heben ist und hinzugeben,
> wenn man willig, durch ein langes Leben
> nur das Eine will und wächst und schweigt.   (SW, I, 637f.)

This poem — which, with its opening invocation to an unidentified 'Du' to come
and ponder on the colours and plenitude of a landscape, probably owes something
to George's 'Komm in den totgesagten park und schau' — contains already the
two closely linked aspects that stand out in the Valais orchard poems: in the first
two stanzas Rilke tells how the orchard (here in the colour of its grass) is filled
almost to the point of identification with human significance, whilst the last two
stanzas present the orchard as a symbol of patient fruition, the two ideas fusing
in the pronoun 'man' and the last two lines — a culmination to which the whole
poem has been climbing as to fruition and the tops of the trees in its one long
sentence from the third line on —, and the whole meaningful activity of the
orchard is summarized in the words 'wächst und schweigt', with which, appro-
priately, the poem ends. These ideas are very reminiscent of the tree
image in Rilke — the orchard here is described as 'Bäume wie von Dürer' — and
it could well be said that the orchard, rather than the forest, is seen by Rilke as a
collection of trees whose significance is compounded of all that the individual
trees signify, rather than having an entirely independent meaning of its own.

The idea of calm organic maturation with which 'Der Apfelgarten' concludes
is fundamental to the Valais orchard poems. It appears, for instance, in the lines:

> Mon beau verger que je sois l'adepte
> de ton silence laborieux . . .   (SW, II, 705)

where the exemplary nature of this landscape feature — already implicit in 'Der Apfelgarten' — becomes explicit. Explicit too is that identity of Ich and orchard that the first two stanzas of 'Der Apfelgarten' had suggested:

> Tout autour veut qu'on l'écoute —,
> écoutons jusqu'au bout;
> car le verger et la route
> c'est toujours nous!   (SW, II, 527)

The main evidence of Rilke's deep fascination with the orchard during the years at Muzot is, of course, the fact that one of the major collections of French poems he wrote at this time is called *Vergers.* Although in fact only a minority of these fifty-nine poems and short cycles are actually concerned with the orchard, all are underlaid with that mood of peace and calm fulfilment that crowned these last years of Rilke's life, and of which the orchard was a supreme symbol. At the centre of this collection is the seven-poem cycle 'Verger' (SW, II, 531ff.), which begins with a statement of Rilke's fascination with this French word for which he could find no adequate translation in German; as the poem shows, it was the landscape feature itself that initially attracted him, but the German language could express it only with too specific a term — 'la clôture qui défend' (such, presumably, as 'Apfelgarten') —, or with one too general — 'un à peu près trop vague' (such as 'Obstgarten'). In the Valais Rilke found both rich and mellow Southern orchards, and the language in which they could be expressed, and, with the idea of organic maturation already prominent in his thought at the time, he took grateful advantage of them:

> Peut-être que si j'ai osé t'écrire,
> langue prêtée, c'était pour employer
> ce nom rustique dont l'unique empire
> me tourmentait depuis toujours: Verger.
>
> Pauvre poète qui doit élire
> pour dire tout ce que ce nom comprend,
> un à peu prés trop vague qui chavire,
> ou pire: la clôture qui défend.
>
> Verger: ô privilège d'une lyre
> de pouvoir te nommer simplement;
> nom sans pareil qui les abeilles attire,
> nom qui respire et attend ...
>
> Nom clair qui cache le printemps antique,
> tout aussi plein que transparent,
> et qui dans ses syllabes symétriques
> redouble tout et devient abondant.

The calm and abundance that Rilke sees echoed in the very sound of the word 'verger' provide the keynote for the rest of the cycle. In the second poem he talks of the forces that attract the orchard — like the tree — both upward and downward; in the third we learn of the meaningfulness of the orchard:

> Jamais la terre n'est plus réelle
> que dans tes branches, ô verger blond . . .

— a meaningfulness compounded of the subtle fusion of permanence and transience in the dappled shadows that the orchard casts together with all its associations of fruitful fulfilment, whilst at the centre of this orchard all is captured in a 'calme fontaine'; the fourth poem tells how all the old forgotten gods are ever busy round the orchard. In the last three poems in the cycle Rilke portrays the poet's relationship to the orchard: in the fifth poem he dominates in a gentle way as a shepherd watching his flock:

> Tu te repais autour de moi, ô troupeau d'abondance
> et tu fais penser ton berger.[11]

In the sixth the image is that of the orchard as a garment, and this time *it* dominates:

> Que de fois, au lieu de promenade,
> il s'imposait en devenant tout grand . . .

In the last poem the balance between the poet and his orchard environment is established; both of them are now seen as equals in relation to the greater environment that surrounds them both:

> Tes dangers et les miens, ne sont-ils point
> tout fraternels, ô verger, ô mon frère?
> Un même vent, nous venant de loin,
> nous force d'être tendres et austères.

Vineyard

Like the orchard, the vineyard is predominantly a feature of Rilke's late works. There are a few early references, derived from the first journeys to Italy, as the poem of 1898 that begins:

> Blendender Weg, der sich vor Licht verlor,
> Sonnengewicht auf allem Weingelände.   (SW, I, 164)

This brilliant sunlight is a feature of nearly all the later vineyard descriptions, and it is the principal distinguishing feature between them and the otherwise very similar orchard imagery — the vineyard too represents rich organic growth and cooperation between Man and Nature, but, with its hot sun and its dry soil, it is lacking in that mood of gentleness that always appertains to the orchard. This emerges clearly from the vineyard equivalent of the *Verger* cycle: the 'Sieben Entwürfe aus dem Wallis oder Das kleine Weinjahr' of 1923.[12] In the two French and five German poems of this cycle Rilke describes the more violent level of this landscape feature's human associations of organic growth and creativity:

> So wie Jakob mit dem Engel rang
> ringt der Weinstock mit dem Sonnen-Riesen,
> diesen großen Sommertag und diesen
> Tag im Herbst, bis an den Untergang.
>
> Der gelockte schöne Weinstock ringt.
> Aber abends, langsam losgelassen,
> fühlt er, wie aus dem Herüberfassen
> jener Arme ihn die Kraft durchdringt,
>
> wider die er, wie ein Knabe, drängte;
> ganz gemischt mit seinem Widerstand,
> wird sie nun in ihm das Unumschränkte ...
> Und der Sieg bleibt rein und unerkannt.   (SW, II, 146f.)

On occasions, though, Rilke portrayed the vineyard in a more gentle light; mention has already been made of his impressionistic picture of the sombre tones of the Capri vineyards in winter (p. 28 above), and in the Valais he could see 'Hänge, gestreift von den Reihen des Weins und später reichlich gekräuselt von seinem Laub'[13] — a sight that inspired him to use imagery akin to the musical and verse analogies of his park and garden descriptions, and thus to show that in this landscape feature too Man and Nature conspired together to produce what was tantamount to an art-work of the highest spiritual order:

> Bientôt ce sera à la vigne
> de se remettre au clair;
> j'attends déjà qu'on aligne
> les échalas comme des vers.
>
> Quel adorable poème
> l'on écrira sur les coteaux!
> Et ce sera le soleil même
> qui le jugera beau.[14]

Road, Path, etc.

The considerable significance that the 'Weg' held for Rilke is attested by the mention of this word at two important points in the Elegies: it occurs first in the Seventh in its list of ecstatically affirmed components of the summer day in the line: 'nicht nur die Wege, nicht nur die Wiesen im Abend', and it appears again in the Tenth as the name of one of the constellations in the sky above the 'Leidland'.

In one of the early poems the 'Weg' is seen as a constrictive feature in the landscape, and it is compared unfavourably with the open 'Wiese':

> Kein *Weg* kann führen. Nur die Wiesen
> sind weite Wege, wie für Riesen,
> und kühl und dunkel um den Schuh,
> und enden nicht bei kleinen Türen
> und führen jeden, den sie führen,
> längst wartenden Gewalten zu . . .   (SW, III, 731f.)

This poem is a typical product of that period when the plain was the dominant image in Rilke's landscapes — the period too in which his youthful pantheism led him to a distinct preference for wild and natural landscape features; the negative associations of the 'Weg' in this poem are quite unique and in the rest of his work the word is decidedly positive. The 'Weg' is that which links, and in Rilke's landscapes it is that which leads Man into and through the environment and establishes his integration with it; this is particularly clear in the poem 'Spaziergang' of 1924:

> Schon ist mein Blick am Hügel, dem besonnten,
> dem Wege, den ich kaum begann, voran.
> So faßt uns das, was wir nicht fassen konnten,
> voller Erscheinung, aus der Ferne an —
>
> und wandelt uns, auch wenn wirs nicht erreichen,
> in jenes, das wir, kaum es ahnend, sind . . .   (SW, II, 161)

Here — unusually — the path is not yet created, and the integration as yet only potential. Normally Rilke's 'Wege' are very much complete elements in the landscape, and the ease with which they integrate the traveller is indicated by the most frequent image with which they are associated: the image of flowing. This image is already present in the story *Der Drachentöter* of 1901 (the same year in which Rilke wrote of the constrictive 'Wege' in the poem quoted above):

Langsam fließen die Wege ins Tal und scheinen nicht anzuhalten bei den weißen Häusern und ziehen leise vorbei als wollten sie sich irgendwo einer stillen Straße vereinen, die geradeaus in Weiten führt, die jetzt offen sind, und in die Nacht, deren erste Sterne wie entfernte Städte an ihrem Ende sich erheben.   (SW, IV, 677)

The same image is used in 'Die Parke', where the whole sixth poem describes how

> . . . keiner von allen
> Wegen steht und stockt . . .

as they flow unceasingly down the terraces and over the park and out into 'den reichen Raum' (SW, I, 606) — providing, as in *Der Drachentöter*, a link with 'das Offene'. This vision of flowing 'Wege' is not confined to Rilke's poetry — he described the streets of Paris in similar terms:

so fließt in kaum merklichem Gefälle die wunderbare Avenue auf einen zu, rasch und reich und wie ein Strom ...   (B, 191; 17 October 1907 to Clara)

Other 'Wege', instead of flowing towards one, carried one along:

... Wege, von denen man jeden einzelnen gehen möchte, so rufend sind sie, so leicht scheint es, auf ihnen weiterzukommen, als ob sie wirklich gingen und man sich ihnen nur überlassen mußte ...   (B, 277; 10 May 1911 to Fürstin Marie)

and in Toledo Rilke talked similarly of 'dieses unbeschreiblich sichere Genommen- und Geführtsein' that he experienced in the lanes of the city (B, 365; 2 November 1912 to Fürstin Marie).

In all these instances, the flowing 'Weg' is a humanized, 'tamed', aspect of the landscape that enables one to enter more fully and more easily into the life of the environment. That this is a typical 'tamed' landscape feature comes out especially clearly when one compares two extreme cases: firstly the 1901 poem quoted above, where the young Rilke sees in the path an instance of constrictive 'overtaming', and secondly the first of the 'Improvisationen aus dem Capreser Winter', where the totally 'untamed' nature of this rugged winter setting leads him to describe it as 'Wildnis, Un-weg', or, alternatively, to show how its paths, where they do exist, far from providing 'dieses unbeschreiblich sichere Genommen- und Geführtsein', overwhelm the hapless victim of their total otherness:

> Weisend greift mich manchmal am Kreuzweg der Wind,
> wirft mich hin, wo ein Pfad beginnt,
> oder es trinkt mich ein Weg im Stillen.   (SW, II, 11)

Such rare extremes indicate by contrast how the vast majority of Rilke's 'Wege' attain the ideal mid-point of being neither over- nor under-tamed.

The 'Weg' is a particularly common feature of Rilke's descriptions of the Valais, and here a new image appears, comparable to the musical and poetic analogies of the rhythmic parks, gardens and vineyards — this is the image of the ribbon:

> Chemin qui tourne et joue
> le long de la vigne penchée,
> tel qu'un ruban que l'on noue
> autour d'un chapeau d'été.   (SW, II, 564)

Or, as Rilke described it in a letter of 26 November 1921:

... schönen, leichten und zugleich spannenden Wege, geschwungen um die Hügel wie Seidenbänder ...   (B, 700; to Gertrud Ouckama Knoop)

The ribbon, like music and poetry, is a non-utilitarian creation of the human spirit at play (cf. 'Chemin qui ... joue'), and thus in these later 'Wege' too Rilke reveals his high estimation of this landscape feature whose 'taming', far from being purely a functional subordination of Nature, has made it free and beautiful, and so filled with human associations that he can joyfully proclaim a total integration with it and the landscape it traverses:

> car le verger et la route
> c'est toujours nous!   (SW, II, 527)

Summary and Conclusions

All the landscape features in this chapter represent a countryside where Man is at home in the midst of Nature, enhancing rather than violating her by his activity, and in no way threatened by any self-assertion on her part. This harmony of Man and Nature is an integration of Self and Non-Self and a balance of part and whole of a degree that is attained in no other landscape features. The attitudes to landscape that emerged in Part One are thus confirmed again when the individual features are examined, for just as there Rilke was found to be particularly favourably inclined to the gently 'tamed' places that he experienced, so here a consistent appreciation accompanies nearly every occurrence of these features in his work.

NOTES TO CHAPTER 4

1.   E.g. SW, I, 81; and SW, I, 113.
2.   SW, I, 603ff. Corbet Stewart, in his study of this cycle, discusses in particular the way in which Rilke, through a metaphorical transformation of the temporal into the spatial, attempts to capture and arrest the transience of these parks. Reinhard Lettau's study is concerned more with the parks' self-sufficient completeness, their bounded and ordered 'Beisichselbstsein'.
3.   The air of gentility is underlined by Rilke's choice of French and frenchified vocabulary: Bosketts, 'chaumière de plaisir', Chambre de Verdure, Intérieurs, Dépandancen, 'Ruine', 'Volière'.
4.   B, 639; 25 November 1920 to Gräfin M.
5.   B, 630f.; 19 November 1920 to Fürstin Marie.
6.   B Nölke, 70; 21 November 1920. Compare the similar statement in B, 639f.; 25 November 1920 to Gräfin M.
7.   SW, I, 606. These tamed landscapes that lead out freely into the open beyond are like symbols of what Rilke mentioned, in a letter of 1924, as the essence of the influence on him of Liliencron and Jacobsen. From them he claimed to have learnt 'wie es möglich sei, von dem Nächsten [sic;= 'nächsten'?], unter allen Umständen vorhandenen Dinge aus den Absprung ins Weiteste zu nehmen' (B, 878; 17 August 1924 to Hermann Pongs).
8.   B Kippenberg, 367f.; 17 August 1919.
9.   Steiner, p. 81. Buddeberg, on the other hand, in equating it with the garden at the end of the Third Elegy, seems to ignore the decidedly negative nature of the Fourth Elegy's garden (Buddeberg, Biographie, p. 565).
10.   B, 786; 19 May 1922 to Lisa Heise. Compare the Sixth Elegy's reference to 'der gärtnernde Tod' (SW, I, 706), which is simply a natural development of the botanical imagery that dominates the first stanza of this work.

11.   The influence of Valéry on these French poems seems to reveal itself here also: these lines are distinctly reminiscent of the eleventh stanza of 'Le Cimetière Marin', where too the poet sits and contemplates a landscape — here a cemetery:

> Quand solitaire au sourire de pâtre,
> Je pais longtemps, moutons mystérieux,
> Le blanc troupeau de mes tranquilles tombes . . .

12.   SW, II, 145ff. See also 'Aus dem Umkreis: *Das kleine Weinjahr*' (SW, II, 480f.).
13.   B. 701; 26 November 1921 to Gertrud Ouckama Knoop.
14.   SW, II, 646. Compare also:

> Les terrasses forment un sonnet
> de leurs gradins qui reculent   (SW, II, 730).

5

THE LANDSCAPE METAPHOR

The Genitive Metaphor

This is the most concise form of metaphorical landscape imagery in Rilke, consisting of the concrete landscape (feature) together with the abstract situation it signifies. The two are joined either in a compound – e.g. 'Herzlandschaft' (SW, II, 286), or, much more commonly, by the genitive – e.g. 'der Liebe Landschaft' (SW, II, 95), 'Dickicht des verwildernden Schmerzes' (B, 790; 16 June 1922 to Gräfin Alexandrine Schwerin). This type of image provides the basis for Rilke's metaphorical use of landscape, and it is often developed into a fully worked out allegorical landscape in the manner of the 'Berge des Herzens' of 'Ausgesetzt . . .', or of the Tenth Elegy's 'Klageland', where, unusually, even the abstract element, the 'Klage', is concretized. These genitive metaphors are not only used to express abstractions: the physical body is quite frequently also portrayed in terms of landscape in such expressions as 'Tal seiner Arme', or 'Laub seines Leibes' (SW, II, 85).

As the structure of the genitive metaphor indicates, Rilke's figurative landscapes are basically anthropocentric in that the landscape is simply there in order to express human characteristics. Instances of the reverse situation in which landscape is seen in human terms – e.g.: 'Umrahmt von Oliven und welkem Gestein erschienen die frisch gebrochenen Flächen wie ein großes blasses Gesicht unter alterndem Haar' (SW, IV, 348) – are very rare when compared with the large number of occasions where Rilke sees humans in landscape terms. This commoner latter type of image takes on three distinct forms: either a *whole* human being is portrayed as a landscape feature, or an exterior *part* of a human being is portrayed in these terms, or – and this is probably the most distinctive of Rilke's landscape metaphors – the *interior* of a human being is portrayed as containing a landscape.

Humans as Landscape

This form of landscape image is predominantly a feature of the early years, the period in fact, before the development of the genitive metaphor. By far the commonest image here is that of vegetation, either in the form of the tree, the garden, or the forest.[1] Vegetation, with its associations of organic growth, of integration, its long flowing stems and vines and branches, is a natural concern for the young Rilke, and it is predominantly the poet's own 'Ich' that is portrayed in this way in such lines as 'ich . . . / möchte blühen mit vielen Zweigen' (SW, I, 192), 'Ich bin ein Garten, und der Frühling schneit' (SW, III, 582), or 'ich bin dunkel und bin Wald' (SW, I, 282). This organic imagery of the earlier years gives way later to more fundamental terrestrial metaphors involving valleys, rivers, and mountains. Here Rilke is less concerned with portraying his own 'Ich', and these three landscape features, in keeping with their associations in the rest of his work, are consistently linked with women, men, and the inaccessible summits of existence respectively.[2]

Landscape in Human Features

These metaphors are concentrated mainly in the works Rilke wrote around the turn of the century, and they may be divided, both temporally and thematically, into two groups. The first group, occurring in stories and poems of the last few years of the nineteenth century, consists of facial landscapes in such lines as: 'sie . . . sah in sein Gesicht, wie in eine weite Landschaft' (SW, IV, 80); sometimes the analogies are developed at slightly greater length:

> und durch der Scheitel dunkle Linien
> dein Antlitz träumte wie ein Land.
>
> Es schlich von deiner Lippen Saum
> ein Lächlich auf verlornem Pfade —[3]

The second group appears in poems written in 1903-4 and consists of the genital landscapes of phrases such as: 'in dem Tal der Scham' (SW, I, 361), or 'in einem blonden Wald von jungen Haaren (SW, I, 349) — an image that is taken up again and developed in the third of the 'Sieben Gedichte' of 1915 with its reference to 'Schamgehölze' (SW, II, 436); the early landscape metaphors of this group are also sometimes developed into a more substantial image:

> wie ein Bestand von jungen Birken im April,
> warm, leer und unverborgen, lag die Scham.   (SW, I, 550)

In general, however, these facial and genital landscapes are, like such similar metaphors as 'Auf meiner Brüste Hügeln' (SW, I, 482) or 'Tal seiner Arme' (SW, II, 85), restricted to short phrases, and it is only rarely that their implications are developed beyond these in landscape terms.

Internal Landscape

Landscapes of this type are found in some of Rilke's most distinctive and most lengthy metaphors. On the whole they are easy to distinguish as it is normally stated quite explicitly that the landscape in question is situated *inside* the person concerned. Thus Rilke mentions in the Third Elegy 'diesen Urwald in ihm' (SW, I, 695), or even talks of 'der inneren Landschaft'.[4] They are restricted mainly to the later poetry, and also appear in some of the letters of this period; one of the very few early references takes the form of a simile rather than a metaphor, showing Rilke experimenting with, but not yet fully realizing the potentialities of the internal landscape:

> jetzt mußt du in dein Herz hinaus
> wie in die Ebene gehn.   (SW, I, 305)

From the point of view of their significance there are, broadly speaking, two groups of internal landscapes in Rilke: at the simplest level there are landscapes whose internal nature is not an inherent part of their significance – that is to say, the image's meaning stems from the associations of the landscape feature in question rather than from the fact that it is internal, and the internalization is merely a metaphorical device to enable the landscape to express a particular psychic state; in the second group of internal landscapes Rilke is presenting an image of an environment that has been 'inwardized', subjected to the process of being transformed into ourselves as described in the Ninth Elegy – here, in other words, the emphasis lies not on the landscape but on the fact of its being internal. A confusion of these two types has led to contradictory statements by Bollnow and Allemann, the former claiming that Rilke's inner landscapes are not examples of 'Weltinnenraum', but merely 'eine Form dichterischer Bildhaftigkeit: die auch direkt faßbaren Eigenschaften der seelischen Welt im sinnlichen Bild deutlicher hervortreten zu lassen' (pp. 74f.), whilst Allemann talks of 'Der Begriff der "inneren Landschaft", der ein Synonym für den Weltinnenraum bildet' (*Zeit*, p. 18). Both of these statements are only partly true: Bollnow, whilst providing an excellent definition of the first type of inner landscape, quite arbitrarily excludes the second; Allemann, on the other hand, does the reverse, overlooking entirely the many inner landscapes that quite patently have nothing to do with 'Weltinnenraum'.

Perhaps the best known of the first group of inner landscapes is that of 'Orpheus. Eurydike. Hermes', where Rilke places the descent of Orpheus into the underworld to reclaim the dead Eurydice into the setting of 'der Seelen wunderliches Bergwerk' (SW, I, 542), an image that harks back to 'das tiefe Bergwerk deiner Seele' in a poem of 1900 (SW, II, 722), and one that permits a metaphorical portrayal in concrete terms of the relationship compounded of love and increasing alienation that exists between the man and his dead wife – a relationship that has

127

its being at the spiritual, i.e. 'seelisch', level, and is thus very effectively con-
cretized in terms of action within the setting of the souls' landscape. The soul,
of course, is not anatomically locatable, and this is true of all Rilke's internal
landscapes: the grotesque situation of having a landscape at some specific point in
the physical body, though sometimes not far away, is avoided by the use of
spiritual inner locations such as 'Seele', 'Brust', or 'Herz', or by simply using the
preposition 'in' without further clarification. 'Brust' and 'Herz', of course, in their
spiritual sense, are already metaphors, and something of their concrete origins is
inevitably present in Rilke's use of the words, a fact that adds to the vividness of
the imagery whilst at the same time a descent into the ridiculous is – just –
avoided by the predominance of these words' metaphorical significance.[5] The
'heart' is, in fact, by far the commonest setting for Rilke's internal landscapes, and,
as in 'Ausgesetzt . . .', the landscape part of the metaphor is normally a mountain
or a valley: thus the poems of the later years contain references not only to the
'Bergen des Herzens', but also to 'mein Herzgebirge' (SW, II, 98), to

> ces monts
> qui forment une chaîne dans le coeur
> en sa partie abrupte et sauvage   (SW, II, 623)

as well as to 'den Tälern des Herzens' (SW, II, 424), whilst a letter of 7 March 1921
contains a reference to 'quelque vallée de votre coeur où il pleut constamment'
(B Merline, 237).

It was in 1914 that Rilke first realized the potential of the internal landscape to
express the product of the Self's 'taming' of the Non-Self, and he talked of

> . . . dem Raume, den ich in mich schaute
> aus dem Weltraum und dem Wind am Meer.   (SW, II, 956)

The two accusatives ('den' and 'mich') indicate an active 'Schauen' that captures
the outside world and lifts it into the observer in an act of 'Einbeziehung', of
creative perception. That this process could be tantamount to a violation of the
Non-Self's integrity was painfully obvious to Rilke in 1914, as the poem 'Wendung'
shows, and the same concern is expressed in his picture of the internal landscape
of its companion-piece 'Waldteich, weicher, in sich eingekehrter –':

> Hab ich das Errungene gekränkt,
> nichts bedenkend, als wie ich mirs finge,
> und die großgewohnten Dinge
> im gedrängten Herzen eingeschränkt?
> Faßt ich sie wie dieses Zimmer mich,
> dieses fremde Zimmer mich und meine
> Seele faßt?
>   O hab ich keine Haine
> in der Brust? kein Wehen? keine
> Stille, atemleicht und frühlinglich?   (SW, II, 81)

128

The problem of finding a gentle internal landscape in which the internalized world could feel at home was solved a few months later in Rilke's discovery of the notion of 'Weltinnenraum', of the gentle realm of 'Bezug' where inner and outer are united:

> Durch alle Wesen reicht der *eine* Raum:
> Weltinnenraum. Die Vögel fliegen still
> durch uns hindurch. O, der ich wachsen will,
> ich seh hinaus, und *in* mir wächst der Baum.
>
> Ich sorge mich, und in mir steht das Haus.   (SW, II, 93)

By the time of the Ninth Elegy the internal realm had become once again a place into which the outside world could be transposed, for now this transposition no longer meant constriction and confinement: once Rilke saw the internal landscape as part of 'Weltinnenraum' he could with a clear conscience again see it as Man's task to 'capture' the outside world through fervent experience and expression. Now the result would not be a violation of the Non-Self, but its liberation, and above all, its heightening, its 'Steigerung':

> Innres, was ists?
> Wenn nicht gesteigerter Himmel,
> durchworfen mit Vögeln und tief
> von Winden der Heimkehr.   (SW, II, 184)

Summary and Conclusions

The landscape features involved in this chapter have, in the main, already been treated individually in the preceding pages, where the significance of each feature was the object of investigation. The object here is thus not a further examination of their meanings, but rather an attempt to indicate some of the more distinctive ways in which they are used by Rilke, in illustration of what Bollnow calls 'die bei Rilke weit verbreitete Gewohnheit, das menschliche Seelenleben unter dem Bild einer Landschaft und anderer sichtbarer Dinge in der Landschaft zu verstehen' (p. 61). The individual features in these landscape metaphors naturally retain their peculiar associations, and these play their part in creating the complex significance that arises when a metaphor brings together two areas of meaning; the important point here, however, is the implications of the technique in general — of the fact that Rilke has metaphorically fused Man and Nature — rather than the meaning of particular instances.

Rilke's use of landscape metaphor shows him experimenting at the figurative level with the portrayal of various aspects of Man's relationship with his environment. In these metaphors he is concerned not only with landscapes that have human associations and humans that have landscape associations, but also with the boundaries of the Self — with an outside world that is situated both on and inside the Self. He is, in fact, putting into practice the theory he expounded in the introduction to *Worpswede*:

Es ist nicht der letzte und vielleicht der eigentümlichste Wert der Kunst, daß sie das Medium ist, in welchem Mensch und Landschaft, Gestalt und Welt sich begegnen und finden. In Wirklichkeit leben sie nebeneinander, kaum von einander wissend, und im Bilde, im Bauwerk, in der Symphonie, mit einem Worte in der Kunst, scheinen sie sich, wie in einer höheren prophetischen Wahrheit, zusammen- zuschließen, aufeinander zu berufen, und es ist, als ergänzten sie einander zu jener vollkommenen Einheit, die das Wesen des Kunstwerks ausmacht.

That this portrayal of Man and landscape, of Self and Non-Self, as the central concern of art may take on metaphorical forms is made clear a few lines later:

Und ein Bildnis machen, heißt das nicht, einen Menschen wie eine Landschaft sehen . . . manchmal scheint der Mensch aus der Landschaft, ein andres Mal die Landschaft aus dem Menschen hervorzugehen, und dann wieder haben sie sich ebenbürtig und geschwisterlich vertragen.[6]

'Sich ebenbürtig und geschwisterlich vertragen' — these words are a concise expression of that ideal relationship that Rilke was constantly seeking in the landscapes of his life, and that he was trying to create in the landscapes of his work. In the former he was concerned with the place of the Self in the midst of the Non-Self, and this was also his predominant concern in the latter too; but nonethe- less the realm of art was not bound by the limits of reality, and in the sizeable body of his metaphorical landscapes he was able to allow 'die Landschaft aus dem Menschen hervorzugehen', and thus to exploit to the full the desired intermingling of Self and Non-Self.

NOTES TO CHAPTER 5

1. Tree: SW, I, 192, 193, 348, 409f., 631; and SW, III, 718. Garden: SW, I, 147, 184, 631; SW, III, 582f., and 602. Forest: SW, I, 282, 283 and 476.
2. Women: SW, I, 541, 676, 696, 707; and SW, II, 220. Men: SW, I, 541f., and 707. Inaccessible summits of existence: SW, I, 689; and B Taxis, 86; 30 December 1911.
3. SW, I, 123. For further instances of facial landscapes see SW, III, 215 and SW, IV, 299.
4. SW, II, 221. Bollnow, in his chapter 'Das Bild der Inneren Landschaft' (pp. 74ff.), examines Rilke's metaphorical landscapes in general, and not only the internal ones that his heading proclaims. There is, for instance, no suggestion in Rilke that the Tenth Elegy — which Bollnow here investigates in some detail — describes an *internal* landscape: the 'Leidstadt' and the 'Landschaft der Klagen' are simply allegorical landscapes, albeit Rilke's most vivid and lengthy.
5. The one instance of a literally located internal landscape — the references to the womb in such lines as 'Doch Hain zu sein und Himmel um die Herme / das ist an dir' in the 'Sieben Gedichte' (SW, II, 435ff.) — is more an example of 'landscape in human features' or 'humans as landscape' than of the (metaphorically) internal landscapes that concern us here.

6. SW, V, 15f. Similar ideas are expressed in the first part of *Von der Landschaft* (SW, V, 516f.). Rilke's rare attempts to express something other than human beings in landscape terms could be disastrous, as in the following passage from a letter of 1900: 'und auf langer schmaler Schüssel etwas blasser westfälischer Schinken, von Streifen weißen Fetts durchzogen wie ein Abendhimmel mit langgezogenen Wolken . . . Große Zitronen, in Scheiben geschnitten, senkten sich wie Sonnen in die goldige Dämmerung des Tees, ihn leise durchleuchtend mit ihrem strahligen Fruchtfleisch . . .' (B, 24; 23 October 1900 to Clara).

PART THREE : CONCLUSIONS

Mention has already been made of the way in which a poet's reaction to, and use of, the landscapes about him can provide a concrete and tangible exemplification of his view of the world in general. Such a key is particularly useful with Rilke, as the subtle and often confusing ideas with which he toyed all his life can sometimes be extremely difficult to grasp. The central thread of Rilke's letters and works that emerges from the preceding investigation is his concern with spatial relationships, both literal and figurative. The various concepts that are involved in this concern – such as the Self / Non-Self relationship, the ideal of 'Bezug', and the idea of 'taming' – in view of their importance in the landscapes seem worthy of investigation at a more general level, and in this concluding third Part I have accordingly brought together some further instances of these and related concepts in an attempt to indicate what light the study of Rilke's landscapes can throw on his thought and its development, as an aid to a greater appreciation of his life and art.

6

THE IMPLICATIONS OF RILKE'S LANDSCAPES

Self and Non-Self

The fact that Rilke's vision of the world is one based largely on the perception and creation of relationships has been noted by a number of critics. Thus Holthusen says: 'Die Metaphern Rilkes sind meistens Raum- und Substanzmetaphern, das heißt Ausdruck einer Welt, in der alles auf alles bezogen ist und alles verwandelt werden kann.'[1] Stahl too sees two basic groups of images in all of Rilke's work, images of 'Not' and of 'Tröstung', corresponding respectively to 'Trennung' and 'Einheit', and it is on these pictures of relationship that he bases his detailed study of the poet's imagery (p. 19 and passim). Others have pointed specifically to the Self / Non-Self aspects of this concern with relationship. Buddeberg, for instance, talks of two constantly interacting lines of development in Rilke: on the one hand there is 'das Verlangen nach Ununterschiedenheit und Versinken im Umfassenden', and this is countered by the desire for 'Gestaltgebung', for an assertion of the Self, which appears in 'die auf Unterscheidung, auf Gestaltgewinnung des eigenen Selbst laufende Richtung' (*Biographie*, p. 112). For Mason the struggle between these two tendencies is portrayed in the *Duineser Elegien* in the form of a protracted attempt to define the proper relationship between the Ego and the environment: 'In den Elegien vernahm man kaum die äußere oder die innere Welt, – das, was man eigentlich wahrnahm, war die sich ewig verschiebende, immer von neuem abgesteckte Grenze zwischen den beiden, und diese Grenze war eben – das Ich des Dichters (*Lebenshaltung*, p. 191). Stein also recognises the importance of the Self / Non-Self relationship in Rilke, and even suggests that the poet's idiosyncratic use of personal pronouns is explicable in terms of this:

It is important that we not be misled in the *Duino Elegies* or elsewhere by the puzzling inconsistency in Rilke's use of pronouns. 'Wir', 'ich', and 'du' are often used interchangeably and with quite unusual connotations. The ambiguity of his relationship to the world, in one sense the negation of individuation, a kind of passive openness, is potentialized by his poet's soul into a dynamic principle of extremest sensitivity to all the non-ego, and becomes thus the opposite of passivity in its usual sense; rather a kind of dynamic passivity. This breaks down the psychological barrier between the ego and the non-ego . . . and seems to result in a less exact grammatical differentiation between the various persons than one would ordinarily expect, even in poetry. This state, coupled with the inspirational, almost frenzied manner of composition of the *Elegies* results in the somewhat baffling use of pronouns.   (p. 278)

Rilke's own awareness of the importance for him of the relationship between Self and Non-Self is attested by a number of theoretical statements, one of the most explicit being the following passage from the introduction to *Worpswede*:

. . . scheint es, als läge das Thema und die Absicht aller Kunst in dem Ausgleich zwischen dem einzelnen und dem All, und als wäre der Moment der Erhebung, der künstlerisch-wichtige Moment, derjenige, in welchem die beiden Waagschalen sich das Gleichgewicht halten.   (SW, V, 15)

The problem was, however, far from being merely theoretical: it was one that Rilke lived and experienced deeply, and often painfully, in every environment he came into contact with:

Sie können gar nicht wissen . . . wie alles [den Künstler] verurteilt, wenn es ihn verlangt, seine innerste Welt zu pflegen und zu vollenden, damit sie das ganz Äußere, alles, bis an die Sterne hin, eines Tages im Gleichgewicht zu halten und, sozusagen, sich gleichzusetzen vermöchte.   (B07-14, 54f.; 24 September 1908 to Rosa Schobloch)

These Paris letters are particularly full of statements on this theme, for here more than anywhere he felt his identity threatened by a forceful and hostile environment: he pictured himself as an over-exposed photographic plate,[2] and talked of 'das Überwiegen des Äußeren', of his 'erbärmlichste und lächerlichste Ausgeliefertsein'.[3] These were the experiences he portrayed in *Malte Laurids.Brigge*, the story of the man who failed in his struggle to control the pressures of the Non-Self, the man whom 'diese Prüfung . . . überstieg',[4] as Rilke described him in 1907, echoing a letter of 1903 in which Rilke's first experiences of Paris exactly prefigure the whole story of Malte Laurids:

Die Stadt war wider mich, aufgelehnt gegen mein Leben und wie eine Prüfung, die ich nicht bestand. Ihr Schrei, der kein Ende hat, brach in meine Stille ein, ihre Schrecklichkeit ging mir nach bis in meine traurige Stube und meine Augen lagen gedrückt unter den Bildern ihrer Tage. (B Lou, 46; 30 June 1903)

Many of Rilke's other major works are also based on autobiographical experiences of the Self / Non-Self problem, often in landscape terms, as in the 'Improvisationen aus dem Capreser Winter',[5] the 'Spanische Trilogie',[6] or the prose passages 'Erlebnis (I)' and '(II)';[7] similar too is the theme of the 1914 poem 'Waldteich, weicher, in sich eingekehrter' and its important companion piece 'Wendung'.[8]

Instances of Rilke's concern with the relationship between Self and Non-Self abound throughout his poetry, and there is hardly a work written by him in which it is not in some way reflected. Any selection of examples from such an abundance of material must be rather arbitrary, but I have attempted in the following to give typical cases of each of the various possibilities that this problem presents. In any relationship between two elements three basic situations are possible: either the first element dominates, or the second does, or both are balanced equally. These three possibilities provide the basis of Rilke's exploration of the relationship between Self and Non-Self: his life and work may be seen in terms of a struggle between the undesirable dominance of either Self or Non-Self in search of an ideal reconciliation of the two.

One of the most frequent images in Rilke for the dominance of the Self is that of its expansion, of its growth outwards to incorporate the Non-Self. This is a particularly common idea in the early poems, where moments of Romantic ecstasy lead Rilke to describe the subordination of the whole world to his exalted mood:

> Wie da die Seele sich schwellt,
> daß sie als schimmernde Hülle sich
> legt um das Dunkel der Welt. (SW, I, 87)

A similar image of the expanding Self is used in the more familar first lines of the second poem in the *Stunden-Buch*:

134

Ich lebe mein Leben in wachsenden Ringen,
die sich über die Dinge ziehn.   (SW, I, 253)

These lines already contain the germ of Rilke's later images of 'Innenraum', as the
following lines from a 1924 poem show, with their distinctly similar picture of the
Self / Non Self relationship:

Raum greift aus uns und übersetzt die Dinge:
daß dir das Dasein eines Baums gelinge,
wirf Innenraum um ihn, aus jenem Raum,
der in dir west.[9]

These last two examples, like most images of the dominant Self, are really instances
of 'taming', and a further discussion of this situation is thus best reserved for
inclusion in the section of that title below.

The most frequent situation in the early work is, however, not the dominance of
the Self, but the other side of the Romantic coin — its passive abandon to the Non-
Self. Thus the early poetry abounds in such sentiments as are expressed in the lines:

Ich bin so jung. Ich möchte jedem Klange,
der mir vorüberrauscht, mich schauernd schenken . . .   (SW, I, 147)

or:

Geheimnisvolles Leben . . .
geschieh mir nur . . .   (SW, III, 748)

Although predominantly a feature of these first works, this totally passive attitude
appears again in the 'Gedichte an die Nacht' of 1914, one of which begins:

Hinhalten will ich mich. Wirke. Geh über
so weit du vermöchtest.   (SW, II, 75)

This passivity becomes formulated in some poems into a principle for the
attainment of integration — the principle of 'geduldig in der Schwere ruhn' (SW, I,
321), a willingness, indeed a desire, to be overwhelmed by the environment that is
particularly an attitude adopted by Rilke in the face of such landscape features as
the spring, the night, the plain, the wind, and, above all, the storm:

Wie ist das klein, womit wir ringen,
was mit uns ringt, wie ist das groß;
ließen wir, ähnlicher den Dingen,
uns *so* vom großen Sturm bezwingen, —
wir würden weit und namenlos. (SW, I, 459)

The abandonment of Self in search of some deeper existence was, like the
dominance of the Self, only one of the possibilities of relationship with the world

135

that Rilke tried in the course of his life. In the majority of his works neither of these two extremes dominates: instead, there is portrayal of the mid-ground, of the struggle to achieve some kind of balance, and nowhere is this described more graphically than in 'Der Magier' of 1924:

> Er ruft es an. Es schrickt zusamm und steht.
> Was steht? Das Andre; alles, was nicht er ist,
> wird Wesen. Und das ganze Wesen dreht
> ein raschgemachtes Antlitz her, das mehr ist.
>
> Oh Magier, halt aus, halt aus!
> Schaff Gleichgewicht. Steh ruhig auf der Waage,
> damit sie einerseits dich und das Haus
> und drüben jenes Angewachsene trage.
>
> Entscheidung fällt. Die Bindung stellt sich her.
> Er weiß, der Anruf überwog das Weigern.
> Doch sein Gesicht, wie mit gedeckten Zeigern,
> hat Mitternacht. Gebunden ist auch er.[10]

The constant tipping back and forth of the scale accounts for much of the subtlety of Rilke's verse, as he attempts continually to define the point of balance, forever adjusting to compensate for an excess of either Self or Non-Self. This subtle and delicate balance appears in such typical phrases as 'bald begrenzt und bald begreifend' (SW, I, 405), 'umarmend und umarmt' (SW, II, 92), where the scale hovers about its mid-point. It appears too in what von Salis describes as Rilke's typically 'ambivalent attitude to his surroundings, and especially to people' (p. 73), that ambiguity of Rilke's love affairs that Buddeberg described as compounded of 'Hinwendung und Abwehr' (*Biographie*, p. 318) and Holthusen of 'Hingabe . . . und Abwehr' (*Selbstzeugnissen*, p. 15) — a duality that Rilke himself portrayed in the closing lines of the Seventh Elegy where he talked of his invocation of the Angel:

> Denn mein
> Anruf ist immer voll Hinweg . . .   (SW, I, 713)

For Rilke the lover and the beloved were central figures in the struggle between Self and Non-Self as they acted out their relationship, now dominant, now dominated, in the emotion they generated and directed one to the other; only that strange, pure and outward-going, 'intransitive' love of *Malte Laurids Brigge* (SW, VI, 898, 930f., and 937) and the First and Second Elegies could provide the resolution to this unhappy turmoil. Indeed, for the lover it was not only the relationship with the other partner that was problematical: in the monologue of 'Die Liebende' the Self's very consciousness of its differentness from the surrounding Non-Self is thrown into doubt:

136

Bis wohin reicht mein Leben,
und wo beginnt die Nacht?

Ich könnte meinen, alles
wäre noch Ich ringsum ... (SW, I, 621)

As the preceding examination of Rilke's landscapes suggests, his lifelong search
for the ideal relationship between Self and Non-Self (in landscape terms the search
for a 'home') seems to fall into three main stages: in the first stage the whole and the
Non-Self dominate in his imagery; the second stage, the period of Paris, Rodin and
the 'Dinggedichte', is one in which the Self and the parts assert themselves – a
period in which, as Rilke put it in his 'Imaginärer Lebenslauf', 'Der Gebogene
wird selber Bieger' (SW, II, 142); the third stage, whose opening is most explicitly
heralded by the resolutions contained in the poem 'Wendung' in 1914, represents
a continuous development of a vision in which the imbalances of the first two
stages are reconciled in an ideal coexistence of whole and part, Non-Self and Self.
Such a generalized schematization of the poet's development is of necessity somewhat
crude, and in any one of these three stages instances may be found of a vision that I
have defined as characteristic of the other two. As I have mentioned in the introduction
to Part One (p. 3 above), it is particularly difficult to define the borderline between
the second and third stages, for, as Buddeberg points out (*Biographie*, pp. 408f.),
both *Malte Laurids Brigge* and the Elegies are products of a lengthy process
of maturation, coming to fruition when Rilke has, as it were, already overtaken
them, with the result that, for instance, the *Requiem* and the first group of
Sonnets, although appearing before each of them, nonetheless reveal a later stage
in the development of his vision. With these reservations, then, it still seems reason-
able to suggest that typical works of each of these periods will be characterized by
the kind of Self / Non-Self relationship indicated. This is certainly borne out by the
kinds of landscape that Rilke experienced and portrayed as his life proceeded: the
unified plains of Russia and Worpswede, the fragmented city of Paris, and the
'constellated' hillsides of the Valais.

'Bezug'

The ideal balance between whole and part, Non-Self and Self that Rilke was
seeking, and that, in the Valais, he finally felt he had attained, was what he called
'Bezug'. The word, though present in the earlier works, does not attain its full
significance until the post-Paris period, when it becomes quite a frequent feature of
Rilke's poetry. As Gebser says of these later years: 'Seine Welt ist nicht mehr die
vorgestellte Welt des Gegenübers, sondern eine der Relationen, der "Übergänge", eine
Welt des "reinen Bezuges" ' ('unsere Zeit', p. 36). The immense significance that
this idea held for Rilke is attested by the deep mood of peace and fulfilment that is

137

evoked in all the poems in which it occurs, and by the consistency with which it is accompanied by such superlative epithets as 'unbeschreiblich' (SW, II, 152, 157 and 230). 'Bezug' is both figuratively and literally 'indescribable', for its subtlety is beyond words; it can only be captured in the form of imagery, and it is this imagery of 'Bezug' that typifies Rilke's later work, and accounts for its delicate nuance.

One of Rilke's favourite and most expressive images for the state of 'Bezug' is that of the constellated stars. Here he saw a beautiful absence of dominance ('Begehren') by part or whole, and in its place a balance in which both sides of the scale were somehow reconciled without any loss of their separate individuality, for in the constellation there was 'überall Lust zu Bezug und nirgends Begehren' (SW, II, 78). Here Rilke saw achieved what he had long seen as the object of all art: 'Einzelheiten in ihrer ganzen Pracht hinzustellen, ohne dadurch den Gesamtwert aufzuheben' (SW, V, 93) — thus in 1902 he described the object of the Worpswede painter Fritz Overbeck. The whole concept of 'Bezug' was in fact present in some of the earliest of Rilke's writings, although the word itself did not enter his terminology until somewhat later, and when it did establish itself it appeared almost entirely in poetic images. The early descriptions of what was later to be seen as 'der unbeschreibliche Bezug' occur, on the other hand, in the numerous articles and essays of a critical and aesthetic nature that Rilke wrote around the turn of the century. Here he already reveals his concern with the whole and the part, writing in 'Zur Melodie der Dinge' of 1898 of life as a combination of 'die große Melodie' and 'die einzelnen Stimmen', and the object of art as the balancing against one another of these two components: 'die beiden Stimmen . . . in das richtige Verhältnis zu setzen und auszugleichen' (SW, V, 418). 'Das richtige Verhältnis' is a direct precursor of 'Bezug', for, as many other statements of the time show, it is a relationship in which neither 'die große Melodie' — the whole, nor 'die einzelnen Stimmen' — the parts, are dominant. Instead, through a heightening of the parts' individuality, a purer and greater unity is established: 'der Künstler hebt die Dinge, die er seiner Darstellung wählt, aus den vielen zufälligen konventionellen Beziehungen heraus, vereinsamt sie und stellt die Einsamen in einen einfachen reinen Verkehr',[11] he wrote in 1900 in clear illustration of Neumann's contention: 'es [geht] Rilke . . . gleichzeitig um den Sinn des Selbst wie um den Sinn des Ganzen' (Neumann, p. 40).

External biographical factors — and not least Rilke's landscape experience — help to explain why this intense youthful concern with what in all but name was 'Bezug' should apparently subside for several years before being taken up again as the cornerstone of the later Rilke's aesthetic vision. It has been pointed out by, among others, Rasch that the a-perspective vision was a typical phenomenon of the art of the late nineteenth century among the *Jugendstil* artists and the neo-Impressionists, and he compares the patterns they created from reality with those that Musil noted in Rilke's work:

Die Verbundenheit der Erscheinungen, die so entsteht, ist von gleicher Art wie diejenige, die Robert Musil in den Gedichten von Rilke wahrnimmt. 'Bei ihm sind die Dinge wie in einem Teppich verwoben; wenn man *sie* betrachtet, sind sie durch ihn verbunden. Dann verändert sich ihr Aussehen, und es entstehen sonderbare Beziehungen zwischen ihnen.'[12]

What Musil sees in Rilke's poetry as he describes it here is, of course, the pattern of 'Bezug'. It is not, however, a particularly prominent feature of the early poetry, in which the parts are very much subordinated to the whole, occurring, as has been said, mainly in theoretical prose works of the time. As the Worpswede writings show, Rilke was coming into contact with instances of 'Bezug' in the artists' colony and was even beginning to use it in his own descriptions, and one could surmise that, had he stayed there, this vision would have developed even more strongly in him. However, he moved to the very different landscape of Paris and the artistic techniques of Rodin. In this world of disparate parts and in the presence of Rodin's accentuation of those parts by sculptural 'Gestaltung' Rilke turned his attention to mastering one by one the separate 'Dinge' around him — a task that left little time for thoughts of the higher 'Bezug' into which they were being raised. But the vision was still present and it asserted itself again during the weeks of the Cézanne exhibition in 1907; here again he saw a transformation of the world in which whole and part were perfectly matched: *'Es ist, als wüßte jede Stelle von allen'* (B, 204; 22 October 1907 to Clara). But more than anything it was probably the experience of the Spanish landscape that fully rekindled Rilke's enthusiasm for the ideal of 'Bezug'; it too, as Gebser suggests (*Spanien,* pp. 48ff. and 91f.), presented him once more in forceful terms with the a-perspective vision that informs the landscapes of the Elegies and prepared him for the climax of his search for 'Bezug' in the Valais. It was thus after his return from Spain in 1913 that the word 'Bezug' established itself in Rilke's poetry and he came to doubt the theories and techniques of the Paris years.

It is noteworthy to what a great extent the idea of a 'Bezug'-type balance and harmony underlies Rilke's thinking in practically every field. It is, in fact, the essence of what Mason calls his 'Weltbild der Nuance' (*Lebenshaltung,* pp. 3ff.), that subtle vision of a world of infinite divisions in what is normally accepted as one and, conversely, of unity in what is normally accepted as different — that world that lies between the crude concepts with which we have divided up our experience, like the midnight 'fente miniscule entre le jour qui finit et celui qui commence' that fascinated Rilke in a novel by Algernon Blackwood (B, 663; 'vers la fin de février' 1921 to 'B.K.'). This was the world of which he had written in 1898 in the lines:

> Fühlst du die vielen Übergänge
> hinzögern zwischen Sein und Sein?   (SW, III, 621)

And it was the world 'zwischen zwein / Widersprüchen' that in 1924 he described as the realm of 'Bezug':

> Mitzuwirken ist nicht Überhebung
> an dem unbeschreiblichen Bezug,
> immer inniger wird die Verwebung.
> nur Getragensein ist nicht genug.
>
> Deine ausgeübten Kräfte spanne,
> bis sie reichen, zwischen zwein
> Widersprüchen . . .   (SW, II, 157)

'Bezug' — though not actually named as such — is equally the ideal behind Rilke's few published pronouncements on politics. He saw the ideal state of the future as being one in which individuals would happily coexist not by 'conforming' but by being fully themselves:

Eine Verbindung von Einzelnen gibt es nur auf einer ganz tiefen und einer höchsten Entwicklungsstufe. Einmal dort, wo jeder nur die Vervielfältigung seines Nebenmenschen ist, und über Jahrtausende hinweg erst wieder zwischen den reifsten und endlichsten Individualitäten, deren jede eine Welt für sich mit allen Mächten und Möglichkeiten darstellt, so abgeschlossen und reich und gesättigt, daß sie einander nicht mehr gefährden.[13]

Nor was it only Rilke's vision of the internal organization of societies that was informed by thoughts of 'Bezug': the same held true of statements he made about external politics. For him the ideal lay in a kind of 'Europe des patries' — but this ideal too was still as yet far away:

Pour qu'un jour (que je crois éloigné encore) nous arrivions à une imprévisible concorde européenne, il faudra que les différents pays s'avancent (en attendant) sur des chemins divers. Il faudra même (comme pour les êtres humains) que chaque peuple, sur sa route particulière, ne pense pas trop au but commun, mais qu'il se concentre, chacun, sur son effort personnel, sur sa tâche, sur sa piété nationale . . .[14]

The 'Bezug' ideal also underlay Rilke's thinking on education, for here too the ideal for him was a system that gave as much free rein to the individuality of the child as was consistent with the coherence of the community. Indeed, from his very first contact with the Swedish educationalist Ellen Key Rilke expressed ideas that were well in the vanguard of pedagogical theory, as is revealed by his enthusiastic account in 1904 of the progressive 'Samskola' in Gothenburg (SW, V, 672ff.), and a letter passage of 1920 shows him still holding the same notions of the object of education:

C'est terrible que nos écoles ne prennent pas comme point de départ les facultés les plus prononcées de chacun de leurs élèves, qu'elles vont jusqu'à les ignorer et même à les combattre, si par hasard elles en découvrent la fâcheuse existence! (B, 653; 31 December 1920 to 'B.K.')

Even his homespun psychology was, in part at least, dependent on the 'Bezug' idea: in 1926 he wrote from the clinic at Valmont of his regret at having finally to accede to the outside 'interference' of medical attention. The various forces and conflicts of his psyche had, he claimed, been held up to then in what amounted to a state of 'Bezug' by his artistic creativity, thus claiming for the artist benefits of a psychological nature akin to the ontological ones conferred on the aesthetically transformed subject of his art: 'Der Trieb zur Kunst', he wrote, 'ist ja nichts als eine fortwährende Neigung, die Konflikte auszugleichen, die unser, aus so verschiedenartigen und einander oft widerstrebenden Elementen sich immer neu bildendes 'Ich' gefährden und spannen' (B Sizzo, 78; 9 May 1926).

Undoubtedly more than anywhere it was in personal relationships that Rilke's need for 'Bezug' affected him most profoundly The constant, and often unsuccessful, attempts at striking the right balance between Self and Non-Self led to such strange Rilkean concepts as 'intransitive love', and to his theory of the ideal nature of marriage – a theory developed and practised as a result of his own unhappy experiences:

Es handelt sich in der Ehe für mein Gefühl nicht darum, durch Niederreißung und Unterstützung aller Grenzen eine rasche Gemeinsamkeit zu schaffen, vielmehr ist die gute Ehe die, in welcher jeder den anderen zum Wächter seiner Einsamkeit bestellt und ihm dieses größte Vertrauen beweist, das er zu verleihen hat. Ein *Miteinander* zweier Menschen ist eine Unmöglichkeit und, wo es doch vorhanden scheint, eine Beschränkung, eine gegenseitige Übereinkunft, welche einen Teil oder beide Teile ihrer vollsten Freiheit und Entwicklung beraubt. (B, 29; 17 August 1901 to Emanuel von Bodman)

In all these various ways Rilke's concern with 'Bezug' played a fundamental – one might say *the* fundamental – part in his life. But as much as anything it was his landscapes that provided him with stimulation to develop his vision, and with imagery in which to express it. He saw 'Bezug' – or its absence – in the relationship of whole and part in them, and he felt it – or again, failed to feel it – in the relationship between the landscape and himself. Thus it was that in 1924, in reply to a question about the 'influences' that had shaped his life and work, he described as of paramount importance a relationship with many landscapes that parallels exactly that 'Bezug'-type combination of loneliness and community that some twenty-three years previously he had set up as his ideal in marriage:

der größeste [Einfluß] bleibt vielleicht zu nennen: daß ich *allein* sein durfte in so viel Ländern, Städten und Landschaften, ungestört, mit der ganzen Vielfalt, mit allem Gehör und Gehorsam meines Wesens einem Neuen ausgesetzt, willig ihm zuzugehören und doch wieder genötigt, mich von ihm abzuheben . . . (B, 861; 26 February 1924 to Alfred Schaer)

141

'Taming'

Where 'Bezug' does not already exist in the relationships between Self and Non-Self and part and whole, then it is the role of Man — and in particular of the artist — to establish it. This, in essence, is the aesthetic theory that accompanied Rilke throughout his life, reaching its climax in the later Elegies. This act of aesthetic transformation is part of the process of 'taming', of giving human significance to the world. Although Rilke hardly ever uses the term himself,[15] it seems to express the common denominator of all the various instances of what Neumann calls Rilke's 'Maßstab menschlich-geistig-ichhaften, sichöffnenden und verarbeitenden, ichbezogenen Sichverhalten [sic; = Sichverhaltens?] zur Welt' (p. 49). 'Taming', it should be stressed, is not always seen by Rilke as a good thing: aesthetic transformation is only its positive side — that type of 'taming' that creates 'Bezug', the 'Sagen' of the Elegies—; in its negative form, which could be termed 'overtaming', the outside world is violated by an act that the Elegies call 'Deuten', and no 'Bezug' is achieved. This ambivalence is, of course, an aspect of that delicate balance between Self and Non-Self that has already been discussed; the ambivalence of 'taming' is particularly acute in Rilke's attitude to words, and it will be examined in greater detail under that heading. First, however, it will be as well to look at some examples of the idea of 'taming'.

As has already emerged, Rilke's landscapes may be divided roughly into two groups: the 'tamed' and the 'untamed'. The adjectives that he used when faced with certain settings make it clear that he himself tended to see landscape in these terms: his poetry contains such phrases as 'die unüberredete Landschaft' (SW, II, 74), and in his letters he talked of the hillsides of Capri as 'Unbewätigtes';[16] similarly, when describing Toledo, he talked of its 'ununterworfene Landschaft,[17] picturing it as 'diese Stadt mitten in ihrer ungebändigten Landschaft'.[18] The activities of the artists at Worpswede were also seen by Rilke in terms of taming — he described Vogeler as a 'Gärtner' (SW, V, 567) — and he concluded his monograph on them with the hope of further taming to come: 'Es ist so vieles nicht gemalt worden, vielleicht Alles. Und die Landschaft liegt unverbraucht da wie am ersten Tag. Liegt da, als wartete sie auf einen, der größer ist, einsamer. Auf einen, dessen Zeit noch nicht gekommen ist' (SW, V, 134). The 'tamed' landscape does, of course, have a lengthy tradition behind it as a feature of poetry in the form of the *locus amoenus*, and Rilke seems to have been aware of this topos;[19] he did not however, explicitly relate it to his own work, or look upon himself as part of this tradition.

The idea of 'taming', although it is often clearest in Rilke's attitude to landscape, is by no means confined to this: although the terminology and intensity tend to vary, it may be found in many different situations throughout his life. In the early years it is a feature largely of the prose works — particularly the aesthetic essays mentioned above —, and when it does appear in verse it tends to take on somewhat extreme forms, as in the conclusion of 'Aber lieber Herr . . .' of 1896, lines that strongly echo Heine and Rimbaud in their prankish yearning for omnipotence over the Non-Self — such a light-hearted 'taming' seems extraordinarily un-Rilkean:

> Essen Sie ruhig Ihr Rebhuhn.
> Sehen Sie, ich habe so Stunden,
> da möcht ich
> die Wolken rupfen,
> mit nachtschwarzen Pappelwipfeln
> dem Mond einen Schnurrbart malen
> und Sterne haben
> im Portemonnaie . . .   (SW, III, 442f.)

On the whole the sympathetic landscapes of Rilke's youth did not arouse in him any great desire to assert his Self and 'tame' them — on the contrary, he found them far more conducive to self-abandon. With the move to Paris, however, the situation changed completely: here was a totally hostile environment that had to be in some way subdued if one were to survive, and the 'taming' concept soon became paramount in Rilke's vision. Here he learnt from Rodin, and later from Cézanne and Van Gogh, to become an 'Arbeiter' and no longer sit passively before Nature (B, 187; 13 October 1907 to Clara), and the active, wilful manner of this new outlook is mirrored in Malte's desperate struggle, which centres around such recurrent terms as 'bewältigen' and 'leisten' (e.g. SW, VI, 929 and 944f.). Now Rilke saw his poetic production as 'eine Bewältigung der Außenwelt',[20] and talked of 'die multiple Aktion künstlerischer Bewältigung'.[21] In his theoretical pronouncements of the Paris period there was almost always something hostile and threatening about the Non-Self that he saw artists confronted with. It was no coincidence that he was fascinated at this time by the acceptance and thus 'taming' of horrible experiences in Baudelaire's 'Une Charogne' and by Flaubert's Saint Julien:[22] this was precisely what Malte tried — and failed — to do through the process of 'Leistung', and it was what Rilke even came to see as an essential component of human existence: 'das Übergroße zur Handlung unseres Herzens machen, damit es uns nicht zerstöre' (B, 187; 13 October 1907 to Clara), thus generalizing what in 1902 he had seen as the philosophy of an individual artist:

Und dieses ist von nun ab das große Grundgesetz der Maeterlinckschen Lebensauffassung: Verinnerlichung, Zusammenfassung aller Kräfte in unserer Seele, Erweiterung dieser Seele zu einer Welt, die mächtiger ist als jene unheilvolle Welt des Schicksals, die dem Menschen so lange drohend und feindlich gegenüberstand. Diesem Schicksal ein Ding nach dem anderen fortzunehmen und es den Menschen zu schenken . . . (SW, V, 539)

In these lines, in fact, the whole of Rilke's vision during the Paris years is perfectly formulated: the definite duality of Self and Non-Self, a Non-Self that is above all else threatening and hostile, and the consequent imperative for the Self to expand and deepen, to 'tame' one by one, just as Rilke did in the 'Dinggedichte', the separate elements of this Non-Self by investing them with a significance that renders them amenable to the human world; significantly 'Bezug' is for the time being forgotten in the face of these more immediate and urgent demands.

In Rilke's later years a new key-word emerges to express the notion of 'taming': the word 'ordnen'. This is the idea that underlies his vision of Orpheus's song — the humanizing on to a higher level of the hostile and destructively transient world:

> Du aber, Göttlicher, du, bis zuletzt noch Ertöner,
> da ihn der Schwarm der verschmähten Mänaden befiel,
> hast ihr Geschrei übertönt mit Ordnung, du Schöner,
> aus den Zerstörenden stieg dein erbauendes Spiel.   (SW, I, 747)

Indeed, this idea of 'ordnen' has been taken by Mason, in his essay 'Die Inspiration und der Begriff des "Ordnens" bei Rilke', as the main creative mode with Rilke. Clearly what Mason is saying in this essay approximates to a definition of taming, but he seems to overlook the negative implications of 'ordnen' — and of 'taming' — when he contends that it is *not* to be equated with 'deuten', saying it is 'nicht . . . das abstrakt-gedankliche Katalogisieren der Erscheinungen durch den Philosophen und den Gelehrten, sondern . . . ihre sinnlich-unmittelbare Gestaltung durch das ordnende Gefühl, durch die ordnende Einbildungskraft des Künstlers' (p. 25). That this is simply not the case is revealed by such references as the distinctly negative 'wir Ordnende' of the fourth of the 'Fünf Sonette' (SW, II, 714) of 1913, and even more clearly by the Eighth Elegy's picture of Man's hopeless attempts to order the world through the false 'taming' of 'deuten':

> Uns überfüllts. Wir ordnens. Es zerfällt.
> Wir ordnens wieder und zerfallen selbst.   (SW, I, 716)

As these examples, together with the one from the Sonnets, show, 'ordnen' may be equated very closely with 'taming', for like the latter it embodies both an ideal and a danger.

The false 'taming' of the 'deuten' type arises from an excessive assertion of the Self over the Non-Self, such as Rilke regretted in 'Wendung'; this is what Steiner calls 'die greifbare Aneignung alles uns Umgebenden',[23] the 'usurpatorischer Zugriff des Innern auf die äußere Welt', for which Holthusen criticizes him *(Der unbehauste Mensch*, p. 84). In landscape such 'taming' resulted not only in such obvious extremes as the dislocated horrors of Paris, but also in more subtly unpleasant environments, such as that of Zurich, which Rilke found unbearably 'tame' (in all senses of the word), talking of its 'zwar gesteigerte, aber unsäglich bürgerliche Landschaft', its 'menschlich-nüchterne Natur' (B Kippenberg, 105; 23 March 1914).

Such a violated world could not, in the ideal of the Ninth Elegy, be 'glücklich', at one and the same time both 'schuldlos und unser',[24] for it had not been, in the words of a poem written six months after 'Wendung', deeply, genuinely, yet unpossessively *felt*:

> [Ihr richtet euch im engen Fühlen ein,
> ihr fühlt euch Zimmer und verschließt den Bau,
> Und darum sagt ihr: *mein* zu einer Frau,
> zu einem Landstrich, einem Lande —. Nein.
> Das ist nicht Fühlen.]
> Daß einer fühlte. Fühlen geht hinaus
> und hat kein Haus. Geht in den Raum hinein
> durchgeht den Stein, ruht in den Toten aus,
> kann alles werden und wird wieder mein.
> Aneignung ist nicht fühlen: fühlen giebt
> zurück und stellt geräumiger die Dinge.   (SW, II, 430)

Here, in a style very reminiscent of the definition of 'Liebe' in I Corinthians 13, the charitable form of 'taming' is defined in terms of 'Fühlen'. It is the opposite of selfish 'Aneignung', of saying *'mein'* to everything and everyone we meet, and thereby constricting and falsifying the world. True 'Fühlen' means empathy rather than dominance, 'Verwandlung' of both Self and Non-Self, a process at the end of which everything is still itself, but now more deeply and more fully so, coexisting perfectly in the open realm of 'Bezug'. Similar ideals lie behind the following poem of 1924, which is probably Rilke's most concise statement of his aesthetic theory and the notion of positive 'taming':

> Nicht um-stoßen, was steht!
> Aber das Stehende stehender,
> aber das Wehende wehender
> zuzugeben, — gedreht
>
> zu der Mitte des Schauenden,
> der es im Schauen preist,
> daß es sich am Vertrauenden
> jener Schwere entreißt,
>
> drin die Dinge, verlorener
> und gebundener, fliehn—,
> bis sie, durch uns, geborener,
> sich in die Spannung beziehn.   (SW, II, 175f.)

The world must not be knocked over by our violation of its integrity, but instead it must be affirmed in all its aspects, from the most solid to the most fleeting. Only thus can it be raised to that higher realm that this poem's repeated comparatives express, and saved from that fate of destructive transience lamented in the Elegies and the Hulewicz-Brief, underlined here by the contrasting comparatives 'verlorener' and 'gebundener'. As in the Ninth Elegy it is Man who stands in the centre as *primus inter pares*, like Heidegger's 'Hirt des Seins', performing his role of 'schauen' and 'preisen'. Only through his agency, through his positive 'taming', can the world

145

be lifted into the higher realm where things are 'geborener', more truly themselves, where they 'sich in die Spannung beziehn'; here alone can they experience that tense harmony of 'Bezug', of the perfect and lasting reconciliation of integration with integrity.

Like 'Bezug', the notion of 'taming' pervaded every sphere of Rilke's life and thought. His gardening activities at Muzot were both figurative and literal,[25] and he celebrated them in the cycle 'Les Roses' (SW, II, 575ff.), but throughout his life, as his letters show, he took great pains carefully to order each new immediate environment that he moved into. Von Salis sees in this a feature linking Rilke's everyday life with his poetic creativity, and notes it as one of his most prominent characteristics:

> For him environment and furniture replaced the missing raw material to some extent, giving him a chance to exercise his creative faculties. . . . This orderliness, this precision with regard to the smallest and least important matters, was one of the most striking features about Rainer Maria's way of life. (pp. 125f.)

For Rilke the poet, however, 'taming' meant using words to create a 'Bezug' of Self and Non-Self, of part and whole; the last element in this aesthetic vision, Rilke's attitude to words, must now be examined.

Words

Rilke's interest in the properties and function of words is a natural one in a poet, and it was certainly one that occupied him at all stages of his life, as his numerous statements on the matter show. Interestingly enough, the majority of these statements occur in poems, which puts him in the ironic situation of commenting on, and not infrequently doubting, the medium in an exalted form of which his comments are expressed. His attitude to words — like his attitude to so many things — is ambivalent, depending on a subtle definition of the type of word in question in any given instance. This ambivalence is the ambivalence of 'taming', for words are the instruments of 'taming' —

> Wir machen mit Worten und Fingerzeigen
> uns allmählich die Welt zu eigen . . . (SW, I, 741)

—and like 'taming', words have both their good and their bad sides.

This awareness of the dual possibilities of the word developed in Rilke at an early age, as the following two poems of 1897 indicate; they were written within fifteen days of one another, and, superficially, appear to contradict one another — an outward paradox that was to culminate in the Elegies' distinction of 'Sagen' and 'Deuten':

> Die armen Worte, die im Alltag darben,

146

die unscheinbaren Worte, lieb ich so.
Aus meinen Festen schenk ich ihnen Farben,
da lächeln sie und werden langsam froh.

Ihr Wesen, das sie bang in sich bezwangen,
erneut sich deutlich, daß es jeder sieht;
sie sind noch niemals im Gesang gegangen
und schauernd schreiten sie in meinem Lied.   (SW, I, 148f.)

* * * *

Ich fürchte mich so vor der Menschen Wort.
Sie sprechen alles so deutlich aus:
Und dieses heißt Hund und jenes heißt Haus,
und hier ist Beginn und das Ende ist dort.

Mich bangt auch ihr Sinn, ihr Spiel mit dem Spott,
sie wissen alles, was wird und war;
kein Berg ist ihnen mehr wunderbar;
ihr Garten und Gut grenzt grade an Gott.

Ich will immer warnen und wehren: Bleibt fern.
Die Dinge singen hör ich so gern.
Ihr rührt sie an: sie sind starr und stumm.
Ihr bringt mir alle die Dinge um.   (SW, I, 194f.)

In the first of these poems Rilke expresses an idea that was quite frequent in his early work: the idea of the poet's reinvigoration of the lost and neglected words of everyday speech: 'Das ist nun gerade das Merkmal der Dichter, ich meine der wirklichen: daß die armen müdgewordenen Worte neu werden bei ihnen und jung, wie noch nie gebraucht und reich in ihrem Unberührtsein.'[26] By the time of the Muzot years this sense of the distinction between the everyday and the poetic use of words had, if anything, grown even stronger; now words were lifted into the realm of magic: 'In das Bereich des Zaubers / scheint das gemeine Wort hinaufgestuft . . . ' (SW, II, 174). This realm is, of course, that of 'Bezug', as the following letter passage of 1922, with its mention of 'Gesetzmäßigkeit', 'Verhältnis' and 'Konstellation', makes clear:

Kein Wort im Gedicht . . . ist identisch mit dem gleichlautenden Gebrauchs- und Konversations-Worte; die reinere Gesetzmäßigkeit, das große Verhältnis, die Konstellation, die es im Vers oder in künstlerischer Prosa einnimmt, verändert es bis in den Kern seiner Natur, macht es nutzlos, unbrauchbar für den bloßen Umgang, unberührbar und bleibend.   (B, 770; 17 March 1922 to Gräfin Margot Sizzo-Noris-Crouy).

In these references to the positive aspect of words Rilke makes little distinction between the word and its meaning, for here the word is a perfect expression of the object it signifies, and the two are virtually identical. Only in the Elegies does he concern himself at all deeply with this matter of the relationship between the

147

positive word and its significance, and in the Ninth Elegy he presents this relationship in a vivid and remarkable image:

> Bringt doch der Wanderer auch vom Hange des Bergrands
> nicht eine Hand voll Erde ins Tal, die Allen unsägliche, sondern
> ein erworbenes Wort, reines, den gelben und blaun
> Enzian. (SW, I, 718)

The word, Rilke suggests, is related to the thing it denotes as the flower is related to the earth: the wanderer, having found a patch of fertile earth in the barren mountains, does not bring back a handful of it to convince those below of its existence; instead he brings them a flower, which is evidence enough, and like words a full and perfect beautiful symbolic expression of that from which it has sprung.[27]

In the false, negative use of words, on the other hand, Rilke is from the very beginning concerned with the relationship of word to meaning, as the second of the poems quoted above shows. Here the words, far from being the perfect expression of the objects, are alien impositions; unlike the flowers that freely and naturally arise, these words are oppressive and heavy (see SW, III, 620 and 654), they are instruments not of liberation but of violation – 'zu grobe Zangen' (SW, V, 435) –, far from heightening they destroy – 'Ihr bringt mir alle die Dinge um'. Rilke's complaint in the first stanza of this poem is directed at the divisive nature of these words: by naming they separate, fragmenting the fundamental harmony of the world into false and procrustean concepts. They ignore that world of nuance that was so important for Rilke:

> Auf einmal lasten alle Namen,
> und unter ihrer Wucht die zahmen
> und zarten Dinge leiden so.
>
> Fühlst du die vielen Übergänge
> hinzögern zwischen Sein und Sein?   (SW, III, 620f.)

The second stanza is concerned with the 'overtaming' effect of these misused words, an effect that was very clearly expressed in a French poem of 1924, where Rilke indicates that 'overtaming' is overhumanizing – endowing something so violently with human significance that it loses itself and becomes 'presque homme':

> Le mot agit, et nul ne le reprend.
> Soudain, à certaines heures, ce qu'on nomme
> devient . . . quoi? Un être . . . presque homme,
> et on le tue, en le nommant!   (SW, II, 649)

The ultimate conclusion of this negative view of the effect of words can only be that things can only truly be themselves when their oppressive names are removed, and this is in fact the conclusion that Rilke explicitly reaches in a poem of 1899:

die Namen, welche auf den Dingen lasten,
sind Bangigkeiten ihres Anbeginns.
Nimmst du sie fort, so *sind* sie nur: sie sind.   (SW, III, 654)

It may seem a far cry from these lines to the Ninth Elegy and its doctrine of
'Sagen', of entry into the higher and more lasting realm that such emphases as
'*sind*' normally indicate — an entry attained by the world precisely by being 'said'
by Man. But in fact, of course, the Ninth Elegy, like the Sonnets, represents the
culmination of that other line of development in Rilke's attitude to words that had
begun with the assertion 'Die armen Worte . . . lieb ich so'. Through 'Sagen' and
the similar Ninth Elegy processes of 'Sprechen', 'Bekennen', 'Preisen', 'Rühmen',
'Zeigen', and 'Verwandeln' the false divisions of the 'gedeutete Welt', of that
world where we 'zu stark unterscheiden', are 'aufgehoben', replaced by the
constellation of 'Bezug'. Here the violated spaces between the everyday world's
concepts, the 'vielen Übergange . . . zwischen Sein und Sein' of the realm of nuance,
come into their own again — though so too does the individuality of the things they
link. Steiner puts very well this perfect balance of whole and part that 'Sagen'
achieves:

Das Wort ist nie des allgemeinen Daseinsgrunds mächtig. Es vereinzelt immer.
Insofern es aber in der Vereinzelung von einer sich auf das Ganze beziehenden,
es wenigstens antönenden Bedeutung geladen werden kann, insofern also es nicht
festlegt und auf dem Festgelegten beharrt, sondern sich lebendig ins Offene hält,
vermag es das Irdische in seiner Gültigkeit wiederzugeben, das je auch ein
Einzelnes ist, seinen Grund und seinen Sinn aber erst vom Ganzen her erhält.
(p. 217)

It is misleading to say, as Stahl does when discussing this Elegy: 'ganz im
Gegensatz zu der hier gepriesenen Rettung des Vergänglichen durch das Wort
steht die Sprachskepsis Rilkes in seinem übrigen Werk' (p. 97). There certainly is
'Sprachskepsis' in much of Rilke's work, but this is always counterbalanced by his
faith in the power of words when properly used. His awareness of the existence of
a good and a bad use of words is paralleled by his consciousness of the good and bad
types of relationship between Self and Non-Self and part and whole, and of the
good and bad types of 'taming'. In all of these the good was the mid-point where
Man met Nature on equal terms, but it was almost invariably a mid-point created
ultimately by Man — Man the speaker, or, in the landscapes of Rilke's life and the
landscape imagery of his work, Man the cultivator.

NOTES TO CHAPTER 6

1.   Holthusen, 'Rilkes letzte Jahre', in *Der unbehauste Mensch*, p. 45.

2. B, 410; 21 October 1913 to Lou Andreas-Salomé.
3. B Lou, 354; 26 June 1914; and 360; 4 July 1914.
4. B, 196; 19 October 1907 to Clara.
5. SW, II, 11ff. See above pp. 28ff.
6. SW, II, 43ff. See above p. 51.
7. SW, VI, 1036ff. See above pp. 29 and 51.
8. SW, II, 79ff. See above pp. 87f.
9. SW, II, 168. A natural corollary of Rilke's image of the expanding Self can be seen in his recurrent image of *eating* the Non-Self, as, for instance, in B, 398; 15 March 1913 to Karl von der Heydt, where, with reference to an account of a journey, he says: 'für Sie ist die Welt, seelisch gesprochen, so wundervoll eßbar und angerichtet, und zwischen den nahrhaften großen Gängen sind immerfort eine ganze Menge kleiner Vorfälle, die Appetit machen'. For other instances of this image see B, 491; 28 July 1915 to Marianne von Goldschmidt-Rothschild, B, 585f.; 2 August 1919 to Lisa Heise; B Lou, 351; 26 June 1914; and SW, II, 549f. One might even go so far as to see the process of 'Verinnerlichung' as akin to 'digesting' the environment.
10. SW, II, 150. The magician is, of course, a representative of the artist. Art and magic are equated in the poem 'Magie' (SW, II, 174f.), written later the same year, and the quasi-magic properties of Orpheus's song are stressed throughout the Sonnets.
11. SW, VI, 1161. Compare SW, V, 474.
12. Rasch, p. 195. The Musil quotation is from *Gesammelte Werke. Tagebücher, Aphorismen, Essays und Reden*, Hamburg, 1955, p. 894.
13. T, 149. See also SW, V, 543. The picture Rilke presents here of a society in which every individual is able to develop to the full is very reminiscent of Schiller's vision of ancient Greece in the *Briefe über die ästhetische Erziehung*. For Schiller, though, society has already been attained once: 'Jene Polypennatur der griechischen Staaten, wo jedes Individuum eines unabhängigen Lebens genoß und, wenn es not tat, zum Ganzen werden konnte, machte jetzt einem kunstreichen Uhrwerke Platz, wo aus der Zusammenstückelung unendlich vieler, aber lebloser Teile ein mechanisches Leben im Ganzen sich bildet' (6. Brief).
14. B Mil, 98; 14 February 1926. See also B Sizzo, 30; 15 July 1922: 'Und wie wäre die Welt zu harmonisieren, wenn Völker sich einander so zugeben wollten, jedes zu seiner Art und der des anderen ehrfürchtig und staunend zugestimmt . . .' The quotation to which this note refers is taken from the longest of Rilke's very rare published political pronouncements (B Mil, 84ff.; 17 January 1926 and 93ff.; 14 February 1926). In it he expresses a distinct aversion to libertarian democracy typical of many of his contemporaries (Lawrence, Yeats, Pound, and the Thomas Mann of the *Betrachtungen*, for instance), and an admiration for the nascent fascist state in Italy. Rilke's politics, inasmuch as, on the available evidence, he could be said to have had any, were, like all his ideas, closely tied up with his aesthetics, which accounts for such dubious manifestations as the (soon disavowed) 'Fünf Gesänge' (SW, II, 86ff.), hailing the god of war in 1914, and his homage to Mussolini. He even briefly, but enthusiastically, acclaimed the Munich soviet of 1918 (B, 562ff.; 7 November 1918 to Clara, 19 December 1918 to Anna Mewes); his enthusiasm soon waned when he realised that the hoped-for regeneration was not forthcoming: 'Revolution hieße für mich ein einfaches reines Ins-Recht-Setzen des Menschen und seiner gern gewollten und gekonnten Arbeit. Jedes Programm, das nicht *dieses* Ziel sich ans Ende setzt, scheint mir ebenso aussichtslos, wie irgendeines der vorigen Regierungen und Herrschaften . . .' (B, 567; 5 January 1919 to Emil Lettré). Mason surmises that there is probably a large body of letters by Rilke on politics and international relations still awaiting publication (*Europe*, p. 195).
15. It occurs in his account of how Rodin familiarized him with the hostile landscape of Paris: 'er brachte es, teilweise gezähmt, dicht an mich heran . . .' (B, 336; 13 February 1912 to Norbert von Hellingrath). It also appears in a French poem describing the contrast between the 'tamed' room and the 'untamed' ('indompté') world outside:

> Fenêtre qu'on cherche souvent
> pour ajouter à la chambre comptée
> tous les grands nombres indomptés
> que la nuit va multipliant.   (SW, II, 590)

16.   B, 152; 1 January 1907 to Clara.
17.   B, 369; 13 November 1912 to Fürstin Marie.
18.   B, 386; 19 December 1912 to Lou Andreas-Salomé.
19.   von Schlözer, p. 47. Compare Wocke, p. 47. For a discussion of the *locus amoenus* in ancient and medieval literature see Curtius, pp. 200ff.
20.   B, 218; 11 March 1908 to Anton Kippenberg.
21.   B, 245; 19 August 1908 to Jakob Baron Uexküll.
22.   See SW, VI, 775; and B, 195; 19 October 1907 to Clara. Similarly B, 245; 19 August 1908 to Jakob Baron Uexküll, and SW, V, 217.
23.   Steiner, p. 214. The word 'haptisch' is used many times by Steiner in this connection.
24.   SW, I, 719. For further examples of happily humanized things see SW, VI, 1065f.
25.   See B, 785f.; 19 May 1922 to Lisa Heise.
26.   SW, V, 464. Compare SW, III, 585; 'Das ist der Zauber: arme Worte finden / und leis sie lehren, im Gedicht zu gehn.'
27.   This image is part of the general pattern of Rilke's mountain imagery. The poet also brings back 'flowers' — the sparse yet beautiful words — that he gathers from the borderland of silence among the largely wordless peaks of his experience.

SUMMARY

As the central theme of the Elegies indicates, Rilke's concern with such notions as the relationship between Self and Non-Self, with 'taming' and the attainment of 'Bezug' is an existential one. The Elegies portray the search for a place for Man in the universe, for a role for him in the scheme of things. They show the investigation and rejection of the conventional answers, and the slow and painful process of winning through to the new vision of positive human activity in the Seventh and Ninth. The search that the Elegies portray closely parallels the course of Rilke's whole life up to the moment of their completion, at which point life and art are united as the ideal is finally attained. Rilke's life was a search for 'home', just as his art was a search for 'Bezug', and the two became more preconditions of one another until they are ultimately inseparable: at Muzot in the constellated landscape of the Valais he found and expressed both.

Rilke's 'homelessness' provides the basis for his art and thought — he saw in his peculiar state a symbol of the general human situation in the twentieth century. The landscapes about him and his reaction to them are thus of immense significance as a concrete key to his all too often intangibly abstract theoretical statements and poetic practice. Just as the Elegies' initial agonized cry at Man's apparent lack of a place in the universe was conceived in the isolated confines of Schloß Duino in its harsh and hostile setting, and their joyful conclusion realized in the happily integrated little Château de Muzot, so were all of Rilke's major landscapes places that provided him with symbolic configurations of a particular stage in his search — sometimes positive visions of the ideal, sometimes pictures of all that was worst in the human situation as he saw it. The landscapes and landscape features he most liked were those in which Man and Nature were acting basically in concert, for in them he saw an image of 'home' and 'Bezug', of a mutual heightening of Self and Non-Self in which part and whole were not only reconciled but even intensified into a superior realm where integrity and integration were no longer incompatible — landscapes in which he saw concretized the product of 'Sagen'. The landscapes he liked least were those where the delicate balance of Self and Non-Self was weighted too heavily on one side — landscapes where Man had over-asserted himself and violated Nature, landscapes that had been 'gedeutet'; or those in which Nature was immoderately dominant.

It is the search for the delicate mid-point between these two extremes that explains the apparent inconsistencies and confusing dualities of Rilke's life and thought: the alternation of attraction and rejection that characterized nearly all his relationships, whether with people or with places; the subtle distinction between 'Sagen' and 'Deuten' and their associated concepts – these result from the constant adjustments that Rilke made to the scales of the Self/Non-Self relationship before he finally found the desired balance.

Rilke's life was a journey through landscape as he moved on from place to place across Europe and beyond, and the various settings he encountered were not merely symbols for him, but decisive inducements to various types of artistic production. The three great periods of his life are dominated by three great landscapes: the open vastness of the plains of Russia and Worpswede, the confusion and constriction of the great city Paris, and the gently tamed hillsides of the Valais. It is impossible to judge the extent to which each of these environments was an 'influence' on him, but it can hardly be a coincidence that Russia provided the setting for so many of his pantheistic neo-Romantic poems, whilst the chaos of Paris was the environment against which he asserted his ordering Self, and in Muzot he serenely and securely expressed his vision of the realm of 'Bezug'. Rilke's vision of Man's place in the world is indeed very well prefigured in the lines he wrote at the turn of the century:

> Und was Du schaust
> und erbaust,
> liebst und verstehst:
> *ist alles Landschaft,*
> *durch die Du gehst.* (SW, III, 397)

BIBLIOGRAPHY

A.   PRIMARY WORKS

The abbreviations under which the books in this section are entered are those used in all the references.

i.   *Rilke's Works*

SW (followed, in Latin numerals, by the volume number) – *Rainer Maria Rilke: Sämtliche Werke*, Herausgegeben vom Rilke-Archiv in Verbindung mit Ruth Sieber-Rilke, Besorgt durch Ernst Zinn, Frankfurt/M, 1955-66 (6 vols)

ii.   *Rilke's Translations*

GW, VI – *Rainer Maria Rilke: Gesammelte Werke*, Band VI (Übertragungen), Leipzig, 1927

Valéry Gedichte – *Paul Valéry: Gedichte, übertragen durch Rainer Maria Rilke*, Wiesbaden, 1949

iii.   *Rilke's Letters*

B – *Rainer Maria Rilke: Briefe* (one volume edition), Frankfurt/M, 1966.
As this is the only collected (though still far from complete) edition of Rilke's letters that is in print and readily available, I have taken it as my basic source for letter-quotations: thus, if a passage quoted appears in this volume, then the reference is given for this volume, irrespective of the fact that the passage might also be found in one, or even several, of the other collections. In order to facilitate cross-reference to other collections I have mentioned the date and, where not already obvious, the addressee of every letter quoted. (N.B. The number immediately following 'B' refers to the *page* – and *not* the letter-number – in *Briefe*.) Where the passage quoted is not contained in B the following abbreviations are used to identify the source; in general reference is made to one of the collected editions other than B only when the letter is not already contained in a specific 'Briefwechsel' edition. (For a discussion and summary of the confusion surrounding the multitude of overlapping, incomplete, and uncoordinated editions of Rilke's letters see pp. 194ff. of Mason's *Rilke, Europe and the English-Speaking World.*) I have used the detailed 'Zeittafel' in B as my basic source of biographical information on Rilke's movements from place to place.

B 92-04 – *R.M.R.: Briefe aus den Jahren 1892 bis 1904*, Leipzig, 1939

B 02-06 – *R.M.R.: Briefe aus den Jahren 1902 bis 1906*, Leipzig, 1930

B 04-07 – *R.M.R.: Briefe aus den Jahren 1904 bis 1907*, Leipzig, 1939

B 07-14 – *R.M.R.: Briefe aus den Jahren 1907 bis 1914,* Leipzig, 1939

B 14-21 – *R.M.R.: Briefe aus den Jahren 1914 bis 1921,* Leipzig, 1937

B 21-26 – *R.M.R.: Briefe aus Muzot, 1921 bis 1926,* Leipzig, 1936

B Gide – *R.M.R. -Andre Gide: Correspondance 1909-1926,* ed. Renée Lang, Paris, 1952

B j. Dichter – *R.M.R.: Briefe an einen jungen Dichter,* Leipzig, 1929

B Junghanns – *R.M.R. -Inga Junghanns: Briefwechsel,* Wiesbaden, 1959

B Kippenberg – *R.M.R. -Katharina Kippenberg: Briefwechsel,* Wiesbaden, 1954

B Lou – *R.M.R. -Lou Andreas-Salomé: Briefwechsel,* Zurich and Wiesbaden, 1952

B Merline – *R.M.R. et Merline: Correspondance 1920-1926,* Zurich, 1954

B Mil – *R.M.R.: Lettres Milanaises 1921-1926,* Paris, 1956 (letters to Duchesse Gallarati Scotti)

B Nölke – *R.M.R.: Die Briefe an Frau Gudi Nölke,* Wiesbaden, 1953

B Sizzo – *R.M.R.: Die Briefe an Gräfin Sizzo 1921-1926,* Wiesbaden, 1950

B Taxis – *R.M.R. -Marie von Thurn und Taxis: Briefwechsel,* Zurich, 1951

B Verleger – *R.M.R.: Briefe an seinen Verleger 1906 bis 1926,* Wiesbaden, 1949

iv.   *Rilke's Diaries*

T – *R.M.R.: Tagebücher aus der Frühzeit,* Leipzıg, 1942

B.   SECONDARY WORKS CITED

Albert-Lasard, Lou, *Wege mit Rilke,* Frankfurt/M, 1952

Allemann, Beda, 'Rainer Maria Rilke', *Insel Almanach auf das Jahr 1967,* Frankfurt/M, 1966, 7ff. (Also as introduction to Rilke's *Werke in drei Bänden,* Frankfurt/M, 1966)
– – *Zeit und Figur beim späten Rilke,* Pfullingen, 1961

Angelloz, J.-F., *Rainer Maria Rilke: L'évolution spirituelle du poète,* Paris, 1936

Batterby, K.A.J., *Rilke and France,* Oxford, 1966

Blume, Bernhard, 'Die Insel als Symbol in der deutschen Literatur', *Monatshefte,* 41 (1949), 239ff.
– – 'Rilkes "Spätherbst in Venedig" ', *Wirkendes Wort,* 10 (1960), 345ff. (Also in *Interpretationen,* Frankfurt/M, Fischer Bücherei, 1969, I, 277ff.)
– – 'Die Stadt als seelische Landschaft im Werk Rainer Maria Rilkes', *Monatshefte,* 43 (1951), 65ff. and 133ff.

Bollnow, Otto Friedrich, *Rilke,* second edition, Stuttgart, 1951

Buddeberg, Else, *Rainer Maria Rilke: Eine innere Biographie,* Stuttgart, 1955

Curtius, E.R., *Europäische Literatur und lateinisches Mittelalter,* fifth edition, Bern, 1965

Damian, Erwin, 'Rilkes Gestaltung der Landschaft', *Zeitschrift für Ästhetik und allgemeine Kunstwissenschaft,* 32 (1938), 152ff. and 214ff.

Demetz, Peter, 'The Czech themes of Rainer Maria Rilke', *GLL,* 6 (1952-53), 35ff.
– – *Rene Rilkes Prager Jahre,* Düsseldorf, 1953

Fletcher, Betty, and Eva Schiffer, 'Island and star: An interpretation of Rilke's "Die Insel" ', *GR,* 27 (1952), 280ff.

Fülleborn, Ulrich, *Das Strukturproblem der späten Lyrik Rilkes.
 Voruntersuchungen zu einem historischen Rilke-Verständnis*, Heidelberg, 1960
Gebser, J., *Rilke und Spanien*, Zurich, 1946
—— ' "Rainer Maria Rilke und unsere Zeit" (Ansprache, gehalten gelegentlich der
 Eröffnung des schweizerischen Rilke-Archivs)', in *Das Schweizerische Rilke-
 Archiv der Schweiz. Landesbibliothek in Bern*, Zurich, 1952
Holthusen, Hans Egon, *Der unbehauste Mensch*, Munich, 1951
 —— *Rainer Maria Rilke in Selbstzeugnissen und Bilddokumenten*, Hamburg,
 1958
Laurette, Pierre, 'Le thème de l'arbre chez Valéry et Rilke' (Dissertation,
 Saarbrücken, 1962)
Lettau, Reinhard, 'Rilkes Zyklus "Die Parke" ', *Monatshefte*, 51 (1959), 169ff.
Mason, Eudo C., *Rilke, Europe and the English-Speaking World*, Cambridge, 1961
 —— *Lebenshaltung und Symbolik bei Rainer Maria Rilke*, second edition, Oxford,
 1964
Neumann, Elisabeth, 'Die Verschiebung des Erlebnisses "Wirklichkeit" in
 mittleren und späteren Dichtungen Rainer Maria Rilkes' (Dissertation,
 Münster, 1935)
Nevar, Elya Maria, *Freundschaft mit Rainer Maria Rilke*, Bern-Bümpliz, 1946
Politzer, Heinz, 'Prague and the origins of Rainer Maria Rilke, Franz Kafka and
 Franz Werfel', *MLQ*, 16 (1955), 49ff.
Rasch, Wolfdietrich, *Zur deutschen Literatur seit der Jahrhundertwende*,
 Stuttgart, 1967
Salis, J.R. von, *Rainer Maria Rilke: The Years in Switzerland*, translated by N.K.
 Cruickshank, London 1964
Stahl, August, *'Vokabeln der Not' und 'Früchte der Tröstung': Studien zur
 Bildlichkeit im Werke Rainer Maria Rilkes*, Heidelberg, 1967
Stein, Jack M., 'The Duino Elegies', *GR*, 27 (1952), 272ff.
Steiner, Jacob, *Rilkes Duineser Elegien*, Bern, 1962
Stewart, Corbet, 'Rilke's cycle "Die Parke" ', *MLR*, 61 (1966), 238ff.
Sugar, Charlotte L. de, *Baudelaire et Rainer Maria Rilke: étude d'influence et
 d'affinités spirituelles*, Paris, 1954
Uyttersprot, H., *Praags cachet: opstellen over Rainer Maria Rilke en Franz Kafka*,
 Antwerp, 1963
Valéry, Paul, *Oeuvres*, volume I, (Bibliothèque de la Pléiade), Paris, 1957
Wocke, H., *Rainer Maria Rilke und Italien*, Giessen, 1940.

C.   OTHER WORKS CONSULTED
It would be impossible to render account of all the works that — often probably
unnoticed — have provided ideas that I have been able to use in this study. Those
actually cited are listed above; the following is a short list of further helpful works
of fairly immediate relevance.

Belmore, H.W., *Rilke's Craftsmanship: An Analysis of his Poetic Style*, Oxford,
 1954
Bentley, Charles A., 'Ein Brief Rilkes an Annette Kolb', *Monatshefte*, 44 (1952),

195f. (The letter in question is dated 21 March 1919)

Betz, Maurice, *Rilke à Paris et les Cahiers de Malte Laurids Brigge*, Paris, 1941

Biese, C.J.A.A., *Die Entwicklung des Naturgefühls im Mittelalter und in der Neuzeit*, Leipzig, 1888

Böheim, J., *Das Landschaftsgefühl des ausgehenden Mittelalters*, Leipzig and Berlin, 1934

Borchardt, R., *Der Deutsche in der Landschaft*, second edition, Frankfurt/M, 1953

Bowra, C.M., *The Heritage of Symbolism*, London, 1943

Brutzer, Sophie, *Rilkes russische Reisen*, Darmstadt, 1969 (reproduction of 1934 Königsberg dissertation)

Buchheit, Gert, 'Die Landschaft der Duineser Elegien', *Der Gral*, 23 (1928-29), 402ff. (Also in *Rainer Maria Rilke*, Freiburg, 1931)

Buddeberg, Else, *Die Duineser Elegien Rainer Maria Rilkes*, Karlsruhe, 1948

Butler, E.M., *Rainer Maria Rilke*, Cambridge, 1941

Clark, Kenneth, *Landscape into Art*, second edition, London, 1956

Darge, Elisabeth, 'Naturgefühl und Landschaftsdarstellung in der deutschen Dichtung seit 1880', *Jahres-Bericht der Schlesischen Gesellschaft für vaterländische Cultur*, 108 (1936), 163ff.

Dargel, Felix Alexander, 'Die Landschaftsschilderung in der erzählenden Dichtung Goethes, Hölderlins und der älteren Romantik' (Dissertation, Heidelberg, 1921)

Dédéyan, Charles, *Rilke et la France*, 4 vols, Paris, 1963

Deschner, K., *Kitsch, Konvention und Kunst*, Munich, 1958

Dornheim, Alfredo, 'Das "Reiselied" Hugo von Hofmannsthals, eine hypoboreische Mignon-Landschaft', *Euphorion*, 49 (1955), 50ff.

Frenzel, Elisabeth, *Stoff-, Motiv- und Symbolforschung*, Stuttgart, 1963

Ganzenmüller, W., *Das Naturgefühl im Mittelalter*, Leipzig and Berlin, 1914

Guardini, R., *Form und Sinn der Landschaft in der Dichtung Hölderlins*, Tübingen and Stuttgart, 1946

Gunert, Johann, 'Landschaft und Naturgefühl in Rilkes Lyrik', in *Festschrift zum hundertjährigen Bestehen der Wiener Stadtbibliothek*, Wiener Schriften, 4 (1956), 273ff.

Hamilton, J.J., 'Landschaftsverwertung im Bau höfischer Epen' (Dissertation, Bonn, 1932)

Hoffmann, Paul T., 'Wie Rilke um die niederdeutsche Landschaft rang', *Der Kreis*, 9 (1932), 342ff.

Kammerer, F., *Zur Geschichte des Landschaftsgefühls im frühen 18. Jahrhundert*, n.p., 1909

Kasper, Alfons, 'Naturgefühl und Landschaftsdichtung im Wandel der Zeiten', *Schönere Zukunft*, 10 (1935), 1082ff. and 1112ff.

Kleinmayr, H., *Die deutsche Romantik und die Landschaftsmalerei*, Strasbourg, 1912

Krech, P., 'Die Landschaft im Sturm und Drangdrama', in *Theater und Drama*, 1933

Kunisch, Hermann, *Rainer Maria Rilke: Dasein und Dichtung*, Berlin, 1944

Langen, August, 'Verbale Dynamik in der dichterischen Landschaftsschilderung des 18. Jahrhunderts', *Zeitschrift für deutsche Philologie*, 70 (1947-48), 249ff.

Leakey, F.W., *Baudelaire and Nature*, Manchester, 1969

Leishman, J.B., and Stephen Spender, *Rainer Maria Rilke: Duino Elegies. Translation, Introduction and Commentary*, London, 1957

Luther, Arthur, *Deutsches Land in deutscher Erzählung: ein literarisches Ortslexikon*, Leipzig, 1936
—— and Heinz Friesenhahn, *Land und Leute in deutscher Erzählung: Ein bibliographisches Literaturlexikon*, Stuttgart, 1954

Mason, Eudo C., *Rilke*, Edinburgh and London, 1963
—— 'Die Inspiration und der Begriff des "Ordnens" bei Rilke', *Sprache im technischen Zeitalter*, 17-18 (1966), 19ff.

Messerschmidt-Schulz, Johann, 'Zur Darstellung der Landschaft in der deutschen Dichtung des ausgehenden Mittelalters' (Dissertation, Breslau, 1938)

Meyer, H., 'Die Verwandlung des Sichtbaren. Die Bedeutung der modernen bildenden Kunst für Rilkes späte Dichtung', *DVLG*, 31 (1957), 465ff. (also contained in the following)
—— 'Rilkes Cézanne-Erlebnis', in *Zarte Empirie*, Stuttgart, 1963

Müller, Andreas, *Landschaftserlebnis und Landschaftsbild: Studien zur deutschen Dichtung des 18. Jahrhunderts und der Romantik*, Stuttgart, 1955

Munro, Donald Farnham, 'Nature Feeling in Modern German Poetry', (Dissertation, Illinois, 1933)

Nadler, Josef, *Literaturgeschichte der deutschen Stämme und Landschaften*, fourth edition, Berlin, 1938-41.

Obermüller, P., and H. Steiner (unter Mitarbeit von E. Zinn), *Katalog der Rilke-Sammlung Richard von Mises*, Frankfurt, 1966

Olivero, Federico, 'The spiritual landscape in Rainer Maria Rilke', *The Poetry Review*, 21 (1930), 257ff.

Oppert, K., 'Das Dinggedicht: eine Kunstform bei Mörike, Meyer und Rilke', *DVLG*, 4 (1926), 747ff.

Orth, Irene, 'Die Landschaft als Lebensraum im deutschen Roman der Gegenwart, dargestellt am Werk Grieses, Pleyers, und Waggerls', (Dissertation, Würzburg, 1941)

Ouwehand, C., and Shizuko Kusunoki, *Rilke in Japan: Versuch einer Bibliographie*, The Hague, 1960

Peters, H.F., 'The Space Metaphors in Rilke's Poetry', *GR*, 24 (1949) 124ff.

Rilke en Valais, Lausanne, 1946 (reedition of special number of *La Suisse Romande* of 1939)

Ritzer, Walter, *Rainer Maria Rilke Bibliographie*, Vienna, 1951

Rolleston, James, *Rilke in Transition. An Exploration of his Earliest Poetry*, New Haven, 1970

Rose, Ernst, 'Rainer Maria Rilke's "Spätherbst in Venedig": an Interpretation', *GR*, 16 (1941), 68ff.

Ruppe, Hans, 'Park und Landschaft von der Anakreontik bis zur Frühromantik'

(Dissertation, Vienna, 1931)

Scheiber, Hedwig, 'Natur und Mensch in der deutschen Lyrik der Gegenwart' (Dissertation, Münster, 1943)

Schlözer, Leopold von, *Rainer Maria Rilke auf Capri: Gespräche*, second edition Dresden, 1932

Schmidt, Albert-Marie, 'Rilke et le paysage parisien', in *Rilke et la France*, Paris, 1942

Schmitt, F.A., *Stoff- und Motivgeschichte der deutschen Literatur: eine Bibliographie*, Berlin, 1959

Schnack, Ingeborg, *Rilkes Leben und Werk im Bild*, Wiesbaden, 1956
—— *Rainer Maria Rilkes Erinnerungen an Marburg und das hessische Land*, Marburg, 1963

Schneditz, Wolfgang, *Rilke und die bildende Kunst: Versuch einer Deutung*, Graz, 1947 (second edition, Salzburg, 1949)
—— *Rilkes letzte Landschaft. 10 Versuche*, Salzburg, 1951

Schwarz, Egon, 'Zu Rilkes Neuem Gedicht "Spätherbst in Venedig" ', *Wirkendes Wort*, 16 (1966), 273ff.

Schwerte, Hans, 'Ausgesetzt auf den Bergen des Herzens . . .', in *Wege zum Gedicht*, edited by Hirschenauer and Weber, Munich and Zurich, 1956, pp. 301ff.

Singer, Herbert, *Rilke und Hölderlin*, Cologne and Graz, 1957

Tecchi, B., 'Rilke in Italia', *Orbis Litterarum*, 11 (1956), 53ff. (originally in *Civiltà*, Rome, 1941; also in *Scrittori tedeschi moderni*, Rome, 1959)

van Tieghem, P., *Le sentiment de la nature dans le préromantisme européen*, Paris, 1960

Wais, Kurt, *An den Grenzen der Nationalliteraturen*, Berlin, 1958

Watson, J.R., *Picturesque Landscape and English Romantic Poetry*, London, 1970

Wessels, P.B., 'Die Landschaft im jüngeren Minnesang' (Dissertation, Nijmegen, 1945)

Wiegand, Carl Friedrich, 'Wandlungen in der dichterischen Wiedergabe des Natureindrucks', *Schweizer Monatshefte*, 20 (1940-41), 279ff.

Wohltmann, Hans, *Rainer Maria Rilke in Worpswede*, Hamburg, 1949

Zermatten, Maurice, *Les années valaisannes de Rilke*, second edition, Sierre 1951

159

PUBLICATIONS OF THE INSTITUTE OF GERMANIC STUDIES

1   *Union List of Periodicals* dealing with Germanic languages and
    literatures in the University Library and in libraries of the colleges
    and institutes of the University
    ISBN 0 85457 005 5   58 pp.   1956   out of print

2   *Schiller Bicentenary Lectures*, ed. by F. Norman
    ISBN 0 85457 010 1   x, 168 pp.   1960   £10.50

3   *Schiller in England 1787–1960: a bibliography*, ed. by R. Pick
    ISBN 0 85457 012 8   xvi, 123 pp.   1961   £8.15

4   *Theses in Germanic Studies, 1903–1961*, ed. by F. Norman
    ISBN 0 85457 015 2   viii, 46 pp.   1962   £1.90

5   *Hofmannsthal Studies in Commemoration*, ed. by F. Norman
    ISBN 0 85457 018 7   xii, 147 pp.   1963   £10.50

6   *Hauptmann Centenary Lectures*, ed. by K. G. Knight and F. Norman
    ISBN 0 85457 021 7   167 pp.   1964   £10.50

7   *Essays in German Literature*, ed. by F. Norman
    ISBN 0 85457 023 3   viii, 166 pp.   1965   £10.50

8   *Medieval German Studies* for F. Norman, ed. by A. T. Hatto and
    M. O'C. Walshe (reprint of 1965 edition)
    ISBN 0 85457 057 8   x, 302 pp.   1973   £14.00

9   *German Language and Literature: select bibliography of reference
    books* by L. M. Newman
    Second enlarged edition
    ISBN 0 85457 077 2   x, 175 pp.   1979   £2.50

10 *Theses in Germanic Studies, 1962–67*, ed. by S. S. Prawer and
    V. J. Riley
    ISBN 0 85457 032 2   vi, 18 pp.   1968   £1.25

11 *Probleme mittelalterlicher Überlieferung und Textkritik —
    Oxforder Colloquium 1966*, hrsg. von P. F. Ganz und W. Schröder
    (in collaboration with Erich Schmidt Verlag, Berlin)
    ISBN 0 85457 033 0   196 pp.   1968   £10.75

12 *Essays in German Language, Culture and Society*, ed. by S. S.
    Prawer, R. Hinton Thomas and L. W. Forster
    ISBN 0 85457 036 5   x, 244 pp.   1969   £14.00

13 *Probleme mittelhochdeutscher Erzählformen — Marburger Collo-
    quium 1969*, hrsg. von P. F. Ganz und W. Schröder (in colla-
    boration with Erich Schmidt Verlag, Berlin)
    ISBN 0 85457 048 9   287 pp.   1972   £15.25

14 *Goethe and the Scientific Tradition*, by H. B. Nisbet
    ISBN 0 85457 050 0   xii, 83 pp.   1972   £7.00

15 *Essays in German and Dutch Literature*, ed. by W. D. Robson-Scott
    ISBN 0 85457 051 9   viii, 191 pp.   1973   £13.50

16 *Three Essays on the 'Hildebrandslied'*, by F. Norman, ed. by A. T.
    Hatto
    ISBN 0 85457 052 7   x, 84 pp.   1973   £7.00

17 *Theses in Germanic Studies, 1967–72*, ed. by W. D. Robson-Scott
    and V. J. Riley
    ISBN 0 85457 055 1   vi, 18 pp.   1973   £1.20

18 *Stefan George: Dokumente seiner Wirkung. Aus dem Friedrich
    Gundolf Archiv der Universität London*, hrsg. von L. Helbing and
    C. V. Bock mit K. Kluncker (in collaboration with Castrum
    Peregrini, Amsterdam)
    ISBN 0 85457 060 8   318 pp.   1974   £12.75

19 *Studien zur frühmittelhochdeutschen Literatur — Cambridger Colloquium 1971*, hrsg. von L. P. Johnson, H.-H. Steinhoff und R. A. Wisbey (in collaboration with Erich Schmidt Verlag, Berlin)
ISBN 0 85457 062 4   359 pp.   1974   £20.15

20 *Selected Essays on Medieval German Literature*, by K. C. King, ed. by J. L. Flood and A. T. Hatto
ISBN 0 85457 063 2   x, 219 pp.   1975   £13.50

21 *Althochdeutsche Glossen zum Alten Testament*, hrsg. von H. Thoma (in collaboration with Max Niemeyer Verlag, Tübingen)
ISBN 0 85457 067 5   xiv, 28 pp.   1975   out of stock

22 *Deutsche Literatur des späten Mittelalters — Hamburger Colloquium 1973*, hrsg. von W. Harms und L. P. Johnson (in collaboration with Erich Schmidt Verlag, Berlin)
ISBN 0 85457 068 3   315 pp.   1975   £19.00

23 *Germanistik in Festschriften von den Anfängen (1877) bis 1973.* In Zusammenarbeit mit dem Institute of Germanic Studies bearb. von Ingrid Hannich-Bode und Siegmund Heidelberg (in collaboration with J. B. Metzlersche Verlagsbuchhandlung, Stuttgart)
ISBN 0 85457 072 1   xii, 441 pp.   1976   out of stock

24 *Karl und Hanna Wolfskehl: Briefwechsel mit Friedrich Gundolf, 1899–1931*, hrsg. von K. Kluncker (in collaboration with Castrum Peregrini, Amsterdam)
ISBN 0 85457 074 8   319, 349 pp.   1977   £26.80
                      (2 vols.)   (plus postage)

25 *August Stramm: Kritische Essays und unveröffentlichtes Quellenmaterial aus dem Nachlass des Dichters*, hrsg. von J. D. Adler und J. J. White (in collaboration with Erich Schmidt Verlag, Berlin)
ISBN 0 85457 078 0   208 pp.   1979   £11.00

26 *London German Studies I*, ed. by C. V. Bock
ISBN 0 85457 095 0   1980   (*in preparation*)

27 *Theses in Germanic Studies, 1972–77*, ed. by C. V. Bock & V. J. Riley. [With a cumulative subject-index to earlier lists, covering the period 1903–77]
ISBN 0 85457 081 0   vi, 57 pp.   1980   £4.90

LIBRARY PUBLICATIONS

The following titles are in print. A complete list is available on application.

LP 1 *Hugo von Hofmannsthal-Ausstellung Katalog*
ISBN 0 85457 013 6   32 pp.   1961

LP 2 *Gerhart Hauptmann Exhibition*: catalogue
prepared by H. F. Garten
ISBN 0 85457 016 0   22 pp.   1962

available on application (s.a.e.)

LP 9 *Periodical Holdings 1970*
ISBN 0 85457 038 1   92 pp.   1970   £0.90

LP 13, *Periodical Holdings* (supplements 1971, 1972, 1973
15, 18 supplied gratis with *Periodical Holdings* 1970)

LP 20 *German-language Literary and Political Periodicals, 1960–1974*
ISBN 0 85457 064 0   60 pp.   1975   £1.90

LP 28 *An Outline Guide to Resources* for the study of German language and literature in National, University and other libraries in the United Kingdom
ISBN 0 85457 084 5   vi, 53 pp.   1978   £1.00

LP 31 *Theses in Progress at British Universities and other institutions of higher education* with theses completed in 1979, work published in 1979 and work due to be published in 1980, as known on 1 January 1980
ISBN 0 85457 091 8   vi, 47 pp.   1980   £2.10
(previous lists — 1967 onwards, except 1973 issue, which is out of print — available on application)

BITHELL MEMORIAL LECTURES

Handling charge: £1.50 per copy

1975 *'Wine that maketh glad . . .'*
The interplay of reality and symbol in Goethe's life and work, by
L. A. Willoughby, MA, DR PHIL, D LIT
Emeritus Professor of German in the University of London
ISBN 0 85457 086 1   iv, 64 pp.

1976 *The neglect of the past and the price it exacts*, by Geoffrey
Templeman, CBE, DL, MA, PH D, D TECH, FSA, Vice-Chancellor of
the University of Kent at Canterbury
ISBN 0 85457 079 9   iv, 18 pp.

1977 *Brecht's misgivings*, by Roy Pascal, MA, LITT D, FBA, Emeritus
Professor of German in the University of Birmingham
ISBN 0 85457 082 9   iv, 19 pp.

1978 *Contemporary historians of the German Reformation*, by A. G.
Dickens, CMG, MA, D LIT, LITT D, D LITT, FBA, FSA, Emeritus
Professor of History in the University of London
ISBN 0 85457 088 8   iv, 27 pp.

1979 *Some German memories, 1911–1961*, by W. H. Bruford, MA,
LL D, D LITT, FBA, Emeritus Schröder Professor of German in the
University of Cambridge
ISBN 0 85457 097 7   iv, 38 pp.

1980 *The man who wanted to know everything,* by L. W. Forster, MA,
LITT D, DR PHIL, LIT DR, D LIT, DOCT DE L'UNIV, FBA, Emeritus
Schröder Professor of German in the University of Cambridge
ISBN 0 85457 102 7   *(in preparation)*

BITHELL SERIES OF DISSERTATIONS

BSD 1 *E. T. A. Hoffmann and the rhetoric of terror*, by Elizabeth Wright
ISBN 0 85457 087 x   viii, 307 pp.   1978   £8.00

BSD 2 *Figures of transformation: Rilke and the example of Valéry*, by
R. F. Cox
ISBN 0 85457 092 6   viii, 199 pp.   1979   £8.00

BSD 3 *Names and nomenclature in Goethe's 'Faust'*, by Ann White
ISBN 0 85457 093 4   vi, 176 pp.   ·   1980   £8.00

The following are in preparation:

BSD 5 *The authority of the source in Middle High German narrative
poetry*, by Carl Lofmark
ISBN 0 85457 098 5   *(in preparation)*

BSD 6 *The banal object: theme and thematics in Proust, Rilke, Hofmanns-
thal and Sartre*, by Naomi Segal
ISBN 0 85457 099 3   *(in preparation)*

BSD 7 *Hermann Broch and the symbolic mode. Aesthetic theory and
literary practice*, by Fergus McGauran
ISBN 0 85457 101 9   *(in preparation)*

Prices, which are for U.K. only, include postage, and are effective from 1 January 1980.
They are liable to adjustment without notice. For overseas orders, add 20% to the price
quoted. This list, which supersedes all previous lists, is based on current stock.

All publications are obtainable on application to the Institute of Germanic Studies,
29 Russell Square, London WC1B 5DP.